THE DEVIL'S
DISCIPLES

*The Truth
About Rock*

by Jeff Godwin

Published by Chick Publications
P.O. Box 662, Chino, CA 91710
Printed in the United States of America

Published by Chick Publications
P.O. Box 662, Chino, CA 91710
Printed in the United States of America

ISBN 0-937958-23-9

194/C

DEDICATION

This book is dedicated to God the Father, Jesus Christ — the King of kings and to the Holy Spirit of the Living God.

INTERNATIONAL DISTRIBUTORS

Comic-Traktate-Versand
Postfach 3009
5632 Wermelskirchen 3
West Germany

Christ Is The Answer, Inc.
Box 5167, Station A
Toronto, Ont. M5W 1N5, Canada
(416) 699-7800

Chick Publications Distributor
P.O. Box 50096
Porirua, Wellington, New Zealand

Penfold Book & Bible House
P.O. Box 26
Bicester, Oxon, England OX6 8PB
Tel: 0869-249574

Evangelistic Literature Enterprise
P.O. Box 10
Strathpine, Q'ld., Australia 4500
Phone: (07) 205-7100

Published by Chick Publications
P.O. Box 662, Chino, CA 91710
Printed in the United States of America

TABLE OF CONTENTS

PARENTS!

Is YOUR child in this picture?

CHAPTER 1

In the Beginning

"My people are destroyed for lack of knowledge."   Hosea 4:6

"I look at Rock like a religion."[1]
                                        Blackie Lawless

"Rock has always been the devil's music. You can't convince me that it isn't." So said David Bowie, one of the most influential Rock stars ever, in 1976.[2]

From a sneering, hip wiggling hillbilly named Elvis Presley to a blood drinking, bat biting maniac named Ozzy Osbourne, today's Rock Stars have the full blessing of Satan in the work they do. Using that titanic power to topple our society is one of their main objectives.

They won't rest until they have achieved their goal.

To many, Rock & Roll means a wonderful, dreamy, nostalgia-filled memory of record hops, bobby sox, and weekend cruises down Main Street.

To many others, a different vision appears, just as real,

but much more alarming. Riots, police with tear gas and water cannon, male singers wearing heavy mascara and lipstick, fondling themselves while hissing demonic lyrics at a mesmerized audience.

Today, very real health problems can be directly attributed to the savage environment at the typical Rock concert, where decibel levels surpassing that of a jet plane taking off are common. Teenage liquor consumption and mind altering drug use run wild at these events.

According to testimony given at the Parents Music Resource Center hearings before the Senate Commerce Committee on September 19, 1985, teenage suicides have gone up a whopping 300% in the last 30 years while the adult rate has stayed the same.

According to Dr. Thomas E. Radecki of the National Coalition on Television Violence, 35% of 1300 Rock videos monitored contained explicit physical violence, averaging 17.9 acts of violence per hour. 13% of violent videos contained "sadistic violence." Violent Rock lyrics from songs in the Top 40 have increased 115% since 1963. And those statistics don't even take into account the smutty sex, alcohol abuse, and satanic themes of most Rock videos of today!

Testimony from Dr. Joe Stuessy, a professor of music at the University of Texas at San Antonio, brought out the fact that for the first time ever, Rock & Roll music, especially Heavy Metal, has become a mean-spirited music filled with one central point as its overriding theme: HATRED.

What mysterious power causes millions of young people world wide to shower their favorite Rock stars with money and fanatical, slave-like devotion? Why the ever increasing thirst for the doubtful benefits of Rock music's strange, hypnotic spell?

The answer lies partially in the beat. The most famous of all Rock bands, *The Beatles,* chose their name precisely because it showcased that word. Most Rock tunes are in 4/4 time, four beats to the measure. This coincides exactly with the time signature of the human heartbeat. Thus, Rock music hits ALL listeners right in the guts, oozing its way like a ravenous leech into the most basic systems of the human body.

Secondly, repetition is the key to the commercial success of any Rock tune. "Hook lines" etch themselves into our brains every time we turn on the car radio. Words, choruses, and certain instrumental parts of the songs are repeated over and over again to the point of saturation. In its entirety, the typical Rock song can best be described in one word: HYPNOTIC.

Rock's young addicts are actually being hypnotized and brainwashed by the music they adore so much!

The message is one of evil, gloating despair dripping with sexual double meanings, or, in some cases, an outright glorification of death, satanic greed, and hate. The bands, both old and new, who have hit the mother lode of commercial success by pursuing this theme are legion. Some of the best known names include: *Black Sabbath, Nazareth, The Rolling Stones, The Doors, AC-DC, Fleetwood Mac, Ted Nugent, Alice Cooper, Judas Priest, Ozzy Osbourne, The Plasmatics, KISS, Iron Maiden, Ronnie James Dio, Motley Crue, Twisted Sister* and *W.A.S.P.*

As the "Stars" of this insanity get richer, our sons and daughters end up losing everything important to their own rational development. Their innocence and trust are freely traded for a lustful, concentrated pursuit of instant self-gratification at any price. Like a huge sprawling parasite, the institution of Rock & Roll squats over our childrens' future, intent on sucking up the last remaining shreds of their respectability.

For those old enough, the hazy, bygone days of 1954 are widely remembered as the birthdate of Rock & Roll. Elvis Presley had just recorded a song called "That's Alright Mama," ushering in the age of Rockabilly. Two years later his swaggering, sneering, hip shaking profile decorated thousands of TV screens on the "Ed Sullivan Show" for

9

which he was paid an unprecedented $50,000. Rock was growing up, and doing it quickly.

Slowly the realization dawned on parents throughout America that their children no longer belonged to them, but instead had pledged allegiance to this greasy, leather jacketed symbol of rebellion and delinquency. Not until a score of years later was the ugliness revealed behind the Presley myth. In the end, Elvis lay fat and dead on the bathroom floor of his Tennessee mansion, his heart blown apart from years of massive drug abuse. With millions of dollars at his fingertips, and the awed worship of a planetful of fans behind him, Elvis Presley died as miserably as any skid-row derelict, alone and pitiful.

From the initial idea of simply providing an energetic emotional release for the pent up frustrations forced on the young by a rigid and uncompromising society, Rock very soon became corrupted by its own power. That initial premise was a lie; Rock was rotten from the beginning. Why did we fall for it?

Concert tours, record albums, magazine interviews and television appearances soon translated into one common denominator: MEGABUCKS. Begun in comparative innocence, within ten years Rock & Roll had become big business, just in time for the British Invasion which would eventually catapult it to the status of (anti) "social art."

The Beatles blasted onto the Rock scene early in 1964, and the world our young people live in has never been the same. Soon after came *The Rolling Stones,* a band of depraved, drug addicted Black Magicians still going strong through the Eighties.

Since 1964, the *Stones* followed closely in *The Beatles'* wake, always striving, but never quite attaining the global success enjoyed by the Moptops. *The Stones'* concerts, music, and image were almost the exact opposite of the Fab Four. Fans often rioted before the high altar of *The Rolling Stones,* sometimes ripping out seats in the theater or auditorium where they stood and hurling the debris at the stage.

Emotionally peaking fans swan dived off balconies onto the crowds below. Police hired as security for the concerts cracked bleeding heads as they went down before an irresistable tide of screaming, frothing teenagers struggling to reach the stage in order to be closer to their "stars."

What were the *Stones* doing during this pandemonium? They simply continued playing as long as possible, coldly noting the chaos they had brought about, occasionally leering at one another. Lead guitarist Keith Richards smashed fans in the face with his boots when they got too close to the stage.

1967 marked a turning point in both *The Beatles'* and *Stones'* careers. LSD had rapidly become the drug of choice among young people worldwide. Ignoring informed warnings about chromosome alterations, brain damage, and mutated offspring, teenagers everywhere were ingesting this explosive chemical about which almost nothing was known.

Soon after LSD had blown a million minds (much to Satan's delight), many of Rock's biggest stars began dying like flies, helpless victims of their dealings with the Devil. By far, the vast majority of these martyred maniacs to the movement were killed by drug overdoses. In the world of Rock & Roll, violent, drug drenched lifestyles sooner or later always beget violent deaths.

"For the wages of sin is death, but the gift of God is eternal life through Jesus Christ our Lord." — Romans 6:23

There is no such thing as a graceful old age retirement from the college of Rock. Overnight superstars awake one day to find their fickle audience has deserted them, taking their potential millions elsewhere. After a lifetime of excessive debaucheries with no thought of the consequences, some of Rock's biggest names suddenly find their health shattered by the time they're 40. Examples include Eric Clapton, hospitalized with bleeding ulcers, Pete Townshend, deaf in one ear and nearly dead from alcoholism, and 50's Rocker Jerry Lee Lewis, who fought

11

for his life in a hospital bed, his stomach ruptured, and his chest wall a mass of abscesses.

Like a disposable plastic glass from McDonalds, these people who have slavishly devoted their lives to the practice of Rock & Roll are discarded onto the trash heaps of hospital beds and TV talk shows. All their money, fame, cars, houses, drugs and jewelry can't buy them one more minute of time as they die or fade from sight — miserably, violently, pathetically.

The decade of the Seventies saw the rise of Punk Rock's ugly head, a trend that continues to thrive today. Groups like the *Sex Pistols* and the *Plasmatics,* as well as scores of imitators, screamed, slashed, bled, and vomited at their teenage audience. Their songs are all about the Devil, death, and destruction. Mixed with the current "Armageddon Rock" of today's Heavy Metal groups, concerned Christians everywhere are up in arms over the state of Rock & Roll in the Eighties.

We now have the advantage of looking back down thirty-two years of Rock & Roll history. Let's put the entire phenomenon into its proper perspective.

Probably the most deceptive period was during the Fifties when Rock seemed most innocent — bratty and fun loving. The Sixties revealed the next step in the satanic plan — drug induced occultism mixed with strong social and political song statements about society's many problems. 1970 began a decade of vulgar extremism, an over saturation of the American dream meets Rock & Roll. Rock stars were never richer, weirder, or more disgustingly contemptible of society's moral laws and sexual taboos.

We are now well into the decade of the Eighties, and thus far Rock shows no signs of slowing down. Today's "new" trends are simply stolen bits and pieces from all the previous eras, with each new group outshocking the last through a never ending parade of outrageous displays of sick, warped, psychotic behavior.

We are witnessing the destruction of our society, but it's

not over yet. When Christians stand up and make their voices heard loud and clear, the Rock stars MUST take a back seat. When mothers and fathers and children delivered from Rock's curse begin shouting the truth boldly for all to hear, the walls of Rock WILL come crashing to the ground. All they need is the truth about Rock, and that's why this book was written. Ephesians 5:11 says: "And have no fellowship with the unfruitful works of darkness, but rather reprove them."

May God help us to put an end to this Rock & Roll blasphemy once and for all!

CHAPTER 2

The Rock Concert

> "Thou shalt have none other gods before me."   Deuteronomy 5:7

> "We are your Gods . . . "   *The Godz*[1]

> "The road around the stadium looked like it had been the scene of a war. Broken glass was everywhere. Trash, ankle deep, filled the curbs, and true to every outdoor Rock show I've ever been to, patches of vomit laced the sidewalk . . . "[2]

Exactly how are our children sent spinning through the Rock brainwasher? What steps lead them into this maze of hatred, drugs, and dissipation? The process often begins at Rock concerts.

People die at Rock concerts. It's a plain fact. Several members of the audience of 500,000+ died December 6, 1969, when *The Rolling Stones* played at Altamont,

California. Fans were beaten, clubbed, shot, stabbed, and run over by motorcycle gangs gone crazy on booze and drugs.

Eleven young people died in December of 1979 when *The Who,* (contemporaries of *The Beatles),* played a concert at Riverfront Coliseum in Cincinnati, Ohio. They were stomped and trampled to death by a crazed mob of six thousand, driven berserk by the urge to Rock & Roll.

Let us examine what your son or daughter actually sees when they make the fateful decision to attend their first Rock concert.

The following facts and illustrations are drawn from the ten long years that I was wholeheartedly under the evil spell of Rock & Roll. I saw some of the biggest bands ever. I was a part of the mass hysteria which has claimed so many young souls and ruined countless teenage lives.

I was there on the forecourt of Cincinnati's Riverfront Coliseum where those eleven people died waiting to see *The Who.* I saw with my own eyes thousands of teenagers driven insane with the Rock obsession. I was trapped inside that raging mob for half an hour, fighting for a little space to breathe, carried along by the uncontrollable force of the riot, my arms pinned helplessly to my sides and my feet barely touching the ground.

Some insidious force possessed those thousands of people that cold December night. The force was of satanic origin, conceived by the Devil and birthed by the band that served him, *The Who.* It drove those young people to such heights of frenzy that they became a mindless stampede of spooked cattle. They were so anxious to see their Rock gods that they ignored the screams and death gurgles of their eleven innocent victims lying crushed and bleeding beneath their trampling feet. (Note: December 3, 1979 — News articles about this event can be found in any major newspaper or magazine of that period.)

Standing all logic on its head, the popularity of *The Who* increased ten-fold overnight. They became more popular and sought after than ever before in their fifteen year history as a group. This is the scope of the problem we face today.

Here is what happens to too many teenage travelers trekking toward their Rock & Roll meccas.

During the long ride, beer, hard liquor, marijuana, and pills of all varieties are consumed like candy. To avoid car wrecks teenagers often appoint a "straight" friend, (one who does not get high), as driver for the evening in order to insure that they all return home alive. Unfortunately, many concert goers have no straight friends willing to drive for them. The police blotters of any major city where concerts are held stand in mute testimony to this sad fact.

Having completed their long drive, the typical group of teens is quite high when they pull into the huge parking lot of the major arena hosting the concert. Security is very lax, with perhaps a dozen police with flare batons directing the thousands of cars past the parking attendants collecting fees through the drivers' windows.

Once successfully parked, everyone quickly finishes the rest of their drinks and "joints" and melts into the hordes streaming toward the arena. Every conceivable drug from "poppers" to morphine is being peddled outside the building. A kind of cotton-candy-hot-dog-carnival atmosphere exists as these youthful vendors hawk their illegal goods. Ticket scalpers are everywhere.

Inside the arena itself, the hazy, smoke filled bathrooms are literal drug stores. The amount of illicit and mind bending chemicals changing hands here is frightening. Joints are smoked openly with impudence. Big, scar-faced dealers wearing biker denim strut past. Huge billfolds chained to their beltloops are stuffed with twenties and fifties. There is no age limit to buy drugs here. No ID is required.

Many of the youngsters turning their money over so eagerly to the pusher in the bathroom often get more than they bargained for. What appears to be cocaine may actually be PCP, a corrosive chemical used to tranquilize hogs. PCP has been found to cause brain lesions, among many other horrible side effects. Unfortunately, the young drug abuser has no way of knowing exactly what he or she has bought until after it is ingested. By then it may be too late. Loss of consciousness, violent vomiting and catatonic stupors all keep ambulance drivers and stomach pumpers busy whenever a major concert hits their town.

Though all concert promoters hire special security forces to patrol the area, no policeman in his right mind is going to enter a smoky bathroom packed with a hundred primed and drugged teenagers in order to make a "bust." At most concerts the police simply look the other way. The widespread abuse is just too massive to control. The sight of 20,000 frothing teens milling aimlessly about like so many drugged cattle is a sobering one indeed. Every cop knows that one arbitrary arrest could be the spark to set off the stampede.

I can clearly remember excitedly looking forward to my first Rock concert. I was fourteen. I had been invited to see one of the premier Heavy Metal bands by two of my friends, Mark and Eddie, one of whom had volunteered to drive the forty-five miles to the concert site. I entered the Dayton, Ohio auditorium with my friends an hour later. Usually reserved for basketball and hockey games, the huge space quickly filled with people. Since this particular concert was general admission with "festival seating," no one bothered to check their tickets for a seat number. Instead, masses of people began swarming over the open expanse of floor directly in front of the stage. This is the "Mega Death" section, as close as a fan can possibly get to his beloved stars. It is here that the ear destroying triple digit decibel levels from the bands' mountains of amplifiers are at their deadliest. A typical fan spending the majority of the evening exposed to such noise may still have his ears ringing days after the event.

Large wooden two-by-fours brace a barricade separating stage from audience. Paid and volunteer security forces man the gap in between, facing the crowd. It is their job to see that no over-zealous fans get past them. Fights, tramplings, and faintings from heat exhaustion occur frequently in this small area where upwards of 2,000 people may be crammed shoulder to shoulder. Any type of fire or evacuation emergency would surely mean the death of most of these Rock disciples. Once securely settled in the "Mega Death" section, it is nearly impossible to fight a path through to the exits until the end of the show. Compounding the already shockingly dangerous atmosphere, bottle rockets, sparklers, firecrackers and M-80's are set off regularly in the midst of this crowd by whooping, drunken troublemakers. The prevailing mood at the typical Rock concert is complete, total, insane anarchy. Or, as the Heavy Metal band *Black Sabbath* says in one of their song titles, "The Mob Rules."

I was persuaded to join the swelling ranks of doped teenagers massing in front of the stage so as to be as close as possible to the "action." Hundreds of glazed eyes and blank, empty faces stared back at me as I found my way slowly through the crowd. With drooping eyelids and slack jaws, many appeared to have no more soul than a department store mannequin.

A great cloud of Marijuana smoke rose slowly, hanging thickly in the air until it reached the signs suspended from the sixty foot ceiling: "ABSOLUTELY NO SMOKING IN THE ARENA BY ORDER OF THE STATE FIRE MARSHALL." This law was no more enforceable than the others.

The phenomenon we are witnessing here is in actuality a subliminal, pagan religious ceremony. The CONGREGATION consists of the thousands of Rock worshipers waiting to be instructed further in their chosen religion. The SACRAMENT is essentially marijuana or some other mood elevating or consciousness altering substance taken to make the worshipers more receptive to the forthcoming lesson. The HIGH PRIESTS, or administrators of the faith, are the group actually headlining the concert. They are the ones instructing their followers in the correct means of obtaining grace through the saving power of The Great God Of Rock & Roll — SATAN.

When the congregation masses at the front of the stage, they are gathered together at an altar for worship. But what exactly is it that they are idolizing so hysterically? Is it utopian freedom of expression? Is it love of one's neighbor? Or is it Rock & Roll itself, a tribal celebration?

It is none of these.

What these poor, drunk, drugged, and duped young people are actually worshiping is PURE EVIL.

This evil may take the form of wanton destruction. One of the biggest Heavy Metal bands of the last decade, *Deep Purple,* used to climax their shows by blowing up stacks of expensive Marshall amplifiers, leaving a smoking, debris littered stage behind them as they made their triumphant exit, fists held high in the air. The effect of such a spree on the fans is awesome. Like a pack of howling, bloodthirsty wolves, the crowd screams and bellows for more. "DESTROY . . . DESTROY . . . "

Sometimes this arcane evil hides behind the guise of sexual posturing mixed with outright contempt for any kind of authority. Sweaty, bare chested Rock stars swagger around the stage, sticking out their tongues, jutting their hips and pelvic regions at the audience as they curse and shout lewd dialogues into their hand microphones.

David Lee Roth, former lead singer for the phenomenally rich and popular *Van Halen,* is a prime example of this kind of crude behavior. Roth was detained by authorities after a *Van Halen* show in Cincinnati, Ohio, for openly encouraging the crowd to "light up." (He wasn't talking about cigarettes.) Onstage in Indianapolis, Indiana, in 1980, Roth actually stopped the other *Van Halens* mid-song in order to smoke a joint given to him by a fan, creating near riot-like conditions in the arena.

In the mid Sixties, the late Jim Morrison of *The Doors*

19

many times publicly cursed police security forces at his concerts, calling them "pigs." Once in New Haven, Connecticut, Morrison was maced by his own security for his vulgarity and refusal to obey directions before being dragged from the stage, kicking and fighting. The fans went wild. Morrison's claim to the Rock & Roll Hall Of Fame lies in his arrest and subsequent 1969 court trial for publicly exposing himself during a concert in Miami, Florida.

In the Fall of 1975 at St. John's Arena in Columbus, Ohio, a concert I attended featuring top draw acts *Aerosmith* and *Ted Nugent* very nearly ended in a mass riot. The fans refused to refrain from lighting matches, lighters, paper, and anything flammable every time the house lights dimmed to start the show. A worried management, desperately trying to conform to the State's Fire Code, repeatedly warned that any further audience pyrotechnics would result in cancellation of the concert. The lights went out; the fans set everything within reach afire, and lead singer Steven Tyler and his band *Aerosmith* hit the stage with their opening song.

In reaction to the flaming carnage, the house lights blazed on again. Enraged, Tyler screamed through the band's thousands of watts of vocal amplification, "Turn those !*?%!&* lights off! Turn 'em off!!"

And off they went.

When young people see first hand the immense and instant power wielded by Rock stars, what else can our children do but worship and hunger for the sickness of that warped, unnatural lifestyle?

Increasingly, this PURE EVIL abandons all disguise and simply presents the concept of Evil itself. Satanism sells records. It's a sad and demoralizing fact, but it's true. Bands such as *The Rolling Stones, Black Sabbath, Fleetwood Mac, Motley Crue* and *AC-DC* have built monolithic careers on their mysterious devilish images. It is only when these demonic practitioners of musical Magick occasionally let

20

their masks down a little too far that the numbing reality of their true goal really hits home.

Forces far more powerful than the mere humans involved are being unleashed at these satanic conclaves masquerading as Rock concerts. I have stood in the middle of the Devil's camp and felt his power explode. I felt it at the first concert I attended as well as every one I've been to since. Here is what it's like:

The lights begin dimming. The crowd noise is up. Standing directly in front of the stage, I could almost touch the electricity crackling through the air from the crowd surrounding me. Ten minutes earlier, I had seen a young boy fall to the floor with a bloody broken nose, the result of another young man who went berserk, throwing punches at everyone around him as he screamed nonsense.

Was this a "freak out?"

Even though the boy on the ground was obviously in severe pain, his face bloody and wet from tears, not one person out of the hundreds surrounding him made a move to help him to his feet or to summon aid. The most strenuous action anyone mustered was to get out of his way as he fell. Looking around, I noted the many different expressions on the nearby faces. Amusement, shock, icy, jaded callousness, rage, fear, but absolutely no trace of any kind of empathy or compassion. What a hard and severe generation we are raising! Their heroes are Heroin addicts with guitars. Their toys are liquor bottles and Pot pipes.

A monstrous roar bellowed out from the crowd as the lights went off. A bottle rocket whizzed over my head to explode in a shower of sparks on the ceiling. Sixty seconds went by while the crowd worked itself up to a fever pitch of anticipation. There were two bands playing that night, the Heavy Metal headliners, and the opening act, (usually an up and coming band with either a new Top 40 Single on the national charts, or some kind of outrageous stage gimmick which has given them the attention necessary to allow them to tour).

Shadowy figures took the stage. I could see their sil-houettes moving against the tiny red pilot lights of the amps. An occasional flashlight beam snapped quickly on and off by one of the band's stage crew making last minute checks on the equipment. More intense seconds of waiting went by. At this point, the tension in the air was thick enough to cut with a knife.

A tremendous dynamite explosion rocked the arena at precisely the same second the band's banks of colored floodlights split the dark. The entire stage was brilliantly il-lumined in greens, reds, and purples, revealing the five members of *"Skyjacks"* (the band's name has been changed) an Australian group on their first tour of the United States. Any thought of conversation between mem-bers of the audience was quite impossible, given the jet engine roar of *Skyjacks'* "music." We were inside it and it was inside us.

My eyes opened wide as I stared at the all male band members. The guitar player on the right was wearing a woman's red dress split up the side. He appeared to have just had his hair done at the local beauty parlor. Lipstick smeared his mouth, and a pearl necklace encircled his throat. The other guitarist, stage left, was dressed up in a green and yellow striped jumpsuit. His full facial makeup was a yellow-sepia tone. His lips were black. A silver fright wig topped his head. The bass player was a nondescript col-lege type with no makeup, close cropped hair, and a serious-ly determined expression on his youthful face. The drum-mer had a white burlap mask with eye and nose holes cut in it over his head. His uniform was a black leotard with man-nequin hands sewn onto the outside.

During *Skyjacks'* first "song," the only lyrics decipher-able from the deafening mush were "Give it to me baby, Let me have it ALL . . ." Toward the end of the tune, the singer forced the bass player to his knees, and, using his micro-phone as a prop, proceeded to simulate homosexual acts. The audience roared its approval.

During the standard drum solo, the weird percussionist abruptly quit playing, ran from behind his drum kit, and began rolling about on the stage. The other members of the group stared stupidly. The one with the fright wig smiled. After five minutes of jumping and falling, the "drum solo" was apparently over. Four more lackluster songs went by. The band was now ready for their final tune. With no melody to speak of, and certainly no earth shaking lyrical content, one must wonder how it ever reached the Top 40 charts. Perhaps the ugly rumors about money and drug payoffs to key market radio station managers and disc jockeys in return for airplay are true.

As soon as the song was over, another thunderclap bomb blast signalled the band's exit. Ten foot flames leaped from special "flamepots" spaced strategically around the edge of the stage. The lights abruptly went out, leaving us in total darkness.

Arena personnel manning the Super Trouper spotlights in the very top of the building must have seen an undulating ocean of pinpricks of light far below them. Virtually everyone in the audience had lit something handy and held it high. Bic lighters, full flaming matchbooks, sparklers, burning paper, even an occasional flashlight. It looked like a full scale Christmas Eve candlelight service down there. This is the fans' way of demanding an encore, and for an unknown group like *Skyjacks,* that was quite an honor.

After five minutes of tramping feet thundering above the titanic noise of the crowd in the dark, the band triumphantly returned to blast through a speeded up version of an old *Rolling Stones'* tune.

Final farewells with much waving, and *Skyjacks* was gone for good. This time the house lights stayed on. A prerecorded tape of Rock music by various well known groups began blasting through the massive P.A. of the arena, not as loud as *Skyjacks* had been, but still pretty unbearable from six feet away.

Ignoring the persistent ringing in our ears, my pals and I

started fighting our way through the milling crowd moving away from the stage area. Searching for the main floor exits, Mark loudly heaped excited praise on the audacity of *Skyjacks'* show.

"The music was pretty good, too."

The rest of this gargantuan gathering of 20,000, (their drugs and drink "buzz" beginning to wear off), moved aimlessly about. Like dim-witted sheep just let out of a dark pen, they blinked and stared stupidly.

A tall, wild-eyed man of about thirty came up next to Eddie and asked him if he wanted to buy some Speed. "No thanks." The man, who could have made good use of a shave and a bath, refused to take no for an answer.

"Come on, Man," he said loudly, "This stuff is some clean Black Beauty. It won't give you a stroke like some of that cheap !*?%!&* that's been going around lately."

(Reports on the CBS Evening News have detailed the chilling facts behind a growing black market fake amphetamine industry on the West Coast. Cutting their placebo mixture with a highly volatile but legal chemical, the poison was then peddled as "Speed." Unpredictable in the extreme, this chemical provoked fatal strokes and heart attacks in many teenage purchasers.)

Seeing a break in the crowd, Eddie walked quickly away from the man, who declined to follow. Besides, he was already busily working on another "customer."

While the audience went in search of soft drinks, pizza, posters and T-shirts in the vast arena lobby during intermission, members of the bands' road crews remained on stage, removing *Skyjacks'* equipment, and substituting that of the evening's Heavy Metal stars, *"Bleeding Nun."* (Again, the band's name has been changed.)

One of the biggest in its field, *Bleeding Nun* boasts of having played before more than one million people in the last year. Their third album, (whose cover was decorated with a skeletal fanged monster clutching a dripping hatchet over a dying victim), sold half a million copies in its first two weeks of release.

"The Nun," as they are called by legions of rabid fans, always seem to come up with a more outrageous climax to their shows with the beginning of every new tour. For every fresh obscenity, another thousand records are sold.

The first phase of the Rock concert was now complete. The audience was properly dazed and mentally bombarded, "softened up," in preparation for the main attraction. They were also primed to the gills by the long cycle of waiting, darkness, first band, intermission, more waiting, more darkness.

This vicious cycle has been all too carefully calculated to wring the last possible dollar from the too-full pockets of today's teenager. He buys programs, ($6.00), posters, ($7.00), and shirts, ($15.00). It also is meant to elevate the audience to its utmost height of feverish anticipation, building more and more restless tension to see the main attraction.

During the lengthy intermission, the crowd took full advantage of the time to go outside or to the restrooms where they would pop more pills, swig more booze, and smoke more joints. Like so many thousands of ravenous locusts, the fans stripped bare the many concession stands, leaving smiling peddlers gleefully counting their take.

Uniformed police patrolled the corridors in ones and twos, but seldom did they arrest or even talk to anyone, though many different types of illegal activity were taking place around them at once. These activities included smoking joints, drinking from barely concealed bottles, sniffing various and sundry illicit controlled substances, and openly hawking drugs for sale. Lots of concert goers could care less about the police there, no matter how visible they may be. Stoned on drugs and booze, a false euphoria grips them; they feel as if no authority can reach them. Sometimes outnumbering the police ten to one, they also feel a certain safety in numbers, the New Generation versus the Old Guard.

The sad thing is they're right.

25

The taped music abruptly stopped, signalling the end of the intermission. My friends and I, loaded down with hot dogs, posters, and programs, beat a hasty retreat back inside the auditorium. We decided to sit in the mezzanine rather than fight our way back to the front of the stage again. Too hot, anyway. This new view was completely different from the one we had before. Now we had the advantage of looking down at the stage and the hundreds of people crammed before it like so many sardines. We had barely taken our new seats when the lights were extinguished. A tangible thrill of anticipation shot back and forth across the auditorium.

The teasing five minutes of black silence went by again as the fans held their breath like a pressure cooker waiting to blow.

An earthquake hit the arena.

Twin thunderclaps burst over the astounded heads of the audience just as the 190 decibel buzzsaw scream of over-amplified electric guitars blasted through their brains. (The human pain threshold begins somewhere around 100 decibels.)

Skyjacks had been loud, but nothing like this!

A brilliant white floodlight beam sliced through the dark, hanging at the left side of the stage for thirty seconds. Gunning the engine of a mammoth black 1340 cc Harley Davidson motorcycle, the lead singer of *Bleeding Nun* roared out to center stage, swinging the thousand pound bike around in rubber scorching circles while blue exhaust filled the air.

The crowd absolutely lost its mind.

The sound of 20,000 screaming humans combined with the supersonic din of a Heavy Metal band has to be felt to be clearly understood. They call such fans "Headbangers," and it's not hard to see why.

Dumping the bike on its side, lead singer Rock Skar plucked a microphone from a nearby stand, and let out an ear piercing shriek which could easily have been heard two miles away. Then he punched the mic stand with his fist, knocking it off the stage. Skar's hair was cropped close to his bullet shaped head, military style. A tiny pearl earring adorned one earlobe. His hard, lined, clean-shaven face was twisted into a cruel scowl of disdain. He was dressed like a refugee from Berlin's Gestapo headquarters. Black leather jacket, thick silver-nail-studded belt and wrist bands, knee high jackboots, dangling handcuffs, biker gloves and a long riding crop completed his shirtless costume.

Tearing off his mirrored sunglasses, he screamed a torrent of profanity at the audience.

"I don't know how much the !*?%!&* tickets cost, but I didn't have to pay for 'em!"

The other four members of the *Nun* stood out in a sea of red spotlights. They also sported neo-Nazi metal and leather regalia, but had long, womanish hair, and Fu Manchu moustaches. The two guitar players and the bassist stood a respectful distance behind the singer, letting him harangue the delirious crowd while they continued churning out bone crunching guitar chords. The drummer was nearly hidden amidst his set, but the primal subterranean thump of his bass drum could clearly be felt in the building's shaking windows and rattling door frames.

A huge forty foot viewing screen behind the band came alive with pictures of the *Nun* riding motorcycles through a red flaming Hellscape interspliced with scenes of hydrogen bombs exploding. The half dozen flame pots set into the stage floor belched out pillars of fire on a periodic three second cycle. The viewing screen also showed nothing but a wall of fire. Seemingly enveloped in licking flames, Rock Skar wailed out the dirge-like lyrics of *Bleeding Nun's* first song.

"We walk among you . . . We live within you . . . " he chanted, his voice cracking.

Like a bunch of hypnotized zombies, the other band members joined in on the chorus. The bass player was wearing an upside down cross round his neck. His glazed

27

eyes stared straight ahead into space as he stiffly repeated the words, "We are watching them arrive ... "

Whereas *Skyjacks* had seemed to be bizarre, rather tongue in cheek jokesters, the *Nun* were total professionals. They simply RADIATED the intensity of an obsessive concentrated glorification of evil sneering power. This was not entertainment. This was not a show. This was very serious business.

The basic ugliness at the root of the *Nun's* music sickened some of the more sensitive members of the audience, who proceeded to head for the exits. But they were definitely in the minority. Besides, as far as the promoter is concerned, the entire audience can walk out; they've already paid their money. The majority of the crowd was standing spellbound, rooted to the spot by the creepy vibrations coming from the stage.

The color combination of so much red flame, black spandex and leather touched some basic core in the pit of my stomach, making me feel physically sick. The stunning reality of evil uncovered in its most basic form was affecting various members of the audience differently. Some swayed and yelled in orgasmic pleasure. Other faces registered a primal fear or a blank incomprehension.

When Rock Skar dropped to his knees and produced a long glistening knife stuck through half a dozen dollar bills, a hundred pairs of hands reached out to him immediately, heedless of the blade's razor edge. Several people choked and gasped for breath when the foaming mob behind crushed them into the security barricades. Should someone lose consciousness from the heat or lack of oxygen, they would probably be blindly trampled to death in the mass rioting.

Bleeding Nun's first tune ended with a crashing of guitars and drums that sounded like two freight trains colliding in a garbage can factory. The audience was screaming so loudly Rock Skar could not make himself understood through his microphone, even with 50,000 watts of vocal amplification backing him. (Enough to power a small radio station.)

Now began the second phase of the Rock concert:

HYPNOTISM. Through the application of blinding colored laser light shows, huge viewing screens squirming with violently erotic self-produced images, and voodooishly repetitious music, the *Bleeding Nun* soon had this congregation in the palm of their hand, disoriented, mesmerized, completely open to the heavy subliminal auto-suggestion of their message.

What is that message? Why, it was written all over Rock Skar's hate-distorted face as he smashed a $1,500 Les Paul guitar to bits on the floor of the stage. It was just as plainly stamped on the vacant features of the bass player who stared straight ahead at nothing, a zombie. It was even more obvious in the flushed, sweaty faces of the riot-crazed audience jumping up and down, screaming their lungs out.

Destruction for destruction's sake. Rebellion. Mindless hate. Blind fascist death worship. All done to the backdrop of sizzling laser beams.

Laser light shows are a standard part of today's ultra-sophisticated big time Rock tours. *Blue Oyster Cult* (one of the first groups to develop such effects), has been banned from using theirs in certain parts of the U.S. because of possibile damage to the unprotected eyes of their audience. After this initial flap subsided, the go ahead was more or less uncertainly given to such shows, a windfall the big groups quickly took advantage of before anyone in authority changed their mind. When millions of dollars are at stake regarding tour dates and the successful completion of those dates on time, as advertised, city councilmen can be bought off, and high pressure promoters threatened with bankruptcy in order to insure that the tour runs smoothly.

Consequently, not only are our children being hypnotized en masse by an extremely sophisticated and manipulative series of flashing laser lights, they may also very well be blinding themselves at the same time.

Destroyed hearing. Destroyed vision. Destroyed mind and soul. So far, the Rock concert doesn't seem to have very many positive things going for it.

The fans, bathed in green, revolving, ribbon-thin beams of pulsating light, looked on with amazement as Rock Skar drew a short bladed knife across his palm, then his wrist. Was he bleeding? No one could really tell in the weird half-light. *The Nun* was busy crashing through the best known song on their newest album, "Sin Follows Sin." The two guitar players slid their instruments off their shoulders and formed a cross with the necks. When they rubbed the electrified strings against each other, a noise was created which sounded much like artillery shells hitting an Army ammunition dump.

An imposing thirty foot tall crucifix-question mark edged with winking neon lights rose slowly behind the band. This logo appears on all their albums. Air raid sirens wailed while the flame pots belched out plumes of fire. Rock Skar raised his head to the ceiling and howled like a wild beast.

Here was the third and final phase of the Rock Concert: UNBRIDLED INSANE MADNESS AND ANARCHY. Wanton destruction. Total bombardment of the senses till pandemonium ensued, an apt description meaning "place of demons." Technically, that is what all this carefully con-trived folderol had been leading up to, the wild unleashing of each persons' private demons, the ultimate in intense celebration of wicked licentiousness.

Flames lick out toward you. Bombs explode in your face. Searing lights blind your eyes. Your ears are deafened from the titanic buzzsaw roar. Somewhere in front of you a drool-ing Nazi in Gestapo drag cackles and points at you insanely. What is there left for this audience to do but scream?

The pace quickened from there. Playing with the height-ened emotions of the crowd, singer Rock Skar bellowed out the song that made him famous, "Rock & Roll Damnation." His wheezy screech reached new heights of snottiness when he yelled, "You're gonna live in sin . . . You're only young, but you're gonna die . . . "

A firecracker thrown from the floor exploded near his face. He ignored it.

Twirling his heavy mic stand around his head, Skar brought it down to the stage with a splintery smash. He then beat it into the wood until it was no longer functional. This was a signal to the rest of the band, who immediately followed suit with their own instruments.

Smoke poured from the bass player's guitar; he whipped it off and threw it at Rock Skar, who proceeded to dismember the instrument, using a sputtering McCullough chain saw. Wood chips and sawdust flew. The drummer kicked his set over. Drums and cymbals tumbled off the ten foot elevated drum platform, barely missing one of the guitarists below. Floor toms and bass drums bounced, smashed, and rolled across the stage.

A stack of Marshall amps blew up, a sizzling shower of sparks erupting from the smoking speaker cabinets. Police sirens and a dozen high powered strobe lights turned the stage into a surreal slow motion horror movie.

The two lead guitarists, with both hands grasping each of their instruments like baseball bats, planted their feet firmly and stared fixedly at each other. A gut wrenching swing, and they smashed the guitars together with a car crash blast of whining concussive force. Shattered over-amplified pickups and split melted wiring created a monstrous feedback scream that could have made dogs howl in pain.

Smoking, sparking debris littered the stage. *The Bleeding Nun,* in full glory and conquering triumph, raised their arms in Nazi-like salutes. Skar even goose stepped.

Pandemonium reigned supreme.

A dry ice manufactured fog eerily suffused the scene, crawling over and around the musicians until they were mere ghosts in the mist. Finally, they disappeared from sight altogether. Twin red spotlights trained on a hulking, demonic horned face drifted eerily eight feet above the stage, the atypical artist's conception of Satan, complete with green glowing eyes. The complex piece of machinery turned scarlet through the thick clouds of fog. Its mouth worked, and a great booming voice filled the arena.

"We are your Gods," it intoned in a deep, shivery, bone chilling bass. "We are your Gods!"

Twenty thousand candidates for the madhouse took up the chant, yelling it at the top of their lungs, "WE ARE YOUR GODS!!!"

The artificial mist thinned, blown away by ventilators at either end of the stage platform. The red spots snapped off, replaced by one lone gargantuan white floodlight which illuminated a battered 1969 Buick automobile center stage.

A grinning Rock Star, his mirrored sunglasses scintillating in the glare, held what appeared to be a sizzling stick of dynamite. Tossing it in the front seat of the Buick, he bolted for the exits. Members of the stage crew were holding their ears.

The car blew up with a muffled boom. Thick black smoke poured from the shattered windshield.

This was the finale, something the star-struck teenagers in the audience would rave about for a week to their friends at school.

"Wow, man, the *Nun* blew up a car at the end of their show. You should have seen it!"

Even though the frenzied fans stomped, screamed, wailed and lit matches for a full ten minutes, the *Nun* did not return for an encore.

After checking with their road manager about the evening's take, (about $75,000 for an extremely brief hour long set), the band was already heading for their opulent suites at the local Hyatt Regency or Hilton Hotels. Chauffeur driven limousines whisked them out of the arena grounds to their destination, stopping only long enough to pick up three willing teenage females waiting outside the arena's service entrance.

Once safely settled in their plush rooms, drunken sexual debaucheries will get under way with the band, their thirty man road crew, and the swarms of eager under-age girls lining the hotel corridors, anxious for a glimpse of their beloved stars. Occasionally, as the decadent orgy loses momentum, band members and their sycophants may begin destroying anything in sight to relieve the pressure and boredom of being rich Rock stars on the road.

Color TV sets fly from balcony windows to land in the pool below. Expensive stereos are submerged in bathtubs, while room service food trays are flung from one end of the hall to the other. One band member sprays anything that moves with his fire extinguisher. Naked men and women chase each other through the mess, howling and screaming. Three rooms down, the drummer is busily working on the exquisitely wallpapered bedroom of his $100 a day suite with a sledgehammer.

Back at the arena, the fans finally got the message that the show was over. Mark, Eddie, and myself joined the thousands of others evacuating the auditorium.

The arena's maintenance people spent the next few hours cleaning up the mind boggling mess of vomit, blood, urine, discarded clothing, broken glass, cigarette butts and joint "roaches," empty food and drink containers, and hundreds of liquor bottles.

On my way outside, I noticed that many fans were leaning on their friends or lovers, too drunk or stoned to walk by themselves. Soon enough they wouldn't have to worry about walking properly; they'd be behind the wheel of a car instead.

Mile-long lines of automobiles began forming; drug and drink shortened tempers flared as impatient drivers leaned on their horns or shouted out obscenities at the sluggish traffic. A skeleton crew of half a dozen whistle blowing police pointed the cars out of the parking lot. No attempts were made to stop weaving drivers as long as they didn't hit anyone. Those overworked cops simply wanted to go home and call it a night.

And so, my first Rock concert was over. Even though we didn't realize it at the time, my friends and I had been treat-ed to a brain bashing display of smut, profanity, destruction, Satanism, and lewdness, not to mention the eye popping scenes of homosexuals kissing and holding hands, whiskey guzzling youngsters, half undressed young ladies, and dope smoking on a scale that has to be seen to be believed.

What did we and the thousands of other young people there learn from this experience? What practical, positive benefits emerged from this situation?

Well, we all knew where to go to buy drugs. We knew how easy it was to smuggle booze in under the very noses of the police. We knew how to lie to our parents about what went on at the concert. ("Oh, nothin' Mom."). And Eddie even knew what he wanted to be when he got older.

"I'm gonna have a band when I turn sixteen," he was bragging to Mark during our ride home. "I'm gonna be a !*?%!&* Rock Star . . . "

CHAPTER 3

Demons in the House

"For we wrestle not against flesh and blood, but against principalities, against powers, against the rulers of the darkness of this world, against spiritual wickedness in high places."   Ephesians 6:12

"You get into evil, you're a friend of mine . . ."   *AC-DC*[1]

There is no question that Christians everywhere believe that a satanic conspiracy exists solely for the purpose of bending and warping our young people's minds to its insane wavelength through the medium of Rock & Roll. Our children's very souls are the stakes in this fiendish game. The case of a mass murderer, the "Night Stalker," is a perfect example. (Los Angeles, 1985)

For all the social apologists and die-hard Rock worshipers out there who say that Rock & Roll is simply a harmless and healthy outlet for violent urges and pent up frustrations, I submit this case.

"The Night Stalker" killed 20 innocent people and attacked two dozen others by a variety of methods including gunshots, stabbings, strangulation, and torture. Children were molested in the course of his nocturnal prowlings, and some victims were raped as they lay dying, their throats slashed and their eyes gouged out. What's all this grisliness got to do with Rock & Roll?

Pentagrams were drawn on the walls of the dead victims' homes. The words, "AC-DC" and "Jack The Knife" (from a *Judas Priest* song) were also inscribed on the walls in the rooms which became torture chambers as a few feet away mutilated bodies gasped out their last breaths.

One of *AC-DC's* songs from the "Highway To Hell" LP called "Night Prowler" described this method of stalking and killing to a "T" — 6 years before the murders occurred! Here are some of the lyrics from *AC-DC's* "Night Prowler:"

"I'm you're Night Prowler
I sleep in the day
I'm your Night Prowler
Get out of my way . . .
Too scared to turn your light out
Cause there's something on your mind
Was that a noise outside the window
What's that shadow on the blind
As you lie there naked, Like a body in a tomb
Suspended animation, as I slip into your room . . . "

Police have, at the time of this writing, in custody a suspect whom they think is the killer. His name is Richard Ramirez. Ramirez claims his favorite Rock group is *AC-DC*. Ramirez painted and had tattooed on his body a pentagram. (Just like the necklace dead *AC-DC* singer Bon Scott wears on the "Highway To Hell" LP cover, and just like the ones used by virtually every Heavy Metal Devil-Rock band around.)

This alleged "Night Stalker" came from a generation-gapped home and raised himself as so many young people do today. It is reported that he got into drugs, Heavy Metal music and Satanism. Besides *AC-DC* and other Heavy Metal groups, *Judas Priest* is also reported as being one of Ramirez' favorites.

AC-DC tells young minds how to vent their frustration and rage on the helpless; how to seek more satanic power through music. Rock music encourages them to open all the doors of their souls through drugs, thereby inviting into their bodies and minds every unclean thing that is out there. As he sat in a California courtroom during his trial in the Fall of 1985, the accused killer, Ramirez, shouted out in a loud voice for the spectators to hear, "HAIL SATAN!"

> "I've got my bell
> I'm gonna take you to Hell
> Gonna get ya
> Satan get ya
> Hell's Bells . . . "
> — "Hell's Bells" by *AC-DC*

Satan snatching kids' souls through Rock & Roll? The Devil dictating musical murder?

These are rather strong statements to swallow. Few people today, preoccupied with surviving in the ultra-complex world of the 1980's, believe in Satan as a living arcane force of mind bending power, much less in a world-wide conspiracy to enslave whole generations of innocent, curious young people. This very rejection of the reality of evil is Satan's greatest strength and stronghold.

Many Spirit-led Christians understand that Rock music is a part of a worldwide satanic web of intrigue. (See Appendix A) Some of the best known Rock tunes are based on ancient Druidic melodies and dirge-like tones, a hypnotic blend of evil rhythm and lewd lyrics which surround the listener's mind, blocking out any but Satan's secret messages.

The Lord has also revealed to some Christians that incarnate demons from the netherworld actually are members of some of the most popular bands, gleefully steering the human Rockers into new paths of evil licentiousness, spurred on by their own greed and lust for fame and power. Thousands of innocent listeners as well as the band members who make the music are corrupted by Satan's songs.

Though at first glance this idea seems quite absurd to some, let's take a closer look at some of today's premier Rock bands and their music.

Rock groups today have already surpassed the wealth, fame, and public adoration of the Hollywood megastars of the Forties. With an arrogant, sneering, cynical depravity, they thumb their noses at the fans who made them famous, treating them like feudal serfs serving the almighty king.

Our young people enjoy this masochistic self-abuse immensely. The money they earn from part-time jobs, babysitting, paper routes, and allowances is squandered immediately on some form of musical entertainment, whether it be records, tapes, concerts, posters, music books, or Rock magazines.

We are witnessing a bizarre sociological phenomenon here: tens of millions of dollars are stuffed into the pockets of the latest trendy Rock group while the fans who spent that money wait like vultures to see how long it takes for the band to self-destruct. Some groups fall quickly by the wayside, pathetic victims of their artificial lifestyles. Others, like *The Rolling Stones,* seem to go on forever, almost as if they had a blood-stained pact with the Devil. They do! Eternal youth and incredible wealth are traded for infecting millions with the sick message at the heart of Rock & Roll.

Still other Devil-worshiping groups add and drop members right and left, changing and transforming the bands they leave, and enter into even greater strongholds of satanic strength.

For example, occult witchcraft enthusiast Ritchie Blackmore quit Heavy Metal forerunner *Deep Purple* to form his own band, *Rainbow.* A pompous little leather-lunged singer named Ronnie James Dio joined Blackmore's new outfit, using his strong writing ability to pen songs about the mystic power of the pyramids, witches, warlocks, and werewolves. After quitting *Rainbow* with four albums under his belt, Dio replaced the disgusting Ozzy Osbourne as *Black Sabbath's* lead vocalist. The name of the album he debuted on: "Heaven And Hell."

Here are some quotes directly from Dio:

> "At least I understand something about the occult, which is more than I can say about certain bands that use pentagrams and upside down crosses as their emblems..."[2]

> "In order to write logically and sensibly about a subject, you have to learn about it. I'm INFORMED about the darker side of our lives..."[3]

Who's doing the informing? Dio is not Ronnie James' real name. His last name is actually Padovana. Dio means "God" in Italian. This guy calls himself and his band God!

THE ROLLING STONES

As the absolute reigning Kings of the satanic world of Rock, however, *The Rolling Stones* would win any contest hands down. Even though its members are well over thirty, (one is almost fifty!), *The Stones* now hold sway over a devoted listening audience so huge as to boggle the mind.

Having survived suicides, riots, murders, nervous breakdowns, heroin addiction, massive drug usage, jail terms, divorce, and the contempt and disgust of a large portion of society, *The Stones* roll on, indestructible and that much stronger for having come through such adversity intact. Death is their spoor, but their money, fame and power continue to grow with every year the band stays in existence.

Twenty years at the top of their profession have taken a heavy toll on the band members, however. The lines in Mick Jagger's face are deeply etched; Keith Richards, his hair streaked with gray, has false teeth, his natural set having rotted away years ago from heavy prolonged cocaine abuse. Former rhythm guitarist Mick Taylor required a plastic insertion to be surgically implanted in his nose to correct a perforated septum (the cartilaginous partition between the nostrils) burned away by massive cocaine use. He eventually quit the band because of the surreal drugged lifestyle he saw himself slipping into as a direct result of being a *Rolling Stone.*

Both Jagger and Richards are virtually men without countries, their drug and criminal records keeping them from establishing permanent residences throughout the world.

Keith Richards particularly has carried the brunt of the band's misfortunes over the years. (Some would say he deserves every bit of it.) His young daughter was born with a deformed mouth and now lives with Richards' mother in England.

Keith's long-time mistress (until the mid 80's), was Anita Pallenberg, a former heroin addict like himself. During the recording of the smash *Stones'* album "Emotional Rescue" in 1980, Keith worked in Paris as Anita added another bizarre chapter to the already bloated anthology of weird *Stones'* catastrophes.

A seventeen year old caretaker at the Richards' New England estate was found shot to death in Anita Pallenberg's bed. Anita was home at the time. A subsequent police investigation and court appearance by Pallenberg resulted in her being fined for possessing an unregistered hand gun, (the "suicide" weapon).

An article reprinted from the English pulp newspaper "Midnite," quoted a Ridgefield, Connecticut police officer named Michael Passaro as having investigated "strange singing" coming from the woods a quarter mile from Keith

Richards' New England mansion, (the same house where the teenage caretaker was found dead).[4]

According to "Midnite,"

> "There have been several bizarre satanic rituals in the area over the past five years. A local reporter attributed the outbreak of occultism to 'rich people taking Acid.'"[5]

To fully comprehend Pallenberg's eerie devilish relationship to the disasters which seem to constantly befall *The Stones* and their entourage, some background on this self-proclaimed sorceress might be helpful.

Anita first met *The Rolling Stones* in 1965, during the initial wave of their enormous popularity. She refused to reveal any details of her life, and really, such things were unimportant, given her stunning beauty and obviously sophisticated intelligence. She would only say that she was a European actress. Pallenberg soon began an intense relationship with founding member Brian Jones, a neurotic and sadistically cruel man whose sexual and narcotic appetites were quickly reaching legendary proportions. This relationship ended ultimately in Jones' miserable death in 1969, caused in part by Anita's desertion of him for Keith Richards as her new lover.

Brian Jones had been in need of psychological help for years, according to early *Stones'* mentor Giorgio Gomelski, who gave them their first steady job at his Crawdaddy Club.

> Brian was "A boy who should have had treatment; his responses were never those of a normal person," Gomelski is quoted as saying in George Tremlett's *The Rolling Stones.*[6]

In terms of pure evil incarnate decadence, Lewis Brian Hopkin-Jones holds no peers.

Here is his philosophy on life:

> "What has proved to be the ruination of many people has been the making of me. I went against everything I had been brought up to believe in."[7]

Jones had several illegitimate children before meeting Pallenberg. He simply ignored them and their mothers. Shortly after inviting Anita to live with him, Jones refused to even see one of his former girl friends who was begging him for some kind of child support. He and Anita giggled inside his apartment while the girl and her baby cried helplessly outside the locked door.

Jones carried a dog chain with him. He often used it to beat his women. Sometimes he would break a bottle over a table edge, then carry the jagged neck in his pocket when he went out, waiting for the right opportunity to slash anyone who annoyed him. He once bragged of sleeping with sixty women in one month, which was no big deal to someone as drenched in sexual debauchery as he.

His graceful charm and wickedly ageless features enabled Brian Jones to scale heights and mount conquests in the ultra chic London society of 1965 that would never have been available normally to a man of his lower middle-class background. His private life was much different from the public persona, however. Misery and self-doubting paranoia dogged him all the days of his short life, like a demon at his back. Not content to send his own soul to Hell, Jones constantly felt the need to drag his friends down into the abyss with him. In Anita Pallenberg, he found a perfect partner for his brutal games. With Pallenberg a willing helper, these two evil creatures descended to depths of druggish depravity better left unsaid.

Pallenberg and Jones used LSD and practiced Black Magic. The mind-eating drug quickly became the focal point of Jones' sordid lifestyle, marking the beginning of the end of his brief career. The evil spells they cast together opened the door to a series of weird events still not fully understood twenty years later.

The next few years would find Jones a near vegetable, his mind blown from abuse of nearly every drug known to man. Busted time and again by police, sentenced to prison, fined unmercifully many times in court, he still stubbornly refused to change his decadent ways. Instead, he retreated further and further within himself until, at last, the final crushing blow to his wasted life fell. Beaten and degraded once too often, Anita left him for Keith Richards.

Brian Jones' whirlwind descent into misery and suicidal self-destruction had begun. Many times *The Rolling Stones'* guitarist would seem to regain control of his drug shattered existence only to slip back into the self-inflicted churning whirlpool that was eating him alive.

After an aborted attempt to drown himself at Keith Richards' English estate at Redlands, Jones seemed to snap out of his suicidal nightmare momentarily. He flew to North Africa for a long vacation where he met Bryon Gysin and recorded "The Pipes Of Pan At Joujouka," an album featuring primitive devil worshipers using music to call up demons.

Bryon Gysin was a photographer who was intimately acquainted with the Joujouka tribe. When their paths crossed, Jones' excitement at capturing an authentic demon calling ceremony on tape knew no bounds. With his insatiable appetite for the occult, he was immediately transfixed by Gysin's description of the primitive tribe's weird activities.

The two travelers soon set off for the mountains. A European sound man with an expensive Uher tape recorder tagged along. They arrived at Joujouka just before the Rites Of Pan Festival, a yearly event in which the natives worked their infernal magic while under the influence of masses of psychedelics. Mesmerized by the music of the voodoo ritual, the tribesmen spun in circles and fell to the ground like epileptics having fits. Their bodies were painted to represent ancient primeval forces like the Greek god Pan.

Jones and his friends stood in the middle of the screaming, sweating throng, their microphones held high and their tapes rolling while all around them the natives howled and leaped as the power of Satan's demons washed over them.

Days later, Brian Jones become convinced that a goat sacrificed by the Joujoukans was meant as a curse of death aimed directly at him. He wasted no time in packing up his sound equipment and returning to London. With his demonic tapes in hand, he entered a recording studio to expand on the hellish sounds of the Joujouka ceremony. Listening to the tapes backwards and forwards, Jones used sophisticated studio techniques to add electronic overdubs to the music, eventually releasing the finished product as an album.

Not content with simply producing a cursed record of actual demon-calls, he quickly incorporated much of the Joujouka musical styles he had memorized into the next *Rolling Stones* album as well.

Its title: "Their Satanic Majesties Request"

This project was the beginning of the end for Brian Jones.

As he was growing more and more dependent on his masses of pills and powders, Brian became proportionately less and less dependable to the other *Stones*. Showing up late at studios too stoned to play, his traveling visas revoked because of his many drug trials and convictions, unable to tour with the band he had originated, a whining, sobbing, emotional wreck, Jagger and Richards finally had no choice but to fire Brian Jones, the man who had started *The Rolling Stones* in the first place. They agreed to pay him $240,000 per year for as long as the group stayed together as compensation. He took the news well and set about auditioning members for a new band. Much time was also spent improving and renovating his newly purchased English estate at Cotchford Farm, former home of "Winnie The Pooh" creator A.A. Milne.

At midnight on July 2, 1969, Brian Jones died.

His death is still shrouded in mystery, nearly eighteen years later. The official police report states that only three other people were present at Cotchford Farm that evening. Yet Keith Richards himself said in a later interview with Rolling Stone Magazine that, according to his sources, a wild party had been in progress at the estate the night of Jones' death.

> "Some very weird things happened that night Brian died . . . there were people there that suddenly disappeared . . . And someone called us up at midnight and said: 'Brian's dead' . . ."8

Though he suffered from occasional asthma attacks, and an asthma inhaler was found by the swimming pool the next day, the autopsy report stated that no evidence of an asthma attack had been found in the dead man's lungs, only that he had drowned in what was officially labeled "Death By Misadventure."

Even though he was often extremely paranoid, even psychotically so, Brian did not take his own life, swears Alexis Korner, the man who discovered singer Mick Jagger. An old friend and confidante who knew all *The Stones* as well as anyone on earth, Korner spoke at length about Brian's death:

> "I really think it was a mistake. I don't think he deliberately planned to commit suicide . . . because he was happy at that time. At least he died when he was beginning to feel happy . . ."9

If Brian Jones didn't commit suicide, then exactly what were the circumstances surrounding his death? In his surreal world of orgiastic parties and massive, uncontrolled drug intake, could the Rock star have simply fallen into his own swimming pool and been too stoned to get out? Or is it possible that some person or persons wouldn't LET him get out of the pool, holding his alcohol and drug devoured body under the water until he stopped breathing?

The only evidence to support such a theory is the fact

that a few days after his death, someone entered Jones' house, using a key, and stripped it of everything of any value. Furniture, expensive rugs, musical instruments, recording and sound equipment — nothing was left.

Jones was a firm believer in astrology and the occult. His insatiable thirst for fiendish explorations into the darker side of human nature opened the door to forces beyond his control. Some of his closest friends were practicing Satanists. Were demon spirits unleashed that hot summer night to put an end to the former *Stone?*

Brian Jones was convinced a curse had been placed on him during his stay at the voodooish village of Joujouka — a curse of death which relentlessly followed him across two continents. This evil man died at just the right time for *The Stones'* career to really take off. Having served his purpose guiding the band through six years of garish, exhibitionist, immoral anarchy, court trials, and screaming newspaper headlines, (which only served to catapult them to ever higher levels of popularity), this dangerous madman died, thereby ensuring THROUGH HIS MARTYRDOM that *The Rolling Stones* would become the biggest, most influential Rock act the world has ever seen.

The Stones also have a member who probably holds the world's record for avoiding drug prosecution: Keith Richards. This man has been known to kick fans at the edge of the stage in the face and knock photographers down flights of steps.

Advocating complete decadent amorality for the better part of twenty-two years, Richards was Brian Jones' apt pupil during *The Stones'* heyday in the early Sixties. Having surpassed his late mentor in hedonistic debauchery long ago, this miserable wretch wrote what surely must be the final chapter in a long wasted life of brutal excess. Under Canadian indictment for heroin trafficking in 1977, Richards, a hopelessly addicted junkie, had his ENTIRE BLOOD SUPPLY transfused with a fresh eight pints by a Florida doctor flown to Switzerland especially for the occasion. Thus, no more heroin addiction for the court appointed tests . . . until the next fix. Richards has allegedly undergone this operation several times, replenishing his drug decayed body with the fresh blood of innocent donors.

The following is some of the wit and wisdom of Keith Richards:

> **On the power of evil:** "Kenneth Anger told me I was his right hand man. . . Once you start, there's no going back . . . "[10]

> **On drugs:** "If you're gonna get wasted, get wasted elegantly."[11]

> **On law and order:** "I mean, your laws don't apply to me . . ."[12]

> **On Rock & Roll:** "Rock & Roll starts from the neck down . . . Nukes may obsess your brain, but they really don't obsess your crotch. It's a few minutes when you can forget about nukes and racism and all the other evils God's kindly thrown upon us . . . "[13]

An extremely sickening scene is depicted in the book *Keith Richards — Life As A Rolling Stone,* by Barbara Charone, giving us a glimpse into just how a Rock star relaxes at home between concert tours and recording dates. Keith's favorite pastime was staring at TV or into the fireplace of his English estate, Redlands. When boredom became too unbearable, he would inject heroin into his body. Anita Pallenberg, also a junkie, would spend most of her day changing clothes, snorting cocaine, and alternately babbling nonsense before flying into a screaming rage. The couple's young boy, Marlon, (judging by photographs, Marlon appeared to be about seven years old at the time), was a constant witness to everything.

Keith would bring out his "works," a needle, syringe, rubber tube to tie off the vein, the packet of heroin, of course, and a spoon to hold the powder as it was turned into liquid prior to injection. This man, the adored idol to millions of youngsters not much older than his own son, would sit in the living room in front of his little boy and shove a needle into his arm. Imagine Marlon watching his father remove the syringe, then slump back in his seat as the "Smack" knocked him out momentarily, his eyes rolling up in his head and his mouth drooling.

"Unto the pure all things are pure: but unto them that are defiled and unbelieving is nothing pure; but even their mind and conscience is defiled." — Titus 1:15.

In performance during the heroin years, (roughly 1971 to 1979), Keith Richards was an eerie, shambling monster on stage, with his vacant skeletal grin and drug-dimmed, lackluster appearance. He wallowed in his image as the amoral druggie outcast, bragging of his fascination with illicit chemicals and Black Magic on many occasions for fawning interviewers and writers anxious to please the famous Rocker.

Discussing Keith Richards brings up an interesting topic — are Rock stars as stupid as they appear? Just to look and listen to them, one would think that they were barely smart enough to tie their own shoes. My opinion is that sometimes a few of them are indeed functional idiots, but more often than not, they are possessed of a high, (or perhaps HIGHER) intelligence. Mick Jagger, Keith Richards, and Anita Pallenberg are all extremely astute and knowledgeable people, but jaded and unwholesome in their intellectual scope. The vast quantities of psychoactive drugs they have ingested over the years, combined with their life in the fast lane existence has smartened them up above and beyond the norm. What good has it done them, except to insulate them from the real world and plunge them into a paranoid, totally self-indulgent prison of their own making? Instead of trying to help others through the knowledge they possess, they continually plow it all back into the perpetuation of Rock & Roll, a dead-end street if ever there was one. These people are the road crew of the Highway to Hell.

Keith's flirtation with the Black Arts was greatly advanced by the woman he had stolen from Brian Jones: Anita Pallenberg. The whole affair very quickly got completely out of hand. How? In the late Sixties Anita became acquainted with one of the foremost warlock-satanists of this century — Kenneth Anger. A pioneer in avant-garde cinema, film maker Anger is not your run-of-the-mill movie director. He completed a movie about incest before his twelfth birthday. The film that launched his career, "Fireworks," was made when he was seventeen. It contained scenes of startling and grotesque sexual imagery, such as a sailor's sex organ exploding into a 4th of July fireworks, and a man's body being torn apart to reveal pulsating insides and a gas meter heart.

Anita was fascinated by Anger's self proclaimed powers of darkness. She practiced witchcraft under his teaching, casting spells on her personal enemies with great success. She kept old bones, roots, and pieces of animals locked away in a bureau for safekeeping, to be used later during her devil worshiping rituals. She wore garlic round her neck when sleeping to ward off vampires.

Here is Kenneth Anger's personal opinion on both Anita Pallenberg and Brian Jones, a man he knew well, as printed in an interview conducted by David Dalton and Richard Henderson which later appeared in Dalton's exhaustive study of the Stones:

> Anger: "I believe that Anita is, for want of a better word, a witch . . . The occult unit within *The Stones* was Keith and Anita . . . and Brian. You see, Brian was a witch, too. I'm convinced. He showed me his witch's tit. He had a supernumerary tit in a very sexy place on his inner thigh. He said: 'In another time they would have burned me.'"[14]

In 1969, Kenneth Anger released an eleven minute film

49

he had spent his life working on: "Invocation Of My Demon Brother." Mick Jagger contributed to the music for the score; his brother Chris acted in the infamous mass of celluloid, as did Mick's girl friend at the time, Marianne Faithfull. The actor portraying Lucifer was a young Californian named Bobby Beausoleil, a former member of the West Coast Rock group *Love*. After months of filming, Beausoleil went berserk, stealing Anger's car and several prints of the devilish film. He then fled London for California.

Shortly thereafter, Beausoleil carried out a grisly murder in Los Angeles. Left behind was a mutilated, butchered corpse and the words "Political Piggy" dripping in blood down the wall of the victim's apartment. Tried and jailed for the crime, it would be months before a chilling fact would come to light: Bobby Beausoleil's closest friend was mass murderer Charles Manson!

Here is Kenneth Anger's own description of "Invocation Of My Demon Brother:"

> "The shadowing forth of our Lord Lucifer as the Powers of Darkness gather at a midnight mass."[15]

Playing His satanic Majesty in the film was Anton Szandor La Vey, author of a satanic Bible and head of San Francisco's First Church Of Satan.

What a coincidence it is that *The Rolling Stones* had released a record in 1967 titled "Their Satanic Majesties Request." Nightmarish and dreamy songs, combined with a mystical, occultish concept for the LP's cover and inner sleeve, marked the record as a thoroughly drugged piece of negativism. *The Stones* had originally wanted a picture of a naked Mick Jagger hanging on a cross to adorn the inside of the album, but this idea was later discarded.

Everyone associated with Kenneth Anger has suffered from that association in one way or another.

Keith Richards and Anita Pallenberg, originally close

friends with the satanist, later fearfully backed out of having Anger marry them in a pagan wedding ceremony, frightened by his powers. They were convinced he had the ability to enter their home in spirit form whenever he wished, bypassing the heavily locked doors and multitudes of sophisticated alarm systems installed throughout the mansion.

Kenneth Anger talked with the man who killed John Lennon — Mark David Chapman — six weeks before the murder took place in late 1980. Chapman was attending a film lecture given by Anger in Hawaii where Chapman lived at the time. Lennon's killer met with Anger after the lecture, pumping the demonologist with questions about John and Yoko.

Six weeks later, Lennon was dead.[16]

Anger so excited *Led Zeppelin* guitar genius Jimmy Page with tales of the legendary psycho-sexual necromancer Aleister Crowley (1875-1947), that Page immediately bought Crowley's ancient abandoned castle on the shores of Loch Ness, Scotland. The next few years would find *Led Zeppelin* fighting off disaster after tragic disaster until the group finally disintegrated over the untimely death of their drummer in 1980.

Kenneth Anger claims to belong to the same demonic secret society as his depraved mentor, Aleister Crowley, the self proclaimed "Beast 666." The society is called "The Order Of The Golden Dawn," and both Anger and Crowley bear the title of "Magus," the loftiest ascension possible in their occult Brotherhood. Anger himself played the part of Magus in "Invocation Of My Demon Brother." It should be obvious that the demon brother in question was the dead Aleister Crowley.

At Crowley's English funeral at Brighton in 1947, his followers were instructed to recite his self-composed poem, "Hymn To Pan" as his body was set afire. Pan was the musical sex-god of the fields, according to Greek mythology. His upper torso was that of a man; his legs and cloven hoofs were those of a goat.

51

This morbid, dangerous fascination with the dead mystic Crowley doesn't stop with *The Stones* and *Led Zeppelin,* however. Other prominent Rockers have also discovered the evil Black Magician, using his name to promote their own insanity. Ozzy Osbourne, for example, the former lead singer for satanic Rock group *Black Sabbath,* has a song on his 1981 "Blizzard Of Oz" album entitled "Mr. Crowley."

Flying from continent to continent and country to country, the ancient evil of Satan has swallowed up more than one Rock star foolish enough to dabble with the Devil. *The Rolling Stones* were both victims and vessels for this arcane power to flow through.

Beginning in 1967 with "Satanic Majesties," *The Stones* have mined the sulphurous mother lode of Rock & Roll demonism with a vengeance. Their blockbuster LP "Goat's Head Soup" featured a pull out poster of a rotting goat's head swimming in a boiling cauldron. (See figure 2.) The songs on the album were laced with references to witchcraft, such as burning "your bell, book, and candle" on "Winter," and a meeting with a decayed corpse in a graveyard in "Dancing With Mr. D." The title of their 1969 live album, "Get Yer Ya Ya's Out," was taken from an African voodoo chant.

On December 6, 1969, *The Rolling Stones* held a free concert at Altamont Speedway, in California. The next day the world was shocked to hear of the brutal stabbing of a member of the audience at the infamous event. A disaster in every sense of the word, the concert was an ill-planned, last minute affair which reached fruition only by the megalomanic demands of Mick Jagger. He wished to have a film of a concert to rival Woodstock, with *The Stones* as head gurus. Having hired the California Hell's Angels as "security" for the concert in return for $500 worth of beer, *The Stones* looked on helplessly as the Angels sadistically beat members of the audience with pool cues, threatened them with knives and guns, and drove their motorcycles through the dazed crowd on bets, heedless of who they ran

Figure 2

Goat's Head Soup.

over. One young black man named Meredith Hunter was seen waving a pistol at the stage where *The Rolling Stones* cavorted, spinning their insane tapestry of musical violence, a few feet away. Half a dozen Hell's Angels jumped on the unfortunate boy, stabbing him to death and grinding a bucket into his eyes.

When the deadly concert was at last over, Mick Jagger left the stage after thanking the Angels profusely for their "protection."

A young writer named Stanley Booth was traveling with *The Stones* all through the Altamont period, gathering material for a book that eventually was published in 1984 titled, *Dance With the Devil.* Booth himself was backstage at Altamont, and also shared in the sins of *The Stones'* sick lifestyle while on the road with them. There are two accounts in his book that paint a perfect picture of just what it was like to be a guest in *The Stones'* evil empire at that time.

Petty criminals that they were, *The Rolling Stones* recorded one of their biggest selling albums of all time, "Sticky Fingers," ILLEGALLY while on their 1969 U.S. tour. None of *The Stones* were members of any Musicians' Union at the time, and didn't want to be, either. The band sneaked in and out of recording studios all through the South in the dead of night. Rather than pay a simple paltry fee and abide by the law, *The Stones* thumbed their noses at America and made a smash record without abiding by any of the rules lesser mortals must follow.

Another revealing insight into the sexual side of *Stones'* tours also comes from Booth's book, where a young female fan says,

> *"The Stones'* third tour, when I was 18, opened my eyes to — everything . . . Men with men, girls with girls, I walked into this room and all these people were fornicating right out in the open . . . "[17]

Finally, Stanley Booth interviewed Brian Jones' father after Brian's miserable death. The elder Jones summed up the total philosophy of his son, the other *Stones,* and millions of kids around the globe when he said,

> "Brian was obsessed with music . . . These records were playing morning, noon, and night. I saw it as a positive evil in his life, undermining a quite good career. Maybe music was his eventual downfall, but at the time I saw it as an evil because he was so obsessed . . . But to him — a religion it was, he was a fanatic . . . "[18]

54

As *The Stones* roll on through the Eighties, they show no signs of discarding their Black Magic persona. It's proven far too valuable for them commercially, and who knows, after twenty years of such demonic posturing, perhaps it is no longer "just an image," (in reality, it never was — see Appendix).

To promote their 1981 LP "Tattoo You," *The Rolling Stones* embarked on a standing-room-only sellout tour which would, by some reports, gross them well over $80,000,000. Eternally youthful, more popular than ever, the devilish pact *The Stones* made almost two decades ago is working still, its power undimmed by the passage of time. As they rally whole new generations of ever increasing converts under their decaying, demonic, drug drenched banner, it becomes obvious that their sickening goals haven't changed one bit over the years. "Tattoo You" is the most recent example.

The inner sleeve of "Tattoo You" is a black and white photo of a cloven-hoofed goat's foot in high heels.

The Rolling Stones' massive, far reaching influence is not limited simply to untold legions of rabid fans, however. Countless scores of Rock bands anxious to mimic *The Stones'* success have hit the big time riding the same pale horse of devils, drugs, and destruction. A prime example is Richard Ramirez' favorite group, the phenomenally popular *AC-DC*.

AC-DC

A raunchy quintet from Australia, *AC-DC* has been known from their inception as a pulverizing rhythmic bull-dozer musically, with the late singer Bon Scott howling and screeching of the joys of sexual and drunken excess. Scott died miserably in February of 1980 in the back seat of a friend's car after a night of heavy drinking. He choked to death on his own vomit. His death came at an extremely bad time for the group, having had their first taste of Top 40 radio play with the release of their sneering bow to devil worship, 1979's "Highway To Hell." (See figure 3.)

On the cover of "Highway To Hell," the group's faces all have a sickly yellow-greenish pallor, as if they've been dead for awhile. Lead guitarist Angus Young sports devil horns on his head as he fondles a phallic forked tail. Bon Scott wears a Pentagram round his neck. On the back of the album, the band stands eerily in a wispy fog, with Young cackling demonically, his head thrown back, his eyes alight

Figure 3

The road crew of the "Highway To Hell."

with Hell-Fire. "Highway To Hell" was Bon Scott's last record.

To those who would say that this current disturbing crop of Rock & Roll records are just tongue in cheek incorporations of trendy occult influences, sort of a Madison Avenue approach to the highly lucrative business of selling a particular type of "image" (i.e. demonic) to a gullible public, I would suggest that they listen carefully to the lyrics of every song on the *AC-DC* album "Back In Black," released in 1980. There is absolutely no way that the author of those words doesn't BELIEVE in what he has written. NO amount of poetic finesse, shrewd contemplation of what will sell in the marketplace, or a simple lucky streak of stringing the right words together can disguise the fact that the stamp of CONVICTION lies firmly on every stanza Brian Johnson sings.

Many people, usually those connected in some way to the Rock music industry, shrug their shoulders and say, "So what? *AC-DC,* the kids love 'em! It's just a phase they're going through, like anything else . . . " This way of thinking sounds suspiciously like the average drug pusher's philosophy: "If they don't get it from me, they'll just get it somewhere else . . . "

This "phase" is only the beginning of a much larger problem. It is the initial entry into the glittery world of Rock bands and their self-serving perpetuation of a decadent myth: that through Rock & Roll you, too, can become a superstar with a harem of voluptuous women, pounds of dope, and money to burn. Far too many liberal proponents of today's permissiveness feel that kids flocking to hear and buy *AC-DC* is "no big deal." I truly feel sorry for these people. They refuse to see the danger right in front of their noses: the fact that their kids are being savagely brain-pounded and tricked into running away from God to the tune of thunderous, bashing Heavy Metal guitars.

I have seen countless times with my own eyes ten-year-old children frantically grabbing at the latest *AC-DC* cassettes in the local record shop, exclaiming, "Wow! *AC-DC* has a new one! I'm gonna get it if Mom will give me the money!"

One of the tapes they were so greedily fighting over was "Back In Black."

"Black" has sold millions and millions of copies worldwide. Three singles from the LP blared for months from tens of thousands of radios across the United States and Europe. And with the release of 1981's "For Those About To Rock, We Salute You," (as well as later LPs like "Flick Of The Switch" and "Fly On The Wall"), *AC-DC* is perched at the very peak of success in an industry where all degrees of talent ultimately translate to the dollar sign.

One song on the album "Back In Black" called "Given The Dog A Bone," describes sex at its most animalistic, totally without human emotion or compassion. This seems to be a new trait of Johnson's lyrical experiments, as this theme runs through several songs on the album critics called "Demon-Rock at its best!" Singer Brian Johnson has been quoted as saying, "We believe in the POWER of Rock & Roll . . . "[19]

Yes, but what kind of power?

How did this motley crew of brain bashers rise to this dizzying height of success? Through a combination of luck and fateful accident, they now find themselves with the ability to infect millions of new converts with their perverse primer of sneering sexual degradation of women, violent psychotic thrills, and bowing awestruck worship of hideous Luciferian strength.

Occult spellcasters as well as many concerned Christians accept the fact that Satan is a concrete entity manipulating the careers of groups like *AC-DC* to further the Devil's own infernal objectives. The following, however, is based on some hard, cold, facts.

Ten years ago, *AC-DC* was a relatively unknown group from Australia. They played boring recycled boogie tunes which consisted of over-long, cliched guitar solos coupled with the tuneless caterwaulings of lead screecher Bon Scott, a former limousine driver for the band. They enjoyed a fanatical cult following, to be sure, but world-wide success eluded them at every turn. Four albums had gone by, and *AC-DC* had not had one big hit single on the radio.

Then came "Highway To Hell."

Imagine the group, their manager and PR people sitting in the corporate boardroom of their Atlantic Record Company headquarters discussing the concept for the upcoming album. Deadlines and contract fulfillments are looming. The band's track record to date has been steady, but disappointing. Record company executives don't care about effort and attitude from a group they've invested thousands of dollars in. They want hit singles, and they want a lot of them, and they want them delivered in a reasonable amount of time.

Someone suggests going the Satanism route for the next LP. It's a proven fact that Satanism sells records. After all, the undisputed Kings of Rock & Roll, *The Rolling Stones,* started the trend in 1967 with their "Satanic Majesties" album, and fed the image for the next six or seven years, eventually building it into a multi-million dollar corporation for themselves. Another connection that clearly shows *The Stones'* influence on *AC-DC* is evidenced by the title of the *AC-DC* live album, "If You Want Blood, You Got It," an obvious paraphrase of the classic *Rolling Stones'* LP, "Got Live If You Want It."

Just to keep the entire thing from getting too sinister, Scott is asked if he can provide the occasional tongue-in-cheek lyric for the songs he will be writing. With his cynical, street wise attitude, he thinks there'll be no problem with that.

AC-DC takes off. Singles from the new album jump onto the charts, and fans in bars and record stores everywhere are treated for a full year to the ragged, whiskey-laced voice of Bon Scott yelling, "I'm on the Highway to Hell . . ."

You certainly were, Bon.

Where did the phrase "Highway To Hell" come from in the first place? Why, from the Bible, of course. Matthew 7:13 says: "Heaven can be entered only through the narrow gate! The highway to Hell is broad, and its gate is wide enough for all the multitudes who choose its easy way."

The transition between their previous records and "Highway" is so sharp at this point that something like the above scene must have occurred. Up until this time, Scott's vocal masterpiece consisted of a song called "The Jack," a tune he had written about the time the entire band had contracted VD from having sex with one particular girl who had been sharing their apartment in the early days.

Catapulted from the ranks of thousands of struggling, starving Rock bands to overnight success with the magic touch of one satanic album — who would have believed it? Was it just fate that when the Devil walked in, these drunkards got famous?

AC-DC happily rode the crest of their new-found fame for the better part of a year. By February of 1980, they had completed work on half of their new follow-up LP to the platinum-selling "Highway To Hell." Things couldn't have looked better for a band that had been stagnating miserably just two years before. Then, on February 25, 1980, Bon Scott died of too much drink in the back seat of a friend's car in London, England.

The band was thrown into chaos.

After seeing Scott safely buried, the surviving members of *AC-DC* met to discuss their future, eventually deciding to forge ahead with their prematurely blasted career. In the November, 1980 issue of the teenybop Rock fanzine "Circus," guitarist Angus Young described the intensive auditions which took place after Scott's abrupt demise:

> "We got replies from all over the world from people
> who wanted to audition. And we heard tapes . . . Some
> of them sounded just like Bon. It was eerie."[20]

All the previous prospects went right out the window the day Brian Johnson stepped up to the *AC-DC* microphone, recalls Young. "As soon as he opened his tonsils everyone sort of said, 'WOW!'"[21]

This man Johnson, a hulking, sinister figure, came from complete obscurity singing for an unknown Scotch band called *Geordie* to become frontman for *AC-DC,* one of the biggest Rock acts in the world. He wasted no time in totally dominating the group's "new" sound. Taking up where Scott had left off, Johnson opened up a whole Pandora's box of vocal tricks for the band, spinning the satanic screw a few turns tighter in the process.

"Back In Black" was unleashed to thousands of rabid teens anxious to see if *AC-DC* could cut it with the new vocalist. What they heard astounded fans and critics alike. Cash registers across the land soon stamped the magic words "Platinum Plus" on "Back In Black."

Brian Johnson's lyrics on both "Back In Black" and the following LP, "About To Rock," can be taken in many different contexts. He is a master at manipulating phrases and verbal attacks with disarming speed and blinding agility.

For example: On the surface, Johnson and his band seem to be saying, "I like the Devil, and if you do too, that's cool." Beneath this rather obnoxious proposal lies another layer of meaning entirely, "If you follow our example, you can be as successful as we have," or, for the non-musicians in the audience, "at least free your minds from your stupid parents." Finally, what is at the heart of the *AC-DC* philosophy can be seen bubbling menacingly underneath the surface of the other gaudy Rock & Roll trappings of fame and fortune: "We'll use you to get rich, you fools. So jump on our bandwagon. We're all going to Hell anyway. We may as well have some company when we get there."

Widely thought to be a tribute to the late Bon Scott with its entirely unadorned, black cover, (sort of an LP in mourning for the fallen singer), "Back In Black" also can be taken quite another way. As all occultists know, to be "into the Black" is to hunger for evil and self-aggrandizement, to shun the light of all good works. In this sense, "Back In Black" means, "Returned in full force with the power of Lucifer behind us." It is impossible to be only partially "into the Black" or "into the White;" there is no in between.

AC-DC has clearly stated where their priorities lie.

Other shivery examples of *AC-DC's* occultish explorations include: Bon Scott calling up demons by name at the end of the "Highway To Hell" LP, death knell bells dolefully ringing at the beginning of "Hell's Bells" on "Back In Black," and a deep devilish SOMETHING which speaks as Scott sings on the live version of "Whole Lotta Rosie."

As *AC-DC's* already considerable power steadily increases, apparently so does their detachment from reality. Johnson sums it up nicely in a line from the song "Back In Black" — "Forget the hearse, cause I'll NEVER die . . ."

Another song from the LP called "Shoot To Thrill" is about killing women for fun. "What Do You Do For Money, Honey" points out the problems of having a prostitute for a girl friend, and side one closes with the touching romantic ballad, "Let Me Put My Love Into You, Babe."

We should ask ourselves a question at this point. Do we really NEED groups like *AC-DC* polluting the airwaves and minds of impressionable young people everywhere? Couldn't the world survive nicely without such bands? What can we do to stop this frightening trend?

Presenting an occultish image and supernatural persona is obviously an extremely lucrative stance for any Rock band sitting at the top of their heaps to undertake. The mysterious, teasing quality of the audience never really knowing for sure whether their favorite group or singer is seriously delving into arcane depths or merely engaging in some shrewd, trendy satanic posturing often proves to be a shot in the arm commercially for the jaded and dissipated members of Rock's aristocracy. The problem with engaging in this game of Rock & Roll audience tag is this: Once the band in question begins riding the skyrocketing, runaway roller coaster of magic and witchcraft, who's going to apply the brakes when the whole thing gets out of hand? When the fans begin believing the image as fact, who is left in control? Certainly not the band. They're too busy raking in the dough. Certainly not the audience. They are the ones being duped in the first place.

Who is in control? SATAN!

THE DOORS

The legendary lead singer for *The Doors,* dark, moody, mysterious Jim Morrison, stated many times that he was not in control of his own destiny. Always walking on the thin line between insanity and reason, dissipation and death, Morrison gobbled up psychedelics like so much candy during the early days of *The Doors.*

He wrote songs like "The Changeling," (changelings were, according to folklore, demon children left in human baby beds at night) and "The End," where Morrison screams that he wants to kill his father and sexually ravage his mother. (Morrison was under the influence of 10,000 micrograms of LSD when he first ad libbed these lines at a California Whisky-A-Go-Go *Doors'* performance in the mid Sixties. When "The End" was recorded in the studio months later, the lines stayed, though they were heavily buried in the mix by producer Paul Rothchild.

The chilling web of dark spells and whispered tragedies which dogged Morrison all the days of his short life came to a head on July 3, 1971, when he was found dead in his Paris apartment. No death certificate was officially tendered, and his body was quickly buried without a public ceremony. No one seemed sure whether he had really died, or had just spirited himself away to some other place of his own choosing. His death date was almost exactly two years to the day since the demise of demoniac *Rolling Stone* Brian

Jones. Morrison had even written an eerie, extensive eulogy to Jones upon learning of the devil worshiper's death by drowning.

In 1970, Morrison (who had always considered himself to be more of a poet than a Rock & Roll star) realized one of his most treasured ambitions. He had published a volume of his own poetry titled *The Lords and New Creatures.* Excerpts from this infernal work give us some key to just how deeply Jim Morrison was into the Dark Arts, just how well he recognized the demons who guided him:

> "The Lords. Events take place beyond our knowledge or control . . . We can only try to enslave others. But gradually, special perceptions are being developed. The idea of 'The Lords' is beginning to form in some minds. We should enlist them into bands of perceivers to tour the labyrinth during their mysterious nocturnal appearances. The Lords have secret entrances, and they know disguises. But they give themselves away in minor ways. Too much glint of light in the eye. A wrong gesture. Too long and curious a glance.
>
> The Lords appease us with images. They give us books, concerts, galleries, shows, cinemas. Especially the cinemas. Through art they confuse us and blind us to our enslavement. Art adorns our prison walls, keeps us silent and diverted and indifferent."[22]

Shortly after the publication of *The Lords,* Morrison underwent a pagan wedding ceremony with one of his many female consorts, one Patricia Kennely, in New York City.

According to Jerry Hopkins and Danny Sugarman's book, *No One Here Gets Out Alive,* Kennely was the editor-in-chief of a prominent Rock magazine, and was also the member of a witches' coven which was part of the Wiccans, an ancient, pre-Druidic cult which worshiped something called "The Horned God," also known as "The Lord." A high priest and priestess of Kennely's coven performed the bizarre wedding ceremony by the light of black candles in Kennely's apartment. Morrison and his "bride" then cut each other's arms, letting their blood drip into a chalice of wine from which they both drank. They stepped over a broomstick, exchanged secret vows, and invoked the name and blessings of the goddess of their cult. To seal their union, both Morrison and Kennely signed two hand-drawn documents, one in witchcraft runes. They signed the pact in their own blood.

Jim Morrison, during the rocky, giddy days of *The Doors'* leap-frog to international stardom, incited his audiences to riot, exposed his private parts in Miami, Florida, and screamed at his concert security forces, calling them "pigs." He spoke often, publicly and in performance, about overthrowing the U.S. Government by force, about violent revolution. He was frequently tripping during his concerts, ad libbing great streams of black, hate-filled dialogues meant to inflame his audiences with the same seething evil that controlled his own blasted soul.

He was drafted into the Army, but ingested massive quantities of LSD and other drugs on induction day in order to change his blood pressure and heartbeat for the physical examination. He also told the Army doctors that he was a homosexual, and they wasted no time in rejecting him.

Free to continue his career, Morrison became a full-fledged alcoholic. He destroyed friends' apartments, urinated in public, and smashed up expensive sports cars. He acted as if demons possessed him, claiming he was not of this earth. He apparently thought himself indestructible, like so many of his contemporaries, and proceeded to test his own mortality to the limits by ingesting ever increasing quantities of drugs and booze, by whooshing drunk through the night in floorboarded Ferraris, and by walking on thin ledges of apartment buildings many floors off the ground. Finally, in Paris on July 3, 1971, Morrison's ravaged heart and body gave up — or else he simply disappeared. No one seems to know for sure.

Jim Morrison was the role model future "Death Rockers" like Iggy Pop and Alice Cooper would later imitate. His sickness was to be passed on to a whole new generation of Rock & Roll devil worshipers.

Who was in control of this puppet?

SATAN!

Today, Jim Morrison and *The Doors* have achieved a global cult status of adoration and popular appeal that rivals the super stardom they enjoyed in their heyday during the late Sixties. Morrison's dead face has adorned virtually every major music magazine and newspaper in the country. *The Doors'* long dormant catalog of albums has suddenly found new life as a whole new wave of fans who were too young to appreciate them in their prime have flocked to the record stores, snapping up psychedelic devil operas like "Strange Days" and "Waiting For The Sun."

The evil of *The Doors* lives on and on. The singer is dead. The band is splintered and retired, but still the records sell, and the magazines reprint their dusty interviews over and over again for an entirely new generation to become addicted to. I wonder how many fresh-faced teens, so eagerly listening to *The Doors* for the first time, realize that Jim Morrison was married to a witch, that he was a drunken, pitiful, lying, greedy maniac, the scum of the earth, a man who ate so many psychedelics in his brief life that the only noble thing he succeeded in doing for society was to completely obliterate his own warped and twisted mind. Even the name *The Doors* was taken from LSD pioneer Aldous Huxley and author William Blake's descriptive phrase, "the doors of perception" (i.e. LSD).

We've already looked at the careers of *The Doors, The Rolling Stones,* and *AC-DC.* Only one other band can possibly match them in terms of world wide popularity and mountains of cash: *Led Zeppelin.*

LED ZEPPELIN

Even though their public image has always been that of rowdy, mystic explorers of inner space, (as well as the inventors of Heavy Metal music), *Led Zep* have hurtled down a spinning path of destruction ever since their inception in 1969. Their dabblings in the Dark Arts have always seemed to eerily coincide with personal tragedies and disasters to members of the group and their families.

Let's take a look at the world of *Led Zeppelin*.

A spooky, looming castle sits perched on a rocky, leaf littered slope next to the cold, black waters of Loch Ness, Scotland. As we have already mentioned, this ghastly place was once the home of the man widely regarded as being the most evil human of the nineteenth century, Aleister Crowley, the self-proclaimed Beast 666, who actually believed himself to be the incarnation of the scriptural Anti-Christ mentioned in the Books of I John and II Thessalonians. He spent his entire life researching, experimenting, enlarging and encouraging the practice of evil. To call this wretch a warlock would not begin to define the scope of his power over others. One would think that such a diseased, shunned place as the late Crowley's Loch Ness mansion, Boleskine, would forever remain locked and boarded over, but the fact of the matter is that this creepy, decaying, abandoned castle is owned by super rich and famous *Led Zeppelin* guitarist Jimmy Page.

He lives there. It's his home.

In my opinion, Edward Alexander Aleister Crowley, in addition to his other grisly titles, is the Patron Saint of Rock & Roll. Jimmy Page is not only interested in the master magician, he's obsessed with him. To want to live in a place where the most powerful warlock of the last century held orgies of the damned and sacrificed humans to Satan is not a normal motivation, to say the least. Years after his death the incredibly powerful ancient evil of such a monster is still reaching out to snare poor deluded Rock star saps like Page.

A secret passageway deep in the bowels of Boleskine House leads not only to the chamber where those horrible blasphemous human sacrifices were held, but to the very grave itself of Aleister Crowley! How would you like to go to bed in a place like that, friends? How could anyone want to LIVE there?

Let's dig a little deeper and see just how strong the Crowley-Page connection is. Here are some chilling facts that show that Jimmy Page is not just a curious seeker after occult knowledge, but a devoted acolyte of the "Great Beast's" hellish legacy.

One of Crowley's principal educational lessons to the many eager students of satanic spell-casting who always filled his home was the occult law of reversal. He encouraged and ordered his pupils in witchcraft to intensely practice walking, talking, thinking, and reading in reverse. He also demanded that they PLAY PHONOGRAPH RECORDS BACKWARDS in order to gain insight into the future! Whose future did HE see in 1910 as he sat in his darkened chamber listening to the demonic chatter of records playing in reverse, Jimmy Page's?

Crowley's backwards recording principle has powerfully manifested itself today in backmasked messages of satanic praise on at least two *Led Zeppelin* albums. ("IV" and "Houses Of The Holy"). If Page didn't put those things on his own group's albums, who did?

Another link between Page and his demon mentor is one of the most insidious substances known to man: cocaine. Crowley was intensely fond of the drug; he kept bowls of it sitting around his mansion within easy reach so that anyone who wished could take pinches and sniffs whenever they pleased.

You only have to look at recent pictures of Jimmy Page to see the sharp stamp of severe coke abuse on his wasted face and body. He doesn't smile often in public because his teeth are rotted and hanging. (Prolonged cocaine abuse attacks and destroys the nerve endings in the gums and teeth, making them rot; just ask Keith Richards.) Coke also brings about delusions of genius and an ultra-snobbish feeling of unqualified superiority to "lesser" human beings. Read any of Page's infrequent interviews, and it's obvious the man is way out on a mountain somewhere, completely divorced from reality.

The final proof of Page's slavery to Crowley's power is the weirdest of all.

Aleister Crowley always had a house full of devoted students of Satan, many of whom were beautiful women. His occult experiments with these people included much sexual exploration in conjunction with the witchcraft. Whenever he chose, he would single out one of those women to be his personal sex slave. To be thus chosen by the "Great Beast" was something they perceived as being a glorious honor. Crowley's favorite nickname for whomever he held in sexual bondage at the moment was his "Scarlet Woman."

Jimmy Page has a 10 year old daughter born out of wedlock. Her name is Scarlett.

(Kenneth Anger, an acquaintance of Page's as well as being an avowed disciple of Crowley, wrote a book called *Hollywood Babylon.* In it his written dedication is to the "Scarlet Woman.")

Can you imagine, friends in Christ, having a baby born to you, and then naming it after a hated Satanist's favorite whore? What about letting the child grow up in the very rooms where babies were murdered, where their hot blood was sprinkled on the screaming faces of the murderers? This is a hellish and very serious business. God help us!

Here is a quote from Aleister Crowley:

> "Do what thou wilt shall be the whole of the law. So mote it be."

Shortly after the tragic, pathetic death of *Led Zep* drummer John Bonham, on September 25, 1980, many memorial Rock fanzines flooded supermarket checkouts across the U.S. One of these collector's editions, called "Will The Song Remain The Same?" contained these quotes from Jimmy Page regarding Aleister Crowley:

> "But I mean how can anyone call Crowley an evil man? For a start, he was the only Edwardian to really embrace the 20th Century. It goes without saying that Crowley was grossly misunderstood."[23]

And on the Loch Ness estate both Crowley and Page have owned:

> "It was also a church that was burned to the ground with the congregation in it. And that's the site of the house . . . "[24]

> "The bad vibes were already there. A man was beheaded there, and sometimes you can hear his head rolling down . . . "[25]

> "Of course, after Crowley there have been suicides, people carted off to mental hospitals and such. The house is located near the water, near Loch Ness . . . "[26]

In *The Led Zeppelin Biography,* by Ritchie Yorke, Jimmy Page was asked which person in history he would most liked to have met. His reply:

> "Machiavelli. He was a master of evil . . . but you can't ignore evil if you study the supernatural as I do. I have many books on the subject and I've also attended a number of seances. I want to go on studying it."[27]

In the November, 1979 issue of Creem magazine, it was revealed that Page owned an occult bookstore in Kensington, England named Equinox, which specializes in the published works of Aleister Crowley. In an interview with writer Chris Salewicz in the same issue, Page was asked if his interests in the occult had diminished over the last few years. This was his response:

> "I'm still very interested. I still read a lot of literature on it."[28]

> "Magic is very important if people can go through with it. I think Crowley is completely relevant to today. We're all still seeking for truth. The search goes on. Crowley didn't have a very high opinion of women and I don't think he was wrong."[29]

According to all the major music trades, Jimmy Page's headlong pursuit of the supernatural has resulted in a backlash of personal tragedy for himself and the rest of *Led Zeppelin* over the years. The band was such a huge, monolithic act that the death of their drummer (from an overconsumption of Vodka), was cause for mourning by millions of saddened fans. This event prompted Rock magazines across the U.S. and Europe to insert big, splashy pictures of burly John Bonham into their regular features at the last minute. When researching material for *Led Zep,* and on Bonham's death, I was amazed to find that every magazine, article, and book that I read had something to say about the "Led Zeppelin Curse" and how it related to Page's occult fascinations.

These are the facts:

During their 1973 tour to promote "Houses Of The Holy," Jimmy Page broke his left wrist, seriously hampering his ability to play.

On the eve of their 1975 tour, a train door mysteriously slammed shut on Page's hand, breaking his ring finger (crucial to a guitarist).

Also in 1975, just as the band was about to start work on a new album, ("Presence"), singer Robert Plant and family were involved in a near fatal car accident while vacationing on the Greek island of Rhodes. Plant's right foot and ankle were smashed. Doctors were unsure whether he would ever walk again without the aid of a cane. Through rest and therapy, Plant's injuries healed, and the "Presence" LP was released.

In 1977, again during an American tour, Robert Plant contracted a severe throat infection which threw the entire multi-million dollar concert schedule into jeopardy. During the third night of a Chicago performance on this tour, Jimmy Page collapsed on stage, and was immediately rushed back to his hotel, unable to continue playing. In a 1977 issue of Circus magazine, Page remarked,

> "It's the first time we've ever stopped a gig like that; we always have a go, really, because we're not a rip off band. But the pain was unbearable . . . If I hadn't sat down, I would have fallen over . . . "[30]

As if these grim events were not enough, tragedy once again punched Robert Plant between the eyes. While trying to shake his raging throat infection, the flamboyant singer received the news that his five year old son Karac had died in Wales from a disease doctors had been powerless to diagnose. The boy was dead in less than a week.

The remainder of the tour was cancelled.

Three years went by. Hot on the heels of their comeback album, "In Through The Out Door," *Led Zeppelin* played a handful of European dates which proved, from critical raves and the audiences' thunderous ovations, that the band was bigger than ever before. As they were preparing to begin the American leg of their 1980 tour, with the kick-off concert set for the Montreal Forum, John Bonham died in the bed he was sleeping in. He had been an overnight guest at Jimmy Page's home.

Less than a month later, *Led Zeppelin* disbanded.

Another point that the music magazines I researched made a big thing of was Jimmy Page's vicious attack on Kenneth Anger, a strange man we have already mentioned as having excited Page with tales of the legendary satanist Aleister Crowley.

Page had contributed to the soundtrack of an Anger film, "Lucifer Rising," much the same way as Mick Jagger had been lured into scoring another occult Anger epic, 1969's "Invocation Of My Demon Brother." Apparently, Anger felt that Page had not given his all to the project. The subject of an interview in a widely circulated British Rock paper, Anger accused Page of backing out of his commitment prematurely, partly because of severe drug problems. Page angrily wrote the mysterious film maker off with the following quotes in Creem magazine:

> "This whole thing about 'Anger's Curse;' they were just these silly little letters. God it was all so pathetic . . . I mean I had a lot of respect for him. As an occultist he was definitely in the vanguard . . . It's truly pathetic. I mean, he is powerless — totally. The only damage he can do is with his tongue."[31]

Shortly after these comments appeared in print, Page collapsed from severe, unexplained pain in the middle of a *Led Zeppelin* concert, and Robert Plant's young son died of an illness no doctor could diagnose. Of all people, an avowed occult enthusiast like Jimmy Page should have known better than to sneer at the Devil's power. Perhaps he thought his own satanic spells would protect him from harm. It seems as though Kenneth Anger had the last laugh on Jimmy Page after all.

The philosophy of Jimmy Page is best summed up by these two remarks printed in "Circus:"

> **On life:** "Dancing on the edge of the precipice; you've gotta live like that. Better to live one day as a lion than a thousand years as a lamb, y'know?"[32]

> **And on touring:** "It's good out on the tiles, away from home. It's a stag party that never ends."[33]

In their rare interviews, *Led Zeppelin* have always come

across with an upbeat, idealistic image of themselves as talented heroes who, humbly respecting their fellow man, carry on searching for the great Cosmic truths lying at the edge of the universe.

Nothing could be further from the truth.

Famous Rock promoter-impresario Bill Graham has rated *Led Zep* the biggest concert draw in the world, but the band's reputation as crude, violent boors who take great pleasure in destroying opulent hotel suites and bullying anyone they please is well documented. At a San Francisco concert during the ill-fated 1977 tour, drummer John Bonham, *Led Zep* manager Peter Grant (A huge 300 pound hulk who delights in cultivating an image of himself as a gangsterish thug), and John Bindon, a Zeppelin employee, brutally beat a member of Bill Graham's security force; that group of paid professionals who receive the thankless task of protecting the "Stars" from over-eager fans.

Bill Graham made these comments about the incident:

> "Because of that deplorable event, I will NEVER allow myself the privilege of working with the band again. But still I tip my hat to them because they have more personal pulling power than anybody since Mahatma Ghandi."[34]

Writer Carl Arrington, of Circus Magazine accurately pointed out:

> "In the world of rock music, *Led Zeppelin* is a shrine before which all serious Rock fans must bow sometime in their lives. And at times the worship is blind."[35]

Blind worship of a band who pioneered the "Destroy your hotel for fun and profit, kicks and publicity" routine is truly disturbing. Dead drummer Bonham was the prime "looner" during these rampages. A legend in his own time, Bonham's credits include: having a pool table installed in his suite at New York's ultra swank Plaza Hotel, then smashing it to splinters after deciding it wasn't level; utterly destroying several expensive paintings in the lobby of a posh movie theater by breaking them over a statue's head; holding motorcycle races in the hallway of L.A.'s elegant Continental Hyatt House; and turning elegant hotel rooms into piles of smoking rubble.

A book called *Hammer of the Gods,* by Stephen Davis, strips away the gaudy mystique of *Led Zeppelin,* showing the pathetic reality behind Rock's biggest band.

Jimmy Page was addicted to heroin for 7 years, the better part of *Led Zep's* tenure as a group. When he wasn't shooting up or snorting coke, he was bedding down with 14 year old groupies and posing for pictures draped in animal intestines and dung with one of the groupies kneeling at his feet, pretending to eat the intestines. This was "gentle" Jimmy Page, sensitive guitar genius and beloved Rock idol, a man so cheap he charged Robert Plant and John Bonham for the food and drinks consumed in their first audition for *Led Zeppelin.* They were penniless at the time. Page was rich.

Zep bassist John Paul Jones passed out on a hotel bed with a homosexual female impersonator he had picked up in a bar. The marijuana joint they had been smoking started a fire in the suite, and when help arrived, the homosexual's clothes were undone, his private parts exposed.

And what about lovable "Bonzo" Bonham, nicknamed "The Beast," the dead drummer millions of fans grieved over after his untimely 1980 demise? Instead of the eccentric merry prankster and wry, witty practical joker written about for years in all the Rock magazines, "Hammer Of The Gods" tells us a different story.

A hopeless and degenerate alcoholic, Bonham twice attempted forcible rape on women not part of the *Led Zeppelin* sexual circus. He was pulled off the screaming women, snarling and growling like a wild beast. Punching girls in the face while in the midst of alcoholic rages was also a favorite pastime. At the bar, he drank his drinks 20 at a time, then looked for someone to insult, punch, curse, or verbally abuse. Anyone would do. After passing out in the first class seat of a luxury airliner, Bonham lost control of his bladder and wet his britches like a newborn baby. The stench made everyone around him gag.[36]

So much for the "great" and "mighty" *Led Zeppelin.*

As for caring about the fans who made them famous, Jimmy Page had this to say about the long-awaited *Zeppelin* film, "The Song Remains The Same." The movie's proceeds were donated to charity, and its ideal was supposed to be a gift to fans hungry for a *Led Zeppelin* incapacitated by Robert Plant's 1975 auto wreck:

> "Let's just say that when we weren't viewing the thing as a tax write-off, there was as much commitment and dedication involved as goes into anything we do."[37]

And to writer Cameron Crowe, Page once said,

> "I'm no fool. I know how much the mystique matters, so why should I blow it now?"[38]

Even though they've neatly managed to keep their sweet smelling image intact over the years as a band who really CARES about their feudal fandom, the truth of the matter is that *Led Zeppelin* was usually so busy greedily gobbling up fees of a quarter of a million dollars per concert that they completely ignored the violence they continually attracted like a magnet. What the band has always been about, according to lead singer Robert Plant, is goodness, innocence, and harmony with the universe, love of one's neighbor, and tolerance of the fellow human beings who share this planet earth. Let us expose the brutal lies behind their hypocrisy with the group's own words, as printed in several leading Rock books and magazines so avidly devoured by thousands of young fans starving for new "fax."

Bassist John Paul Jones — "I hope you can appreciate us stoned out of your mind . . . "[39]

Manager Peter Grant — "If someone's being rough with you, you gotta be rough back."[40]

Robert Plant — "The lifestyle of Rock & Roll is to live well and to take a good woman."[41]

Jimmy Page — "Anarchy's all right if you can see where you're going afterwards . . . It's the easiest way out . . . "[42]

Besides these overt messages of hate and callous indifference to anyone outside their own select circle, chilling facts have just recently come to light about some hidden messages and satanic directions buried in *Led Zeppelin's* songs, most importantly in "Stairway To Heaven."

"Stairway" is by far the most requested song on radio today, and has been for many years. The CBS Evening News first broadcast the story in April of 1982 that, when played backwards, devil-fashion, the song revealed a whole slew of pro-satanic communications. This is what is said: "I SING BECAUSE I LIVE WITH SATAN. THE LORD TURNS ME OFF. THERE'S NO ESCAPING IT. HERE'S TO MY SWEET SATAN. WHOSE POWER IS SATAN. HE WILL GIVE YOU 666. I LIVE FOR SATAN."

According to brain researcher James Yarroll, in testimony given at the California legislature, the human brain has the ability to scan, pick up, and translate messages in reverse, even at a subliminal level, eventually incorporating them into the conscious sector of the brain automatically. Thus, "I live for Satan" is actually implanted in a person's brain after listening to "Stairway To Heaven" many times.

What further proof do we need that the Devil and *Led Zeppelin* are working together to poison the minds of our youth without their even realizing it? Those messages of evil didn't just appear out of nowhere. It would be ridiculous and utterly impossible for Robert Plant to sing such a stream of devilish words backwards, consciously or unconsciously. He simply sang his satanic directions normally, and the finished product was then blended backwards into the final mix of the song. Such a process would be quite easy in today's modern studios, where tape machines and skilled engineers are capable of just about anything. Since Plant denies doing this, the only other explanation is that demon voices are singing a duet with him!

One of the last concerts *Led Zeppelin* played was at Knebworth, England, for an audience of over 150,000 people. Even though they are technically no longer a band, the crass money grabbing and occultish meandering mentality of this group will still taint the minds of untold thousands of impressionable teens as long as a copy of "Stairway To Heaven" exists. Those youngsters are just waiting to absorb the legacy of *Led Zeppelin*.

Isn't it time someone put a stop to it?

How much longer can we as a society afford to stand idly by and watch whole generations fall to the rotting, dead-end dreams of the *AC-DCs,* the *Doors,* the *Rolling Stones,* and the *Led Zeppelins?* No concerted effort has ever been made to stamp out such blights upon society, mainly because of the multi-million dollar clout these bands have.

NOW is the time to pursue our right to determine our young people's future development along Christian lines and ideals. Volumes of facts are available to anyone wishing to educate themselves about all the top Rock & Roll acts currently kowtowing to the Devil. At the very least, parents and educators should be able to keep their homes and classrooms free of the trappings of the Rock & Roll menace — the records, the magazines, and the radios and tape players.

Rock stifles the ambition to become better through hard, honest work. It creates a star-crossed dreamland of astrology, Black Magic, and witchcraft. It leaves teens lusty, slavering to win those eager groupies and grip that million dollar brass ring in the sky.

It took ten years for us to realize that satanic messages in reverse were being beamed into our kid's brains all this time. Who knows what's been going on while we all had our backs and ears turned, too busy with our own problems? Who knows what strides evil has made while we've all been napping?

It's time to put a stop to this.

NOW!

CHAPTER 4

Symbols & Signs

"Beware of false prophets, which come to you in sheep's clothing, but inwardly they are ravening wolves. Ye shall know them by their fruits. Do men gather grapes of thorns, or figs of thistles? Even so every good tree bringeth forth good fruit; but a corrupt tree bringeth forth evil fruit. A good tree cannot bring forth evil fruit, neither can a corrupt tree bring forth good fruit. Every tree that bringeth not forth good fruit is hewn down, and cast into the fire. Wherefore by their fruits ye shall know them."
Matthew 7:15-20

"Why don't we sing this song all together, open our heads, let the pictures come. And if we sing this song all together, then we will see where we all come from . . . "

The Rolling Stones[1]

Webster's New World Dictionary of The American Language describes the word "subliminal" like this: "below the threshold of conscious awareness."

In the massively influential, super-sophisticated, highly technical and all pervasive empire that is today's Rock &

Roll industry, subliminal "clues" and messages, many of them openly and blatantly praising Satan, are splashed all over Rock album covers and inserted in far too many Rock songs to be merely some kind of harmless coincidence.

This very minute, record buyers and Rock & Roll listeners all over the world are being unknowingly indoctrinated with Satan's secret messages of hate, despair, fear, and blasphemy. Who knows how long this has gone on undetected, or where it will finally lead?

When young people first get interested in buying Rock albums, many times it's because they've heard a certain song on the radio that they especially liked, or perhaps some of their friends have recommended a particular group or record to them. Maybe, like me, they've recently been to a Rock concert where they were exposed to new songs they hadn't heard before, prompting them to go out and buy the album of the group headlining the concert.

Just as often, unfortunately, a teenager browsing through a record store is strangely attracted to the weird cover graphics of one of the staggering number of Rock LP's now in existence.

Today the cover graphics are every bit as important to the success of that album's sales potential as the music inside the sleeve. Don't forget that the multi-billion dollar record conglomerates are interested in only one thing: SALES, which further translates to dollars. They could care less about what the consumer actually thinks of the album's musical merits once that magic million dollar gold or platinum mountain of success has been scaled. The real motive behind this spree of naked greed is to ensnare as many potential record buyers as possible through a wide variety of lurid, smuttish, controversial and satanic album covers. Proof of this can be found by walking through any record store in the country. Garish, disgusting album covers, (often with occult themes), leap from the record racks at the unsuspecting customer, attracting his attention immediately against his will. Some of these covers are outright pornography.

I well remember myself one day at age fourteen looking through dozens of LP's at the local record shop when I was stopped in my tracks by a copy of *Alice Cooper's* "Killer" album. Done up in neon red, the entire face of the record sleeve was a photograph of a loathsome boa constrictor, its forked tongue hanging out of its mouth. Printed above the snake were the words "Alice Cooper." The album itself folded into a 1972 calendar whose centerpiece was a dead Alice dangling from a hangman's noose. Seeing such an out-rageous cover prompted me to buy the album, which in turn led me to fall in love with Cooper's snarling, psychotic, anti-social anthems. The next step was to anx-iously await the next LP, and so on.

I was hooked.

Mine is not an isolated case. For the better part of six years, *Alice Cooper* was THE most famous and successful Rock band in America. Their records sold in the millions. Their concerts sold out regularly with every new tour, financed from the pockets and allowances of hundreds of thousands of adoring teens eager for *Alice's* own peculiar brand of sadistic thrills.

Would *Alice Cooper* have become the megastars they were without the added push of those disgusting album covers? Early in their career, when media focus and attention were such a necessity to them, would a simple photo of the band pasted on the front of the LP have sufficiently shocked the "straight" music press into recognizing their "talent," forging *Alice Cooper* into the household word it has since become?

Doubtful.

This modern trend of bizarre pictures and photos decorating record sleeves is a fairly recent innovation. It's roots can be traced back to 1967, when, during the heights of the Psychedelic Movement, *The Beatles,* and later *The Rolling Stones,* re-leased their landmark LP's "Sergeant Pepper's Lonely Hearts Club Band," and "Their Satanic Majesties Request."

Prior to this time, a black & white photo splash of the group or performer was about as daring as the record companies got. Liner notes were "in" then, and often the entire back side of an album would be filled with song titles and some glowing account of the stellar achievements or philosophies of the group. This was all that was necessary to sell that particular artist to the public. The music was, after all, the most important thing.

But times changed, and consumers got bored with the same old thing. *The Beatles,* always at the forefront of such major social shifts in taste, rushed to fill the gap.

The age of the "mystic" album cover had been born. Michael Cooper, the man who photographed the intricate, many faceted covers for both "Sergeant Pepper's" and "Satanic Majesties" was to later have severe drug problems after keeping company with *The Rolling Stones.* Cooper died several years ago. The dam burst after these two breakthrough recordings were released in 1967. Suddenly, every Pop group in the industry was selling its product with swirling, psychedelic splashes of color or exotic talismanic symbols and ancient Asian drawings, (Hindu gods and such), the weirder the better. Album lyrics began to be printed on the outside of the record sleeves, (another *Beatles'* first), allowing star struck teens no doubt as to what each individual Rock group REALLY had on its mystical, LSD-laced mind.

JOHN LENNON AND THE BEATLES

The Beatles must bear the brunt of the blame for focusing the record buying public's attention on album cover graphics, setting the stage for the blasphemies that followed, (and the ones still being produced today).

"Sergeant Pepper's" set entirely new standards for concept advertising, to be sure. Words like innovative, breakthrough and landmark, don't begin to describe the far reaching impact this single record has had on the whole of the advertising and recording industries. As with other infernally inspired projects of this nature, there is more here than meets the eye. Beneath the album's garish, psychedelic facade, a series of subliminal "clues" appeared which would continue on other records the *Beatles* released until their breakup in 1970.

Sometime during the late Sixties, rumors were spreading via radio station disc jockeys and common word of mouth that *Beatle* bassist Paul McCartney was dead, killed in a car crash in England. A double was supposedly being used for all *Beatle* photo and recording sessions. Even though he would fiercely deny any active participation in such a callous hoax on millions of teens around the world, head *Beatle* John Lennon himself couldn't come up with any plausible explanations as to how this vicious rumor got started. He had no idea why every new *Beatle* album was being closely scrutinized for the latest "Paul is dead" clue.

Actually, the entire affair has all the earmarks of Lennon's sarcastic cynical sense of humor. A bitter rivalry had always existed between Lennon and McCartney musically —witty, social satirist Lennon versus the fluffy, melodic song-stories of Paul. In fact, John Lennon so hated his own demigod status of popular appeal that he successfully destroyed his image as one of the innocent phenomenal Moptops through a series of "bed-ins," "bagisms," and "peace protests" during the early Seventies. In addition, he was always the "subliminal media man," inserting his "clues" and half-heard vocal tricks into numerous songs as a practical joke on critics and fans alike!

Lennon himself said,

> " . . . I mean we used to have a laugh putting this, that, or the other in, in a light-hearted way. Some intellectual would read us, some symbolic youth generation wants it, but we also took seriously some parts of the role . . ."[2]

Here then we have the roots of what may have been a cruel joke fostered on a gullible, adoring public by a group whose mass appeal was waning after nearly five years at the top. By 1968, Lennon hated his own publicity and false social status, and he intensely disliked Paul McCartney's one dimensional, self serving perpetuation of *The Beatle* myth. (McCartney had taken over as leader of *The Beatles* after the drug death of their manager Brian Epstein in 1967, overseeing rehearsals, the production of movies and records, and the general continuation of the *Beatle* money machine. Up until that time, John Lennon had been the un-disputed leader of the group.)

What, from Lennon's viewpoint, could be better than symbolically "killing" Paul, burying *The Beatles,* and raking in millions of bucks from heartbroken fans at the same time?

If such a plan existed, it totally succeeded.

As they were beginning to slide off their giddy plateau of global popularity, the "Paul is dead" rumors gave the Liver-pool laddies a badly needed shot in the arm. Fans flocked to the record stores to snap up the latest *Beatle* releases; journalists in all the major Rock magazines and even in the so called "straight press" wrote reams about the farce which was bilking thousands of grief stricken teens.

The Beatles were on top once again.

In researching the life of John Lennon for this book, again and again I have found stark inconsistencies between what he said and taught in public and what he read and thought in private. The man's awestruck fawning over pagan metaphysical mysticism was a particular private obsession. Such occult Devil-work as numerology, the Tarot, transcendental meditation, spiritualism, and divina-tion all ruled his every waking hour. His entire schedule, daily, monthly, and by the year were all laid out according to these heathen plans. Yoko Ono was instrumental in de-veloping such fascinations within him, though the ultimate responsibility lies with Lennon alone.

After some initial holding back, he also plunged headlong into the pursuit of psychic experimentation within the astral plane. Let's not forget that non-stop for several YEARS, the former *Beatle* ate some of the most powerful LSD ever produced . By the last stage of his life, Lennon's jaded hallucinogenic palate was more than ready for another huge (and ultimately fatal) dose of demonic doctrine.

The public John Lennon was quite another matter, however. Peace. Love. Wife. Family. Strong belief in the universal brotherhood of man sitting snugly in the hands of a bountiful Creator. THAT was the John Lennon the world saw through the media, all of it tinged with just a dash of Harpo Marx-type zaniness.

Lennon paid a high price for his global superstar status, though. He was shot to death December 8, 1980, in front of his home in the ultra-plush Dakota Apartments by a deranged former Beatlemaniac named Mark David Chapman. In a psychiatric evaluation of Chapman which appeared in an October issue of Rolling Stone Magazine, psychiatrist Daniel Schwartz and writer Murray Kempton made these revealing remarks:

> "He (Chapman) tells me he can feel the presence of Satan's demons around him . . . 'I can feel their thoughts. I hear their thoughts. I can hear them talking, but not from the outside, from the inside.'"[3]

> " . . . He tells me that it was Satan's demons that gave him the strength and the opportunity for the present offense . . . "[4] (Lennon's murder)

Police described the pudgy 25 year old murderer as appearing to be "hypnotized" at the time of his arrest.

Isn't it all too obvious? The real cause behind John Lennon's grisly death is pretty self-evident, it seems to me. By his own admission, Lennon in his youth was a violent, antisocial, thieving street Punk thug with severe emotional disturbances and imbalances. These problems were caused partially by his father's desertion and his mother Julia's accidental death when John was barely into his teens. Lennon would walk down Liverpool streets in his greasy Elvis hair and black leather jacket, hurling curses at passersby and screaming out brutal, sarcastic comments at cripples and invalids confined to wheelchairs. He beat his girlfriends and popped pills and drank hard liquor like it was going out of style; all this before he was 20!

When *The Beatles'* career skyrocketed, so did Lennon's depraved, selfish appetites. Orgies, prostitutes, marijuana, LSD, cocaine, heroin, transcendental meditation; he suddenly made self-destruction the "in" thing to do. Later, his well defined agnosticism would give way to outright pro-Communist speeches, interviews and songs, as well as a thinly veiled contempt for nationalism, patriotism, and abiding faith in God as the Creator of the universe. At this time in his life, (about 1969), John Lennon was indeed a vile and disgusting tool of Satan.

As the decade of the Seventies wore on, Lennon and his wife Yoko Ono had a child, Sean. The former *Beatle* dropped out of sight and quit making Rock & Roll records for five years. In 1980, he and Ono produced their joint collaboration, "Double Fantasy," a record filled with passionate devotion to wife and family. Then demons possessed Mark David Chapman, and John Lennon was murdered, dying horribly and pathetically. His phenomenal life was erased in the wink of an eye. The depraved lifestyle Lennon had cultivated in his youth finally caught up with him. The demons he had consorted with all those many years turned on him and tore him to pieces when he tried to run away from them. Such is Satan's way of dealing with his disciples. Satan simply DID NOT ALLOW IT TO HAPPEN! Lennon had outlived his usefulness as the Devil's slave, and he ceased to exist.

Though he often talked about Jesus Christ, paying him lip service as a great philosopher, I know of no instance where John Lennon ever accepted Jesus as his personal savior. The fruits of his life, though honored by the world's standards, were not those of a Christian.

There should be a lesson for all of us in this pathetic man's life.

New insights into that murky period of semi-retirement just before his death in 1980 have only recently begun to surface, and the picture they paint is not pretty at all.

In *Dakota Days,* by John Green, Lennon is shown hiding from the public out of fear, not personal conviction. Green was John and Yoko's personal Tarot card reader. Yoko especially demanded his fateful advice on a daily basis for every major and minor matter of her life. Green was on an exclusive retainer to the Lennons for several years, even bunking in at their Dakota suite on occasion to be more readily available for odd hour fortune telling sessions. Yoko refused to make many a move without first asking "the cards" what to do. Lennon was more skeptical, but after seeing several successful examples of Green's skill, he, too, wholeheartedly embraced the witchcraft.

Wait a minute, some of you may be saying. Fortune telling's just a harmless game, isn't it? Surely such a popular pastime doesn't qualify as "witchcraft."

I'm afraid anyone asking that question is greatly mistaken. Tarot card reading is the same thing as "divination" or "divining the future." It is a sin forbidden in the Bible, (II Kings 17:17, Jeremiah 27:8-9, Jeremiah 29:8-9, Acts 16:16-24, and Deuteronomy 18:10-14). Anyone that engages in it provokes the Lord to anger.

If we examine this a little more in depth, it should be obvious why God refuses to allow us to consult spirits and unseen forces to reveal the future. It's not that these things don't work; on the contrary, there is very real power involved. But what business is it of ours to know what the future holds? If we knew the struggles and joys to come, why would we need the strength of our God to get us through those hills and valleys? The Lord wants us to put our faith in HIM, not some fortune teller or the forces that make him what he is. God has a plan for each of our lives; He'll reveal it to us step by step as He desires. To want to know the Mind and Will of God beforehand is incredible arrogance, in my opinion. We should also realize that the modern Tarot owes an incredible debt to Aleister Crowley. (Funny how his name keeps popping up, isn't it?) Crowley spent a large part of his life researching and re-defining the ancient Tarot.

In the pages of *Dakota Days* we also find Green and Yoko journeying to South America to consult a bona fide "bruja," or witch. Yoko parted with $60,000 in return for a whole slew of spells regarding career and health. At the end of their sojourn, the witch sacrificed a dove over an altar and demanded that Yoko sign her name in blood on a devilish contract. Terrified, Lennon's wife begged Green to do the honors, which he did, though he signed Yoko's name.

According to John Green, John Lennon's oft repeated "househusband" story was basically a lie. Though he did care for and feed baby Sean, he quickly tired of the routine and resented his responsibilities. He is also reported to have kicked the child in anger, as well as subjecting his wife to the most heartless cruelties and public humiliations, relying on his well known "acid wit" and sarcastic tongue to break her down. The real reason he had dropped from sight was because he could no longer write songs, and didn't know what to do about it.

Now, admittedly, Lennon was an incredibly complex human being thrust into a position few men have ever held before or since — for a few years during the decade of the Sixties, he was worshiped AS A GOD. From roughly 1970 until his death, he was respected as the wisest of philosophers — on a par with the best the Bible had to offer. That's how starved our world was for wisdom. Was John Lennon really that wise? Wise men don't allow every aspect of their lives to be ruled by a single number, as Lennon did. Details?

The number 9 held an incredibly powerful and mystical significance for the former *Beatle,* some of it chilling in view of later events.

Lennon was born on October 9, 1940. His son Sean was

also born on October 9. Shortly after his birth in war-torn England, baby John and his mother Julia moved into a home whose address was 9 Newcastle Road. *The Beatles* began their dizzy roller coaster ride to global stardom when they began playing at the Liverpool Cavern Club in 1961. 9 years later, in 1970, they split up. Lennon married Yoko Ono in 1969. (He met her on November 9, 1966). They both moved from England to New York in 1971. He lived there for 9 years, until his death in 1980. *The Beatles'* last album was recorded in 1969 ("Abbey Road"). Above his bed at the Dakota, Lennon had hung a numeral 9 on the wall. In 1969, he officially changed his name from John Winston Lennon to John Ono Lennon. He then bragged that between John Ono Lennon and Yoko Ono Lennon there were 9 O's. (Yoko urged him to do this so that his numerological number based on the letters of his name would become 9.) He claimed to have seen a UFO while standing on the roof of the Dakota building at 9 a.m. John and Yoko's favorite Tarot card reader performed a pagan nuptial ceremony in 1975 to celebrate their 6th wedding anniversary. They insisted that the ceremony MUST commence at 9 p.m. John Lennon wrote several songs centered around the number 9, the earliest being "One After 909," also "#9 Dream," and the infamous "Revolution 9."

"Revolution 9," (from *The Beatles'* landmark "White Album," was eight minutes and fifteen seconds of wild electronic noise mixed with garbled snatches of spoken dialogue and music gleaned from English radio, all tied together by a clipped British voice endlessly reciting, "Number 9, Number 9, Number 9 . . . " When reversed, that "Number 9" message becomes "Turn me on, dead man," which marked a mad dash by DJs across America to record and play the song in reverse in order to find the latest "Paul is dead" clues. Where did the "Number 9" intonation come from? It was the voice of the audio engineer testing his equipment where "Revolution 9" was recorded . . . Abbey Road studio #9!

All of this could be written off as pure coincidence or a glaring example of John Lennon's weird foolishness if it weren't for Charles Manson. The demented and drug-blasted California-murder mastermind claimed to hear "secret voices" on the "White Album" which he said gave him the go ahead to order the butcherings of beautiful actress Sharon Tate and her friends. The killings occurred on August 9, 1969!

People thought Charles Manson was simply a drug burned-out psychopath when he claimed to hear voices on that record. They didn't know there really WERE hidden messages there! Manson was such a Beatlemaniac he even saw parallels in the Bible of the power of his gods — *The Beatles.* He often read and quoted Revelation 9:7-9 to his followers. Here is the passage:

> "And the shapes of the locusts were like unto horses prepared unto battle; and on their heads were as it were crowns like gold, and their faces were as the faces of men. And they had hair as the hair of women, and their teeth were as the teeth of lions. And they had breastplates, as it were breastplates of iron; and the sound of their wings was as the sound of chariots of many horses running to battle."

He claimed that the faces of men and hair of women were obvious references to *The Beatles,* and that the breastplates of iron and sound of wings was the electric guitars they wore on their chests, with the noise of their music sounding like chariots rushing to battle.

Demented? Probably. Demon possessed? Undoubtedly. Coincidence? Hardly.

There's just one nagging question here: How is it possible or even conceivable that John Lennon's "Revolution 9," written and produced one continent and an ocean away, spoke to the depraved mind of a madman who believed that Revelation 9 was prophecy fulfilled in *The Beatles?*

Revolution 9. Revelation 9.

I believe the hand of Satan stands out clearly in this matter.

In numerology, the number 9 is the FINAL number, the end of the line, so to speak, the last single digit and highest counting number before starting over again with other numerals. It is also 6 reversed, and 6 represents man. The final tragic and creepy irony between John Lennon's wasted life and his occult fascination with the number 9 came on December 8, 1980 when he was shot to death in New York City by Mark David Chapman.

In England, John's birthplace, it was already December 9th!

Here is a tally, album by album, of the clues connected to the "Paul is dead" rumors.

(See figure 4.) "SERGEANT PEPPER'S LONELY HEARTS CLUB BAND:" On the front of the LP, Paul is singled out from his fellow *Beatles* and the crowd of famous people surrounding them by an open hand directly above his head, the Hand of Death. (Note: The bald and baggy-eyed face on the top row, second from the left, is none other than Aleister Crowley!) *Beatle* Ringo Starr later remarked, "We just thought we would like to put together a lot of people we like and admire."[5]

On the reverse side of the record, McCartney has his back to the camera, in marked contrast to the other three Moptops, who are facing forward. As the sleeve opens up to reveal a smiling photo of the Fab Four, a patch sewn onto the arm of McCartney's gaudy uniform reads OPD (Officially Pronounced Dead).

"MAGICAL MYSTERY TOUR:" All four Beatles are wearing strange Halloween masks on the cover of this record. Paul's is that of a walrus, symbol of death in the Soviet Union. On the back cover the group is identically attired in immaculate white tuxedoes. Red carnations adorn their lapels. Except for McCartney's; his is black.

"THE WHITE ALBUM:" the clues on this LP are lyrical, appearing on three of John Lennon's songs, "Glass Onion,"

Figure 4

The beginning of the end.

"Revolution #9," and "I'm So Tired."

"Glass Onion" contains this stanza: "Here's another clue for you all/ the walrus was Paul . . ." "Revolution #9" contains an eerie, disembodied voice saying repeatedly, "Turn me on dead man . . ." Gibberish at the end of "I'm So Tired" says, "Paul is a dead man. Miss him, miss him," when reversed.

(See figure 5.) "ABBEY ROAD:" The cover of this LP has the Beatles strolling single file over an English

Figure 5

"Turn me on, dead man."

crosswalk. John Lennon is dressed completely in white; Paul, in a black suit, is out of step with his fellow *Beatles.* He is also barefoot, (the symbol of a corpse in Hindu mythology). The license plate of a parked VW nearby reads 28 IF, taken to mean that McCartney would have been 28 IF he had lived.

Thus was the "concept" or "message" album begun. From a series of greedy publicity stunts staged by the most famous group in the world, *The Beatles,* a whole new generation of Rock bands would reap the benefits of that deceitful harvest. The unwitting consumer's attention had been intensely focused onto the covers of Rock & Roll records, not just the music contained inside their sleeves. From there it was only a matter of time until a radical slide into blatant satanic occultism took off, reflected in the bright, shiny covers of Rock & Roll records. This grisly phenomenon peaked in the mid Seventies, run into the ground by such "no future" prophets of doom as *Black Sabbath* and *KISS*.

Just when normal, healthy music lovers had breathed a hefty sigh of relief at the final disposal of such garbage by a jaded and bored listening public, the entire nightmare sprang back to life around 1980, resurrected from the dead by such demented Rockers as *AC-DC,* the *Plasmatics,* and Ozzy Osbourne, former lead singer with *Black Sabbath.*

OZZY OSBOURNE & BLACK SABBATH

Ozzy's story is rather a strange one. He doesn't look anything like the popular conception of a Rock & Roll superstar.

Easily fifty pounds overweight, Ozzy's belly threatens to split his tight, shiny, sequined pants when he jumps and squats in concert. His double chin flops up and down when he sings while his long, greasy hair hangs round his fat face like a golden halo. He is missing some teeth in his lower jawbone, and lots of self-inflicted and intricate tattoos decorate his fingers, chest, forearms, and knees. Launched to stardom in 1970 fronting *Black Sabbath,* he became famous by singing about corpses, asylums, drugs, the Devil, and Atomic War. His nasal, tuneless singing style sounds like a raccoon caught in a leg trap.

How did *Black Sabbath* get famous? It seems impossible that such a ragtag bunch of misfits and weirdos could sell ten records to their relatives, much less tens of millions of albums over a 15 year span. Where did the occult influences that dripped from every lyric and guitar note come from?

Ozzy Osbourne, original singer/songwriter/frontman for the group, sheds some light on this subject in Hit Parader magazine. Somehow his comments don't surprise me.

> "We started developing a fascination with the occult. Tony, in particular, was reading every book he could come up with on the subject and Geezer was writing a lot of bizarre lyrics. One day he wrote a song called 'Black Sabbath,' which was inspired by a Boris Karloff movie. The rest, you could say, is history."[6]

Tony Iommi is *Sabbath's* guitarist, and Terry "Geezer" Butler its' bass player/lyricist. By Ozzy's own admission in this article, the early *Black Sabbath* was a bunch of stoned out kids from poor working class neighborhoods who played Blues tunes and covers of *Rolling Stones* songs. It wasn't until Iommi and Butler began a serious study of the occult that things began to happen.

These are the kind of lyrics Osbourne and Butler were writing after the Devil lended a hand:

"BLACK SABBATH:"

"Satan sitting there
He's smiling
Watches the flames go higher and higher
Oh no, please God help me . . . "

"N.I.B." (Nativity In Black):

"Now I have you with me
Under my power
Our love grows stronger now
With every hour
Look into my eyes
You'll see who I am
My name is Lucifer
Please take my hand."

In 1974, *Black Sabbath's* fifth LP, titled "Sabbath, Bloody Sabbath," hit the record stores. There can be no question as to where this record was coming from, not with a cover graphics display such as the one that adorned its gut wrenching outer sleeve. An artist's conception depicts a horrible nightmare; a naked man lying on a rumpled bed writhes before Satan's imps gathered around him. Their horned, evil faces stare intently into the man's own as if waiting for his soul to escape the confines of his body, fair game for the demons. The man is choking to death from a venomous snake wrapped tightly round his throat. Rats scamper over the bedclothes, and the bed headboard has turned into a huge, grinning skull with long arms and webbed talons reaching for the unfortunate sinner. The numbers 666 lie beneath the skull. Because of the nudity we cannot print this picture.

Having cut his teeth on such disturbing trash during his *Sabbath* days, Ozzy Osbourne has plumbed even lower depths in his current solo career.

Dumped by the other members of *Black Sabbath* for being too weird and drug decayed even for them, he went on in 1980 to form a new band and produce an eerie album, 1981's "Blizzard Of Oz." Before embarking on his first solo tour to promote the "Blizzard" LP, a shocking story appeared in all the major music magazines as well as newspapers everywhere. Ozzy, in an attempt to generate some grisly publicity for himself, was reported to have bitten the head off a live dove while at a meeting of some very influential and dignified record company executives, spitting the remains of the bird on the table when he was finished with his "snack."

While such melodramatic hype is not unusual in big time Rock circles, neither Ozzy nor any of his representatives ever bothered to issue a denial as to the truth of the story. On the contrary, Ozzy himself told Rolling Stone Magazine that he had done the disgusting act because he was "jet lagged." And so, the image of the sick, insane Rock Star turned satanist has been played to the hilt. An image built on such shocking cruelty must be taken at face value. How could any self-respecting human being allow himself to be manipulated in this way unless he had become trapped, a prisoner of his own demented addictions?

When Ozzy Osbourne bit the head off that dove and spat the remains on a table before a bunch of startled and sickened record executives, what was really going on there? Of course Ozzy is sick, demented, insane and unnatural — that's obvious — but what message was the unclean spirit that moves in Ozzy trying to accomplish through that incredibly well publicized media event?

Satan loves subliminal symbolism, and the twisting of it for his own ends. What is the symbolic significance of a dove — representing purity, harmlessness, gentleness, monogamy (doves have one mate for life), peace, and cleanliness? The ancient Jews used doves as sacrifices to God because they were considered "clean" animals. They ate grain rather than carrion like birds of prey or scavengers. This is the exact opposite of the powerful predatory image Satan likes to foster. Scripture tells us in Luke 3:21 & 22 that the Holy Spirit of God descended "as a dove" on Jesus at his baptism. I believe the subliminal impact of Ozzy's depraved act was the chewing up and spitting out of the Holy Spirit of God and Christ.

In Billboard Magazine, (the recording industry's Bible), Ozzy bragged of new, eye popping tricks to come at his future concerts. He said "gallons of pig's blood" would be used, and that he himself would blow up at the end of the show, showering the stage with intestines and other organs. A January,1982 ad in the Indianapolis Star for an upcoming Ozzy concert at the huge Market Square Arena, warned the audience not to eat anything before coming to the concert, as Ozzy's antics might just make them throw up. Parental discretion was also advised.

In the February, 1982 issue of Rolling Stone Magazine, Ozzy was reported to have jumped onto a table in a crowded German restaurant during a meeting of CBS Record Company executives. He then proceeded to urinate into a wine carafe, after which he kissed one of the astonished businessmen full on the lips. Soon after this event, Ozzy checked himself into a U.K. sanitarium for three days. After being released from the sanitarium, Osbourne sank to new demented depths at a Des Moines, Iowa concert where he bit the head off a live bat onstage. He subsequently received a painful series of rabies injections, as the headless bat's body could not be found by local Board of Health officials anxious to determine whether the animal had been rabid. (Maybe Ozzy ate the body, too!)

Osbourne's bad luck continued to dog him through the early months of 1982, climaxing in the plane crash death of his twenty-six year old guitarist, (and band backbone), Randy Rhoads.

Some of Ozzy's songs and lyrics paint the perfect picture of the insane ideas bubbling through his blasted brain. For example:

"YOU CAN'T KILL ROCK & ROLL:"

"Cause Rock & Roll is my religion and my law
Won't ever change, you may think it's strange
You can't kill Rock & Roll
I'm here to stay . . . "

"LITTLE DOLLS:"

"Tortured and flaming you give birth to Hell
Living a nightmare
It's a pity you'll pray for your death
But he's in no hurry
Demons and curses that play on your soul
Like something ignited . . . "

"DIARY OF A MADMAN:"

"A sickened mind and spirit
The mirror tells me lies
Will he escape my soul or will he live in me
Is he tryin to get out or tryin to enter me
Voices in the darkness
Scream away my mental health . . . "

Surely we can produce better heroes than this for our

children to imitate! At the very least, concerned Christian parents and other adults in positions of authority should be able to stop sickening trash such as this in its tracks before it goes on to other, even more outrageous lengths.

Ozzy Osbourne's lyrics mirror the covers of his albums perfectly.

Ozzy's LP, "Diary Of A Madman," is truly a landmark in the no-holds-barred glorification of witchcraft and demonic possession. (See figure 6.) A wild eyed, blood-spattered Ozzy, his clothes dusty and ripped, makes strange

Figure 6

A madman or a trapped man?

gestures and signs with his hands and fingers. He is cavorting in a cobwebbed castle chamber, candelabra behind him throwing out elongated, ghostly shadows. An upside down cross hangs on one wall. Nearby, a young boy of about ten (the boy is actually Ozzy's real son) giggles wickedly over an ancient book clearly marked "SPELLS." A black cat spits and arches its back atop a dusty window sill. The boy is pointing directly at the person holding the record. Flip the album over, and behold! The boy is gone; the bloody body

Figure 7

Where's my Alpo?

is collapsed over the "SPELLS" book lying on the table, and omnipotent Ozzy, (now dressed in blinding white), stands triumphant, arms raised, a sickly leer on his beer bloated face.

In both pictures, and especially on the European Extended Play version, one object figures prominently: the limp, lifeless body of a dove on the dusty table. Its neck appears to be broken, its throat ripped and torn as if Ozzy may have been chewing on it. We can only hope that the dove wasn't a real one.

Figure 8

Lunch with Ozzy.

Figure 9

Give ME your children!

(See figures 7, 8 and 9 for more of Osbourne's madness.)
It would be unfair to label Ozzy Osbourne a lunatic without getting his own personal slant on things. After all, some say his well worn image is no more than a slickly running cog in the media machine, a kind of tongue in cheek con game. Here are some of Ozzy's thoughts, as printed in Circus and Hit Parader magazines:

"Let everybody know that I'm just as evil and just as crazy as ever."[7]

"The Devil is within us all the time. It's here. All this is the Devil. Weird things happen to me because I live in a weird house in a weird area. Somebody found that people in the area had been holding Black Mass over at the !*?%!&* abbey. That's why this cross never leaves me . . . "[8]

"I mean one time I wanted to get a !*?%!&* black cathedral built in back of my house. My wife freaked and wouldn't allow it . . . "[9]

"I can say that my album has a lot more musical variety. One of the songs is about this guy named Aleister Crowley. That man was the phenomenon of his time . . . "[10]

"Yes, I feel like I've met the Devil. I feel that I was a servant of his once . . . "[11]

"I have OD'd many times, but I have the will to live . . . I have a mission in this world and that mission is to just Rock & Roll . . . "[12]

"There were these real weird people comin to hear *Sabbath*. These guys were lined up in the corridor dressed in black robes, holding candles . . . "[13] (See Appendix A.)

From "Oui," a skin magazine that features interviews with Rock & Roll stars in between the centerfold spreads of naked women, the following gut wrenching comments were taken from an Ozzy Osbourne conversation:

"I've always been !*?%!&* crazy. When I was a child, I watched this film where a guy got hung on a ship. I wanted to know what it was like, so I tried to hang myself. I put the rope over the thing, kicked the chair, held the rope and let go . . . "

Ozzy: "I spent three years in a slaughterhouse, killing cows and pigs and all sorts of things. It got pretty bizarre — I was figuring out all these different ways to kill these animals. Have you ever drank blood?"

Oui: " . . . What kind of blood are you talking about?"

Ozzy: "Oh, ox blood, pig's blood. I have, and I gotta admit, the first time you do it, you get quite a weird feeling."

Oui: "What was the first time like?"

Ozzy: "Well, you kinda stick a knife in there and hold out your cup. After that I got into the habit and started drinking it rather frequently.",

Oui: "What did your co-workers think?"

Ozzy: "They thought I was totally insane. I once sawed a live sheep's head in half with a hacksaw. I guess that sort of capped it for them . . . "

It was reported on MTV's Music News on November 14, 1985, that Ozzy Osbourne and CBS Records, (his recording company), were being sued by a parent whose son had committed suicide while listening to one of Ozzy's songs titled, "Suicide Solution." Osbourne typically denied any responsibility for such a crime as influencing young minds with his degenerate mush, even though this isn't the first time his lyrics have inspired the young to take their own life.

In the summer of 1984 I personally witnessed an anti-Rock Revival meeting led by Brother Dan Peters of the Peters Brothers Ministries, St. Paul, Minnesota. In the course of his presentation, Brother Peters showed color slides of a young man who had attempted to blow his own head off with a shotgun while listening to a *Black Sabbath* record. After his unsuccessful suicide attempt, this young person spent the next few years in painful plastic surgeries designed to rebuild his face, most of which had been torn away by the shotgun blast. The poor boy's face was a mass of twisted and scarred tissue. Though the Lord spared him from Hell, it was obvious that young man's life would never be the same as before he allowed Ozzy Osbourne and *Black Sabbath* to come into it.

I for one would like to know how Ozzy and others of his ilk can go to sleep at night with the deaths and mutilations of who knows how many young people on their consciences. Could that be one reason why Rock stars drown their brains in booze and burn their bodies with debilitating drugs? Satan allows just enough of their blasted guilty consciences to reemerge in order to drive them further into the depths of hellish self-destruction, dragging millions of fans along as well.

Ozzy Osbourne, sickening and frightening as he is, is by far not the only Rocker making millions by promoting Satanism.

W.A.S.P.

Blackie Lawless, the founder/singer/songwriter/bass player of the demonic L.A. Metal band, *W.A.S.P.*, claims to have been the first to use pentagrams in the logo of one of his earlier groups.[14] Blackie was a member of the *New York Dolls* when they were managed by former *Sex Pistols'* mentor, Malcolm McLaren. Through the *Dolls,* Blackie met *KISS* guitarist Ace Frehley. From Ace, Blackie was introduced to Gene Simmons. Lawless claims Simmons stole the "Il Cornuto". devil sign from him. Another of Blackie's friends was Nikki Sixx, the bass player/songwriter of *Motley Crue.* If what this guy says is true, then he has been a tremendously evil influence on today's Heavy Metal bands. This man should be watched closely!

Lawless' comments:

"We were the first band ever to use a pentagram on a

logo. Our logo was an inverted pentagram; it said 'Sister' through it and it had flames around it."[15]

About the Il Cornuto: "I looked for something because Ozzy got real big doing it . . . "[16]

The article states that Blackie discovered the sign in a photo on an occult book jacket. What a strange coincidence that Anton La Vey's "satanic Bible" features a picture of him making the Il Cornuto sign on the back of the book! The article goes on to say that in 1977 Gene Simmons attended one of Lawless' concerts.

Blackie Lawless: "About three months later, "Love Gun" comes out with him doing it on the jacket. It was the first time the world had seen that. He started doing it live and it caught on . . . "[17]

W.A.S.P.'s stage show features twin skulls 7 feet high and 12 feet wide. Lasers are set in the eyes, and smoke comes out of the nose. Fireworks shoot out from between Blackie's legs, and at some point in the show he pours blood from a human skull into his open mouth. Total cost for their staging: $100,000.

In "Hit Parader," guitarist Chris Holmes tells how he came to join *W.A.S.P.:*

"Blackie saw my picture in the "Beaver Hunt" section of "Hustler" Magazine. That was in 1978. We got together and formed a band called *Sister . . . "* [18]

Dear God in Heaven! Holmes' quotation just floored me. God-fearing Christians may not be familiar with "Hustler" magazine, but it has a circulation of many thousands all over the world. It is probably one of the most disgusting and vile pieces of pornography ever put out. The "Beaver Hunt" section Holmes talks about is particularly disgraceful. It just seems beyond comprehension, but "Hustler" readers, both male and female, send in snapshots of themselves stark naked to this section of the magazine in the hopes of winning a prize, or perhaps just getting a little more "action," or both. They often times pose themselves in lewd positions in order to stand out from the other entries. We know from looking at the clear band of plastic on *W.A.S.P.'s* debut album that the word *W.A.S.P.* itself stands for, "<u>W</u>e <u>A</u>re <u>S</u>exual <u>P</u>erverts." What a horrible reality is unveiled here! What kind of man would look in a "Hustler" magazine, ogle a snapshot of another naked male, then call him up and offer to start a Rock band with him? If that's not perversion, what is? I have a feeling that Blackie and Chris were more interested in getting to know each other than just playing music together.

This whole affair is disgusting, brethren. It's despicable! A perverted pair of Rockers writing songs about the Devil. One guy drinks cow blood on stage. The other one, (Holmes) has a guitar painted with blood dripping down it. His stage outfit is black, red, and yellow flames licking upward all over his body, and his arms are covered with tattoos of skulls. These people must be stopped, and the only way to do it is to expose them in their hateful perversions and Devil-worship. They've got to be stopped now!

Many, many Christians today believe in an imminent Apocalypse, and a return to "the days of Noah." We consider ourselves to be in the midst of the Last Days as foretold in Scripture. And the simple truth of the matter is that these Rock groups are also singing about it, promoting the concept, and branding it into the minds of millions across the globe. They are preparing a new order of callous indifference to decency, and jaded thrill seeking, with a demon hiding behind every bend in life's road. Is it deadly serious soul snatching by satanic envoys, as true servants of Christ know to be true, or merely Madison Avenue advertising run rampant, as many others believe?

Either way, it adds up to the same thing: the spreading of evil.

Compared to the *Plasmatics,* however, *W.A.S.P.* and Ozzy Osbourne are just schoolboys.

THE PLASMATICS

Should a prize be given for the ultimate blasphemous obscenity ever to grace the cover of a Rock & Roll record, the *Plasmatics* would surely walk away with the award. The piece of garbage posing as a record album is the cover of their 1981 release, "Metal Priestess." Here we have an outright glorification of Lucifer, no question about it. Let me describe this album cover to you, then see if you don't agree. It is so disgusting we could not print a picture of it.

Wendy O. Williams, the *Plasmatics'* gravel throated screamer, is standing in relaxed profile, one arm pointing upward to the black, storm tossed sky. Rolling thunderheads mass in the background. Wendy is dressed, or rather undressed, in a Sado-Masochistic leather corset-harness and thigh high boots. Her buttocks are bared from the Nazish costume, as are her breasts. She is standing in front of a gigantic inverted iron pentagram (five pointed star), within a circle. That ancient symbol of necromancy, the Mendes Goat, could easily be drawn within its sharp, triangular lines as it points down toward Hell. This pentagram backdrop is also used in the *Plasmatics'* live shows.

What is the significance of the pentagram being inverted?

In the time of the Roman Empire, when Christian persecution was at its peak, the followers of Christ were often crucified on inverted X's or crosses. Tied or nailed upside down on the structures, (some of which were then set afire), their heads were facing the dirt. It was thought that in this posture their soul would descend directly into the underworld at the point of death. One of Christ's original disciples was tortured in this way.

On the reverse side of "Metal Priestess," two photos of the other band members are featured. One, lead guitarist Richard Stotts, sports blue hair and pointed breasts on his leather studded chest. The other *Plasmatic* is wearing a Dracula cape and is holding a lit black candle, the kind used by witches and satanists in their devil-worshiping ceremonies. Song titles include: "Masterplan," "Sex Junkie," "Doomsday," "Black Leather Monster," and "Lunacy."

The catalogue number of the LP is W.O.W. 666.

The following is just a taste of where the *Plasmatics* are coming from. The lyrics to "Lunacy" and "Doom Song" spell things out pretty clearly.

"LUNACY:"

"Ancient forces from the tomb
Behold the power the full moon
Dichotomy from outer space
Dominates the human race
It comes at night
And takes you out of your head
It shows no mercy when it gets you
Can take the living
And can make them dead . . ."

"DOOM SONG:"

"Behold the power of the night
Curse the filthy hypocrites
Crawl into their beds at night
Ooze from slimy depths below
Scream into their frozen brains
Work thy wretched wrath
Remove all obstacles from our path
I command that these things of which I speak
Will come to be
Behold the Prince Of Darkness here!"

If you ever wondered just exactly what an "incantation" is, the lyrics of "Doom Song" are just that — an actual incantation used by witches to call up a demon to gain revenge on an enemy! (See Appendix.)

Surely even the most skeptical person would have to admit, just from the small amount of information already presented, that the Devil and Rock & Roll are good friends. These few records and album covers previously talked about are just the tip of the iceberg! Volumes could be written about the thousands of satanic references, both lyrical and photographic, that permeate the whole of today's Rock record industry. What is truly frightening about this trend is the fact that it is no longer content with just using references to Satan, Hell, Spirits, and Outer Space. We are sliding into a self fulfilling prophecy of Doomsday thinking. Listening to these Rock records, it's Doomsday this, and Doomsday that. Every song lyric seems to reflect the "forget about tomorrow, live for today" *(AC-DC)* syndrome. Every album cover depicts madness, despair, or has something to do with the Anti-Christ concept these days. Young people are being prepared for the end of the world all right, but they're joining the losing side!

Lest anyone should think that the groups we're talking about here are an insignificant minority, let me set the record straight: *Black Sabbath, KISS, AC-DC, W.A.S.P.,* the *Plasmatics,* Ozzy Osbourne . . . These bands are BIG!

AC-DC alone was paid $552,395 for three sellout shows at the San Francisco Cow Palace, on February 14-16, 1982. I wonder how many of the millions of unemployed Americans today struggling just to get by could make good use of that half a million dollars? I wonder how many starving children or drug addicted young people could have been helped with such a wad of ill gotten loot?

At last count, *AC-DC's* "Back In Black" album had sold 14,000,000 copies worldwide, according to Billboard Magazine, and is still climbing! *The Rolling Stones'* 1981 American tour was reported to have grossed between sixty and one hundred MILLION dollars! These groups are the trend setters. All the smaller fish follow in their wake, trying to repeat their success, (i.e. get rich too!)

When your friend or child takes one of these records

home, the inherent evil and demon spirit contained in that piece of plastic has invaded your household. Your child's going to be looking intensively at that cover, examining it, puzzling over the pentagrams and other occult symbols re-created there. He's going to be playing that record over and over, memorizing the songs.

And the covers aren't the only thing young record buyers are digesting. What about the lyrics hidden inside the records? Up till now we've talked mainly about the merchandising-advertising concepts on the outer sleeves which are used to sell the product. What about the song lyrics themselves? Outrageous as some of these covers are, the lyrics of the majority of modern Rock songs go way beyond the bounds of good taste, bad taste, or any taste at all. Some are so self-explanatory that they can only be taken one way — the way they were intended to be taken: as an outright glorification of hellish satanic strength.

Here's an example: On the *Plasmatics'* "Beyond The Valley Of 1984" album, side one commences with a song called "Incantation." A strange, high-pitched bell rings dolefully in measured cadence for several seconds. Suddenly, many voices, some male, some female, begin chanting. Weird, churchy organ chords ebb and swell behind the eerie chorale. It takes a while to make out what the muted, disembodied voices are saying, as it's in Latin. When the realization hit me, a chill went up my spine.

The *Plasmatics* are saying "Omni Maximus Plasmatics" — All Power To The *Plasmatics!* I wonder where they think that power is going to come from! (This phrase also appears on a *Plasmatics* T-shirt which can be ordered from Creem magazine.)

Depressing funeral bells also mark the beginning of *AC-DC's* "Hell's Bells" on the "Back In Black" album. A sample of the lyrics go like this:

> "Satan's gonna get you
> Gonna drag you to Hell

No one's puttin up a fight
You get into evil
You're a friend of mine . . ."

I used to have on tape a recording of a real Black Mass by the Rock group *Coven.* It began with the long, slow ringing of bells. Unknown chants in Latin followed, and it wasn't long before a voice in English yelled out, "Do you renounce Jesus as the Christ?!" That's as far as I listened, and that was many years ago. The point here is this: There is a certain very describable sound and tone to the bells that started that Black Mass; the easiest way to describe them is to say that they sound like funeral bells, booming, gloomy, eerie. The following Rock songs all start with bells that are virtually identical to those in that Black Mass: "Masterplan" by the *Plasmatics,* "Mother," by John Lennon, "Black Sabbath" by *Black Sabbath,* "Tormentor," by *W.A.S.P.,* "Journey To The Centre Of Eternity," by Ozzy Osbourne, and "Hells Bells," by *AC-DC.* How many more examples are out there, waiting to be discovered?

What does a bell do, anyway? It calls us together to meet, it warns us of impending danger, and it tells us what TIME it is. I believe that the reason so many of these death-bells are in Heavy Metal Rock songs is that Satan is telling young people all over the world, NOW is the time to give me your soul.

Don't listen!

The song, "Hells Bells" is probably the best example of Satan-Rock ever recorded. Pages could be written about the devilish aspects and Luciferian reversals contained in its lyrics and music. One example: the words "If God's on the left/ Then I'm stickin' to the right . . . " is the reverse of what we read in the Bible in Matthew 25:33-46. The passage is about the Judgment Day when our Lord separates the Faithful from the sinners like sheep from goats. Those washed in the Blood will stand at the Lord's RIGHT hand, their destiny eternal life. Those on the LEFT will be doomed to Hell and damnation. I've got news for *AC-DC:* God's not on the left OR the right; He's right in the middle, and everything we do and everything we are depends on His unchanging nature and perfection, not our personal whims or beliefs.

Where will you be on that Day of Judgment, young people, on the left with Angus Young and his band, or on the right with the Saints of God?

Make your choice, because time's running out.

Other songs on "Back In Black" mention Satan directly. For example:

"GIVEN THE DOG A BONE" —

"Goin down to the Devil
Down, down, to 90 degrees."

"HAVE A DRINK ON ME" —

"Don't worry about tomorrow
Take it today
Forget about the check
We'll get Hell to pay . . . "

"BACK IN BLACK" —

"I've got nine lives
Cat's eyes
Forget about the hearse
Cause I'll never die . . . "

AC-DC's 1981 LP, "For Those About To Rock, We Salute You," shows no change from their previously charted territory. Witness lyrics from the following songs:

"C.O.D." —
"Care Of The Devil
Care Of The Devil in me . . . "

"FOR THOSE ABOUT TO ROCK" —
"Stand up and be counted

For what you are about to receive
We are the dealers
We'll give you everything you need . . . "

"EVIL WALKS" —

"Black shadow hanging over your shoulder
Black mark up against your name
Evil walks behind you
Evil sleeps beside you
Evil talks around you . . . "

"INJECT THE VENOM" —

"Got no heart and
Feel no pain
Take your soul and
Leave a stain . . . "

The title of "For Those About To Rock, We Salute You," is a paraphrase of the speech Roman gladiators used to hear from their emperor shortly before being thrown into savage deadly combat in the Circus Maximus which could produce only one survivor — "For those about to die, we salute you."

AC-DC is equating entering the world of Rock & Roll with dying!

They ought to know.

The previous lyrical examples we have just shown have all been straightforward in their homage to Satan. *AC-DC* and the *Plasmatics* certainly don't mince words in their songs when it comes to the Devil. But when it comes to outright demonic praise of Lucifer, they don't hold a candle to *KISS.*

KISS (KINGS IN SATAN'S SERVICE)

One member, Gene Simmons, used to paint his face in gargoyle fashion. He still drools a bloody froth from his gaping mouth in concert, sometimes blowing flames from a lit torch, like a circus fire eater. He also likes to wear a necklace of miniature human skulls, as well as a skull ring, inspired by his idol, *Rolling Stone* Keith Richards. On one concert tour, Simmons, his leathery bat-wing costume trailing behind him, actually flew thirty feet (via a concealed winch mechanism attached to a harness on his back), to land atop a huge tower stage-left where he appropriately bellowed out his signature tune, "God of Thunder."

Gene is writer and singer of the song on *KISS'* "Destroyer" LP (see Revelation 9:11), called "God Of Thunder." At the beginning of the tune little children's voices are heard shouting, "I don't want to go to that place." Part of the lyric is as follows:

> "I'm the Lord of the wasteland
> I gather darkness to please me
> And I command you to kneel before the
> God of thunder
> And Rock & Roll
> The spell you're under
> Will slowly rob you of your virgin soul . . . "

KISS' stage show set new standards for live concerts during the decade of the Seventies. Gargantuan explosions punctuated parts of their songs, (such as one of their more socially relevant numbers, "Rock & Roll All Night, And Party Every Day"), while twenty foot flames shot up around them. In their black nail studded leather and eight inch high stacked heel boots, they appear to have just arrived from the Gates of Hell.

Head death Rocker Gene Simmons openly brags of having a scrapbook stuffed with naked snapshots of the literally thousands of female fans, (some as young as 14!), with whom he had sexual relations during ten years of *KISS* concert tours.

KISS as a group has done more to perpetuate the modern trend of "Shock Rock" begun by *Alice Cooper* than any other band in the last decade. Much of the shock-

ing is contained in the filthy lyrics of most *KISS* songs.
For example:

"CHRISTINE SIXTEEN" —

"She's been around
   But she's young and clean . . . "

"CALLING DR. LOVE" —

"Even though I'm full of sin
   In the end you'll let me in . . . "

"LOVE EM AND LEAVE EM" —

"You lift your dress
   You want to impress . . . "

"GREAT EXPECTATIONS" —

"And you feel what my fingers can do . . . "

"MAKIN LOVE" —

"Put your hand in my pocket
   Grab onto my rocket . . . "

"FITS LIKE A GLOVE" —

"I go through her like a hot knife through butter . . ."

KISS' 1981 LP, "The Elder," contains a song called
"MR. BLACKWELL." One line stands out in particular:

"I'm a sinner who just loves to sin."

Others include:

"Let's drink a toast to the inhuman race
   You're all so weak it really makes me ill
   Don't like you now and probably never will . . . "

The previous examples are just a small part of the overall
picture. Today, there's a whole new breed of *KISS* imitators out there, carrying on the tradition. I want to speak as
sincerely and straightforwardly as I can, friends in Christ,

about the new reigning Kings of Rock's feudal empire:
Motley Crue. I also want to talk about their 1983 LP "Shout
At The Devil," and their strange connection with their war-
lock friends, *KISS.* (See figure 10.)

Figure 10

"It makes me sick when I hear the !*?%!&* people dump on us
because they think we're into devil worship. I can't believe how
stupid most people are." — Mick Mars (far right)

MOTLEY CRUE

This band is worse than *KISS* ever was at the height of their blood-thirsty conquest of world youth in the mid Seventies. It is my belief that, through a complex set of circumstances *Motley Crue* has ascended *KISS's* throne. Some of the factors involved were public appeal, record sales, group personnel problems, changing attitudes and expectations of Rock-hungry youth and an ever more depraved recording industry. *KISS* removed their make-up in 1983, leaving the stage door wide open for *Motley Crue* to walk right through and take up where they left off. Satan and his chief demons orchestrated this event. Mere mortals could never have brought such diverse happenings together so perfectly. Here's how it happened:

KISS had been under extreme pressure ever since their inception (around 1973) to remove their make-up and show their faces to the world. It would have been a suicidal move, career-wise. Their larger-than-life personas represented by that horrible make-up was their main drawing card. To show their naked faces in public would have made them just one more ugly Rock & Roll act, (which is what they turned out to be). All through the Seventies the biggest scoop any photographer could hope for, from whatever variety of newspaper or magazine, was to capture one or more of the members of *KISS* on film unmasked. Few succeeded, so stringent was the group's security.

The question in my mind is, "Why now?" There are many answers. By the early Eighties, *KISS's* popularity was waning. Their albums weren't doing so well. Their drummer, Peter Criss, told them to take a hike, and went solo. (He flopped.) Their record company (Casablanca) folded. Their lead guitar player, Ace Frehley, went off the deep end, either from drugs, drink, or dangerous driving, and was fired. How to recoup the losses and rebound back onto the charts? *KISS's* answer was to pull their last rabbit out of the hat and remove their make-up. They had already hired two new flunkies to replace Criss and Frehley, each with their own stage character already worked out. All four bared their ugly mugs on the cover of the "Lick It Up" LP (See figure 11.)

It's easy to understand the band's motivation for such a move. These Rock stars want everything Satan gives them, and they want to keep getting it forever. Already incredibly wealthy by anyone's standards, their drug bills for ten years would have put a dent in the most fabulous fortune.

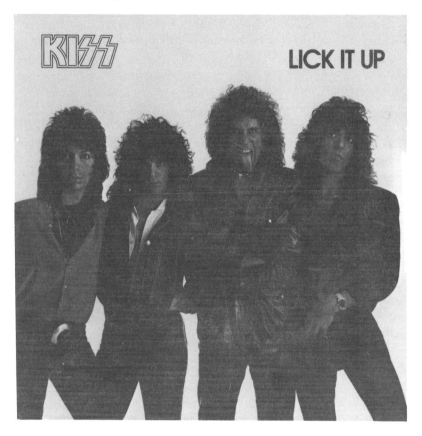

Figure 11

Which is uglier, their faces or their music?

Cocaine's not getting any cheaper, you know. Critics of the group, (myself included), chuckled, thinking at this late date no one could possibly care what *KISS* looked like without face paint. Boy, were we wrong!

"Lick It Up" sold incredibly well, leaping into "Billboard's" Top 100 and resurrecting a band everyone but the fans thought was dead. This brings up another important point: Once a band like *KISS* has made it big, their image and most famous tunes literally achieve immortality. Even if all the *KISSers* were dead and buried , there would still be a copy of one of the records being bought SOMEWHERE by SOMEBODY for the first time. The bands come and the bands go, but their wickedness lives forever on vinyl or tape. The evil that they conjured up in 1975, for example, will still be working its spell in 1995 and beyond on whole new generations of young people. The band doesn't have to physically be intact, or even be alive, for that matter, but if they are, that only adds fuel to the fire. The best example of this is the *Beatles,* the Grandfathers of Rock. Since John Lennon's death, they'll never make another record, but they still sell an incredible number of albums around the world! Lennon is literally selling records from his grave!

Even though *KISS* is old, used up, and past their prime, they're still a considerable force to be reckoned with. The question is, what happens to those millions of boys and girls now growing up who were too young to get into *KISS* in their heyday? It was their older brothers and sisters who paid for *KISS'* drugs and drink through their album purchases. Who will fill the gap for this new breed of Rock-hungry youngsters? If it's not cool for these kids to idolize the same group their older siblings worshiped, who will fill the gap?

The answer is: *Motley Crue.*

Motley Crue looks like *KISS. Motley Crue* sounds like *KISS.* I think *Motley Crue* probably even smells like *KISS,* but there's one important difference between the two.

121

Whereas *KISS* could leave the stage, remove their make-up, and walk down a street like anyone else without being recognized, the *Crue* ENJOY being thought of as depraved, Devil-worshiping delinquents. They brag time and again in Rock magazine interviews that the image they live is not an image. It's their life, and they like it that way! They thumb their noses at society and everything decent, but not in a semi-apologetic, vaguely guilt-ridden manner like Gene Simmons used to do when confronted with his sins by magazine writers. Gene would try hard to justify his insatiable appetite for sexual orgies with 13 year old girls; the *Crue* doesn't care what you think! At least Simmons had the faint stirrings of something resembling a conscience!

Motley Crue is much younger than *KISS* (early 20's); they appeal mostly to an audience of early teens and pre-teenage boys and girls. Their influence is therefore all the more dangerous, since those young people are just beginning to form their ideas about sex, religion, and human relationships. *KISS* gave *Motley Crue* their first big break by allowing them to support their "World Invasion" tour a few years back. Ozzy Osbourne nudged them a step further up Rock's ladder by doing the same thing in 1983. Satan certainly takes care of his own!

Now *Motley Crue* is BIG TIME! Their lipsticked and mascaraed faces leer from the covers of every major and minor Rock magazine in the land, month after month. Their moronic and profane interviews disgrace the pages of those same magazines so often because it's HOT COPY, man! Their philosophy can be summed up thusly: "Beat someone up; have lots of sex, preferably the brutal kind; and God? You still believe in that crap?"

The *Motleys* wear tattered rags on and off stage. Their hair-dos look like the mangy pelts of rabid wolves. Their music is an unbridled, unbroken hymn to Lucifer and his legions. When they say they live their image all the time, they mean it. Blond singer Vince Neil was arrested in Los

Angeles for beating a woman in a bar. He didn't like her comments about his wearing a U.S. Marine uniform, so he beat her. Bassist Nikki Sixx likes to photograph himself and the other band members having sex with willing girls and women in their tour bus. He plays the video tapes back later for everyone's enjoyment.

What brought the *Crue* to the pinnacle of sinful success? *KISS* and Ozzy Osbourne helped, but what elevated a gang of simple-minded perverts into the most popular Heavy Metal band of the day?

The answer is "Shout At The Devil." I want to sincerely warn all parents reading this. If your child possesses this album, you should immediately do two things. Listen to the record ONCE to familiarize yourself with its contents, then destroy it. Burn it, break it, throw it in the garbage, but get rid of it! Your youngster's immortal soul is at stake.

There has never been, in my opinion, a more deadly example of Satan-trap than this record. It is filled with violence, profanity, Devil worship and hate like no other that ever came before it, and that's just what we can audibly hear! The back of the LP contains this statement: "Caution: This record may contain backward messages." What's all this "may contain" business? If a warning like that is printed plainly for all to see, then that album CONTAINS back-masked messages, you can bet on that! What about the songs themselves, what makes them so deadly? Judge for yourself from this sampling:

"BASTARD" —

"Out go the lights
 In goes my knife
 Pull out his life
 Consider that bastard dead . . . "

"10 SECONDS TO LOVE" —

"I got my camera
 Make a star outa you
 Let's inject it

Photograph it
... Just wait honey
Till I tell the boys about you ... "

"RED HOT" —

"The kids scream in fright through the night
Loving every bite with delight
And we blow out our minds with your truth
And together we stand for the youth ... "

"KNOCK EM DEAD, KID" —

"I'm back
And I'm coming your way ...
And I'm primed for hate ... "

"SHOUT AT THE DEVIL" —

"Been tempted by his lie
... He's rage
... He'll be the love in your eyes
He'll be the blood between your thighs
... But in seasons of wither
We'll stand and deliver
Be strong and laugh and
Shout at the Devil."

("Seasons Of Wither" is an old *Aerosmith* song. *Aerosmith* was one of Nikki Sixx's biggest idols in his pre-*Motley* days. One line from that particular song goes like this: "Love for the Devil/ Brought her to me ... ")

Side one of "Shout" begins with a spoken introduction. It's called "In The Beginning," and this piece of perverted prose is nothing more or less than demon prophecy:

"Those who have the youth have the future
So come now, children of the Beast
Be strong
And shout at the Devil."

The narration is done by someone named Allister Fiend. His evil voice drips over the weird organ chords and whirlwind noises behind him as he lovingly caresses each blasphemous word. The name "Allister Fiend" no doubt is in reference to the late Aleister Crowley, patron saint of Rock & Roll.

Another song on this record is titled, "God Bless The Children Of The Beast." It leads directly into a chilling cover version of the *Beatles'* "Helter Skelter," the song that Charles Manson said signalled the Armageddon. And just who are the "Children Of The Beast," anyway? Modern day Rock stars following in the footsteps of Aleister Crowley, his spiritual "children?" Or could it be literally the children of the Beast Rock & Roll, the helpless young people who freely give away their souls to the power of Rock? What a horrible legacy! What a horrible future!

"The Devil" LP opens up to reveal glossy color photos of the *Crue* members. (It's obvious that Elektra, the company that produced this record, invested a lot of money in its design and distribution. Why take such a big chance on a little known band like *Motley Crue?* Because Satanism sells, that's why! And Elektra knew it!) (See figure 12.)

In these photos, the boys are standing amidst flames and smoke. The background looks like every sinner's nightmare of the ferment of Hell. Nikki Sixx displays the Il Cornuto Devil sign proudly, defiantly. The *Crue* makes a big deal out of constantly flaunting this sign. Rare indeed is the picture of the *Motleys* without at least one of them giving the Satan signal. An inverted pentagram adorns the front, back, and inner sleeve of "Devil." Band members also wear pentagrams on their headbands, gloves, drums, and stage set. Poor deluded Rock fans are told by the *Motleys* and others that the Il Cornuto means "Long Live Rock & Roll." Well, that's not far from the truth. As long as Rock & Roll lives, our young people will continue to die.

A former High Priest of the devil named Mike Warnke wrote a book in 1972 called "The Satan-Seller." In it he details the rituals involved in conjuring demons and making flesh sacrifices to Satan. Among them are using spells above a hellish altar so that demon energy appears

Figure 12

**Straight from the Gates of Hell.
Members of the Motley Crue.
(continued next page)**

Figure 12

**Straight from the Gates of Hell.
Members of the Motley Crue.**

directly above a pentagram drawn on a nude girl's stomach. A secret handshake with only the index and little fingers extended admitted a member to the Black Mass and identified him as Satan's servant. (The Il Cornuto!) The successful conclusion of a well-cast spell was finished with the words, "As I will, so mote it be." which is the exact creed, word for word, of Aleister Crowley and his covens!

Warnke also told of receiving and coveting sacred rings as he moved up Satan's ladder, rings of power guarded by demon spirits. Ever notice how many rings Rock stars wear? I wonder how many of those signets came from satanic ceremonies? One thing's for sure, they're not just imitating Ringo the *Beatle!* Vince Neil and Nikki Sixx wear lots of rings; some are Death's Head skull rings like *Rolling Stone* Keith Richards'. What about the others?

Warnke had one other thing to say about his experience that also applies to Rock stars in general and *Motley Crue* in particular. He stated in his book that demons are always searching for suitable human bodies to inhabit. When they find one who is far from Christ, they gleefully enter in. If cast out, they return with legions of comrades. The soul possessed is not always a case like the "Exorcist." Many times the people become hate-filled monsters of egotism and false pride, pillars of blasphemy and engines of destruction to those around them.

I think that perfectly describes *Motley Crue.*

Crue singer/frontman Vince Neil, for example, has finally had to face up to his actions of December, 1984, when his drunken driving killed one man and seriously injured two other people. Neil was ordered to pay over 2 1/2 million dollars to the victims and their families. He also received 5 years probation and a 30 day jail term. Whether all this is worth the price of a human life is debatable, but at least this court case proves that Rock stars are not immune from paying the price for their detestable deeds. Vince is 24 years old. He's got a long time to live with the knowledge of causing another's death. However, Vince hasn't wasted any time mourning the tragedy. Right after the trial, he quickly hit the Rock & Roll tour trail with the other *Motleys.*

Not only do the *Crue* want a young person's soul, they want a continued source of money from the Rock worshiper. Inside "Devil" a sheet of *Motley Crue* merchandise by mail order is found. Logo stickers, shirts, jerseys, gloves, wallets, buttons, armbands, headbands, caps, pins, and posters are all hawked. Average price: $11.00. Most of these items sport the pentagram (probably so Satan's slaves can clearly be marked at the next *Crue* concert). Where did *M.C.* learn about this sort of mass merchandising? Well, I don't know for sure, but *KISS* used to have the same kind of gimmicks tucked away inside their albums. One final note. For $7.00 fans can join *Motley Crue's* Fan Club. What's it called? S.I.N. Club. (Safety In Numbers.) The ad says, "Are you into S.I.N.?"

Parents. Young people. I ask you in all Christian concern to do something about *Motley Crue* within your own sphere of influence. Boycott that concert, destroy that record, tear down that poster, tell your friends what you have learned. Don't be a victim of Satan and his *Crue.* Don't fall easy prey to false teaching and the psychology of hate. I beg you to turn your attention to Christ, not Nikki Sixx. Let Nikki choose his own path and fate. Don't follow him down that fatal road to hell and damnation.

"Hit Parader" gives us some of the wit and "wisdom" of *Motley Crue:*

Vince Neil — "We collect underwear from girls and keep it on our stage amps."[19]

Nikki Sixx — "I stole the first guitar I ever owned."[20]

Mick Mars — "It makes me sick when I hear the !*?%!&* people dump on us because they think we're into devil worship. I can't believe how stupid most people are. Just because they may not understand Rock & Roll, or *Motley Crue,* they assume that everything has some demonic meaning to it. I guess if you look hard enough you can find the devil in just about anything."[21]

In answer to Mick Mars' challenge, I have this to say: I'm not stupid, (plenty of other faults, you bet, but stupidity's not one of them), I completely understand what *Motley Crue* is about, and I also understand what Rock & Roll is about. I also state categorically, here and now, that *Motley Crue* DOES worship the Devil; they worship and serve only themselves which is the same thing as worshiping Satan. If you don't believe me, Mick, ask Anton La Vey's followers, the former head and founder of the First Church Of Satan, and they will tell you that attaining your own "godhead" through your individual potential is the core of Satanism. I do agree with Mick on one point, though, you CAN find the Devil in just about anything, and *Motley Crue* is full of Satan from top to bottom. He reeks from your perverted music, the stench of his evil is splattered all over the filthy and lewd interviews you give, and his stamp is firmly slapped on your wasted faces in every picture of you I've ever seen. You are of the Devil, you belong to him, and only the Almighty Power of Jesus Christ can save you from eternal damnation, if you're willing to accept it!

Motley Crue is just one of many, many groups peddling the same poison. Grisly graphics, hidden subliminal satanic instructions in reverse, lyrical drug and sex lessons galore; it's all there for even the most naive teenager to stumble upon. All he or she has to do is listen to the music; Lucifer will do the rest.

This nightmare has been going on for a long, long time. As far back as 1967, L.A.'s LSD-laced savages, *The Doors,* not only had strange album covers for their records, but the songs inside those psychedelic sleeves contained subliminal communications aimed directly at the ultra-heightened hearing of tripping fans. As *Doors'* producer Paul Rothchild tells it in a 1981 "Bam" interview: "If you listen closely to

Doors' records you'll find hundreds of places where there are vocal things put in that are part of the subliminal rhythm track. You'll hear a 'CH-CH-CH.' Things like that . . . "[22] (See Appendix.)

It has taken ten years just to discover the fact that *Led Zeppelin's* "Stairway To Heaven" was in reality an infernal hymn to Satan. What about the dozens of other *Zeppelin* songs scattered over nine albums? Who knows what devilish orders lie lurking in their depths? At this point, no one really knows for sure just how widespread such satanic manipulation has been in the past, and how extensive the infestation is today. We can only hope that someone has the courage to begin listening to and identifying Rock recordings so that parents can at least recognize the danger before them: the damnation of their precious childrens' souls.

In order to more fully understand just what it is young people are looking at and listening to in the rotten world of Rock & Roll, I have compiled a list of some of the most popular albums in Rock's roster, both new and old. These records are ranked as classics because of their outrageous displays of obscene and satanic cover graphics. Some groups have more than one cover included in this listing. Many bands are continually trying to outdo themselves in terms of sickness and gory deathscapes. All too often, they succeed.

"KISS Alive." (See figure 13.) This is the LP that launched this demented band of conniving charlatans and cradle robbers into the multiplatinum superstar stratosphere. It is decorated with the cover to end all covers, a perfect portrait of both *KISS* themselves and the philosophy behind Rock & Roll: "Blind em, Blast em, and Bilk em."

The gigantic *KISS* logo glows overhead. The two S's at the end of the word are identical to the Nazi SS symbols so hated and feared during World War II. The entire scene combines D-Day, Pearl Harbor, and the eruption of Mt. St. Helens into one big chunk of exploding dynamite.

Figure 13

Kings In Satan's Service (KISS).

The back cover of "KISS Alive" is a photograph of the inside of the arena where *KISS* is performing. It is filled to capacity with thousands of young people. Two teens hold a big, hand-drawn poster of the four members of *KISS*. The band's logo has been copied to perfection. After all, these are the 1980's. No one thinks about the Nazis anymore. (Except the hundreds of survivors who were tortured under their brutal reign.)

An old piece of film, (about 1971), of bisexual Rock star David Bowie playing live shown frequently on MTV features the Bowie band standing under a huge circle above their heads with the "satanic S" lightning logo on it. The lightning bolt looks just like the ones used by *KISS*. We know from reading in Luke 10:18 that Our Lord saw Satan fall like lightning from Heaven. But where did this distinctive jagged slash that's been so widely adopted by demon Rockers come from in the first place? *KISS, Black Sabbath, AC-DC, Raven, Metallica, Krokus, Judas Priest, Keel, Bowie,* and who knows how many others use this sign as their own. Where did it come from?

The answer is in a Time-Life book called *World War II — The Nazis.* In the early stages of the total Nazification of Germany, Gestapo chief Heinrich Himmler, one of the most feared and hated men in the entire nation, undertook archeological excavations in various parts of Europe, digging for clues to the "magnificent" past of the Aryan "super-race." At a site in Bavaria, ancient runic inscriptions were uncovered. Runes were part of a centuries-old Germanic alphabet which possessed mystical significance to the Teutonic tribesmen of that time. One of the tokens unearthed was the lightning bolt "S." Himmler incorporated the sign into the Gestapo, making it the infamous "SS" (for Schutzstaffel). Several other runes were also used in secret SS rituals.

The two letters of *KISS'* logo are identical to those of Himmler's SS; all the other Rockers that use this symbol also must share a spiritual bond with the Nazis, whether they want to admit it or not. From the Nazis, it's only a short distance to THEIR guiding light, SATAN. The horrible irony of this situation, at least as far as *KISS* is concerned, is that Gene Simmons' mother was reported in Circus Magazine to be a concentration camp survivor! I wonder how she and all the other witnesses of Hitler's atrocity feel when they see those terrifying symbols on record covers and concert stages. What do they think?[23]

On a later *KISS* LP, "Love Gun," the cover graphics once again set shocking new lows for the entertainment industry. It is too perverse to print.

By this time in their career, *KISS* had gone from larger than life cult heroes to full blown comic book status. That's right, they even had their very own Marvel comic book. Eight-year-old children were reading about the heroic exploits of Gene Simmons, a man who has been quoted as saying, "Cannibalism has always been of interest to me. I've always wondered what human flesh tastes like."[24] Gene Simmons was also one of the first Rockers to use the "Il Cornuto" Devil sign.

The "Il Cornuto" is a Sicilian sign of the Devil used to cast spells and to ward off the "Evil Eye." This demonic symbol is a trademark of Gene Simmons as well as singer Ronnie James Dio, formerly of the *Black Sabbath* group. When in concert Dio flashes the wicked sign at every opportunity. Dio's album covers also feature the Il Cornuto prominently. (See figure 14.) The Heavy Metal Rock group *"Heart"* displays the Cornuto sign on the back of their 1982 album, "Private Audition," further proof that all these Devil-Rock groups love to share their demon signs with each other and an unsuspecting public. (See figure 15.) *The Beatles* were the first Rock band to use the Il Cornuto on an album cover. (See figure 16.)

Cheap Trick also uses the Cornuto sign. (See figure 17.)

Even pop-rock star Todd Rundgren and group *Utopia* use the twin-horned salute! (See figure 18.)

Rainbow — "Straight Between The Eyes." (See figure 19.) Ritchie Blackmore, formerly the guiding light behind Heavy Metal pioneers *Deep Purple,* is a self-avowed student of witchcraft and occult phenomena. As ringleader of *Rainbow,* he has produced many strange albums over the years. All have dealt in some way with his supernatural obsessions and dark, brooding fears for the future of mankind. Ronnie James Dio, former frontman for *Black Sabbath,* got his big break singing with Blackmore's *Rainbow.*

Figure 14

A reversal of Revelation 20:1-2.

Figure 15

Opening Doors For The Devil.

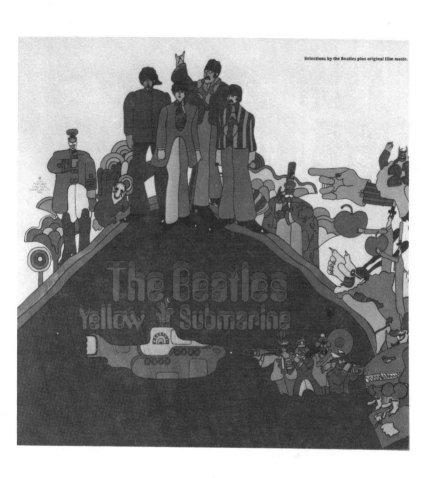

Figure 16

The first group to use the Il Cornuto Devil sign.

Figure 17

The sign of authority.

Figure 18

Satan's plan? World Conquest!

Figure 19

The power of Rock: destruction of the mind.

One song on "Eyes" is called "Power." Some of the lyrics go like this:

> "I can take anything that gets in my way
> I don't worry bout tomorrow, I just live for today
> Got the power when I turn it on
> Gonna get my fill
> Nothin's gonna stop me now, and nothin ever will
> I got the power
> I can feel the power
> Turn it on . . . ."

The cover of "Straight Between The Eyes" shows a guitar smashing into a person's forehead, great chunks of flesh flying in every direction. Subliminal pictures are contained in the eyes themselves.

As of October, 1984, Blackmore had abandoned *Rainbow* in order to reform the original mega-Metal *Deep Purple* line-up of the early Seventies. A reunion album and tour was undertaken, generating millions of dollars for the aging Masters of modern Heavy Metal music. Ritchie refused to take part in the affair until he personally could be guaranteed one million bucks for his effort. That demand was met. A couple of members of the group had become so overweight in their years off that they were shipped to a fat farm to lose some lard. After all, there's nothing very awe-inspiring about an obese over-the-hill Rock star stumbling and sweating about on a stage.

Blackmore makes records in a castle he claims is haunted by a demon servant of the god Baal. The Old Testament is full of warnings and judgments from the mouth and hand of God Himself about having anything to do with Baal worship. The Lord was provoked to anger against the Israelites on many occasions because of their communion with this detestable god and his goddess "wife," Ashtoreth, whose symbol on the hillsides of the land was an Asherah pole. The perfect justice and righteous anger of our Lord broke out against the Jews and Canaanites not only for their sin of idolatry, but also because of the horrifying, sickening crimes which were a big part of Baal worship.

Temples of Baal and Ashtoreth were usually built together, the priests and priestesses of which were prostitutes. Homosexuality and sexual sin were encouraged in the worship ceremony, the climax of which was the ritual murder of babies as a sacrifice to these gods. The poor dead children were then buried in a nearby cemetery. At times "foundation sacrifices" were offered as well, wherein the murdered babes were walled up within the foundations of newly built homes to bring "good luck" to the inhabitants. Is it any wonder the Lord Our God used great men like Jehu to purge such filth from the land of Canaan?

If a servant of Baal indeed controls the environment of the place where Ritchie Blackmore records his songs, doesn't that make Blackmore himself an attendant unto Baal? No Christian would stay for a moment in such a place. Ritchie not only stays, he welcomes the opportunity! If young people worship Ritchie Blackmore, *Deep Purple,* and *Rainbow,* aren't they also indirectly worshiping and lending power to Baal? Obviously "Straight Between The Eyes" was fashioned with a little help from Ritchie's demon friends, the enemies of God.

Perhaps some skeptics may say that the Devil in Rock & Roll is really no big deal, a harmless titter, or even a healthy release of pent up anti-social pressures via therapeutic role playing.

(See figure 20.) I submit the 1982 Rock album "The Number Of The Beast," by Heavy Metal group *Iron Maiden* as evidence that a deadly serious Satan is right now bargaining for the very souls and minds of our children.

Billboard Magazine's full page ads proclaimed the record as being "Forged in the fires of Hell," which it undoubtedly was. The album can only be described as satanic. A horrible, decayed creature appears on the cover of "Beast," manipulating a laughing red Devil, pitchfork in hand, like some gigantic puppet on a string. The Devil in turn has his

Figure 20

Revelation 13:18.

own puppet, a miniature version of the decayed creature. The earth is a sea of flames, and flying taloned creatures with pitchforks and tails are swooping down on the helpless humans awash in the Lakes of Fire.

Isn't the irony here chilling? Isn't it obvious what *Iron Maiden* is trying to get across? *Iron Maiden* is using the Devil even as the Devil is using *Iron Maiden!* To a true believer, the message is crystal clear: It's time to make some choices, for ourselves and for our children. Will it be God's way, or Satan's?

On the back side of "Beast," extensive liner notes tell us that this album is dedicated to "Headbangers, Earth Dogs, and Hellrats everywhere . . . " with "Special thanks to *KISS, Judas Priest,* and *UFO.*" Thanks for what? Paving the Highway To Hell so quickly?

Some of the "Beast's" song titles are equally revealing: "Children Of The Damned," "The Number Of The Beast," "Hallowed Be Thy Name," and "Run To The Hills." As if any further examples of Satan's intent were needed, this quotation from Revelation 13:18 appears prominently on the backside of the album:

> "Woe to you, oh Earth and sea, for the Devil sends the
> Beast with wrath, because he knows the time is short . . .
> Let him who hath understanding reckon the number of
> the Beast for it is a human number, its number is 666."

This verse is repeated as a spoken introduction just before the song, "Number Of The Beast" begins. Here are some of the lyrics to that particular song:

> "In the night the fires are burning bright
> The ritual has begun
> Satan's work is done . . .
> I'm coming back
> I will return
> And I'll possess your body
> And I'll make you burn
> I have the fire
> I have the force
> I have the power to make my evil take its course."

The time IS short. Let's make the most of it while we still can.

"Blackout" by The Scorpions. (See figure 21.) A screaming man with bandages around his head bellows so loud shards of glass are flying through the air. Why is he screaming? Because the prongs of two steel forks are buried in his eyes. "Blackout," get it?

144

Figure 21

Blinded by Rock and screaming to get out.

The groups, songs, and records we have just discussed are only a small portion of the entire Rock & Roll panorama. Nearly every other Rock LP that you or your son or daughter can pick up will probably have some reference to that tried and true formula, sex, drugs and the Devil buried in its lyrics or imprinted somewhere on its cover. The Heavy Metal groups are notorious for fostering these obscenities upon their teen and pre-teen audiences, but this loathsome cancer seems to be so all-pervasive that

145

virtually EVERY Rock band producing records makes some reference to Damnation, Demons, and Druggish Sex.

I have put together a list of the ten most dangerous Rock & Roll bands. They are dangerous in the sense that they have the potential to warp and twist the minds and morals of millions, given their mass popularity. The groups included in this list also seem to have no guilt about fleecing as many fans as possible before their careers derail. They boast openly of their drug busts, their perverse sexual exploits, and their closeness with the Devil. As far as the responsibility to their listening public is concerned, they simply could care less.

(1) *AC-DC* wins the number one spot by a landslide. This band has done more harm than almost any other group around today.

(2) *The Rolling Stones* — They invented Diabolic Rock. Miserable drug-eaten hedonists, their anarchic amorality has become a banner waved by millions of young people everywhere.

(3) *Led Zeppelin* — Even though they broke up when their drummer died in 1980, *Led Zep* still sells thousands of albums a year. A new crop of young fans discover this jaded group of occult thrill seekers annually, digesting their entire catalog of dismal, melancholy dirges and hyped up, Heavy Metal sex operas with relish.

(4) *Motley Crue* — A ragtag gang of foul mouthed and vulgar fornicators who openly brag of their detestable lifestyles, *Motley Crue* is Satan's Pied Piper of the 80's, their siren call dragging thousands of fresh souls down the well-worn ruts of the Highway To Hell.

(5) *KISS* — Not content with the millions of dollars already stolen from an innocent fandom consisting mainly of

146

thirteen year old girls, *KISS* is still far from fading into the Rock & Roll trash heap. 1982 marked the group's comeback with new flashy costumes, images, and TV appearances meant to enlist fresh converts into the ever swelling *KISS* Army.

(6) *Twisted Sister* — This group's blatant ultra-macho, animalistic, "I'll kick your teeth in" attitude combined with a sexual preference that is anybody's guess make them one of the weirdest, sickest, and most dangerous of the 80's Slime-Rock groups. Avid worshipers at the shrine of *Alice Cooper,* they have succeeded in carrying *Alice's* degeneracy far beyond the realm of eye makeup and headless baby dolls.

(7) *Judas Priest* — Flying saucers, Nazi biker glory, smash-em-up and spit out your teeth. Violence, violence, violence. The world is insane enough without this disgusting group of Rock & Roll fascists.

(8) *Black Sabbath* — With frontman Ronnie James Dio, this thudding, downer witch-Rock band of aging necrophiles signed a new lease on life a few years ago after dumping former singer Ozzy Osbourne. Even without Ozzy, *Black Sabbath's* songs remain the same: Death and Demons and Magic. Dio also quit to go solo, but *Sabbath* vowed to slog on.

(9) And speaking of Ozzy Osbourne, he surely deserves a place on this list due to his repeated, disgusting, brainless acts of vulgar depravity: (Public urination in a restaurant, and biting the heads off live animals like some sort of demented circus geek.)

(10) *W.A.S.P.* — Deserves a place on this roster for their unvarnished appeal to the basest and most perverse elements of today's Rock. Their name means "We Are

Sexual Perverts" and their music proves it.

For anyone wishing to see for themselves the handiwork of the bands mentioned in this chapter, a trip to the local record store could be a very enlightening experience. Most of the albums listed, both new and old, are just sitting there in plain sight, waiting for someone to buy them.

SUMMING THINGS UP:

It was in the late Sixties, when the drug LSD began to proliferate wildly, that record covers first started incorporating secret messages into their graphic arts, helped along by the biggest Rock act of all time, the *Beatles*. What we are witnessing today is a natural extension of the seed that was planted in 1967. Messages are being drilled and ground into the heads of young record-buyers whether they consciously realize it or not. Drugs, backmasks and contact with spirits are advertised in nearly every song's lyrics or album covers. All of this is surely having some kind of subliminal impact on the growing minds of young listeners. The Devil has left his brand on every kid that listens to this stuff!

The final, deciding factor as to whether we shall continue to allow this to go on should be from the Scriptures themselves. What does the Bible say about talking with spirits? What does it tell us about other forms of witchcraft?

>"And the soul that turneth after such as have familiar spirits, and after wizards, to go a whoring after them, I will even set my face against that soul, and will cut him off from among his people. Sanctify yourselves therefore, and be ye holy: for I am the Lord your God." Leviticus 20:6 & 7

>"A man also or woman that hath a familiar spirit, or that is a wizard, shall surely be put to death: they shall stone them with stones: their blood shall be upon them." Leviticus 20:27

CHAPTER 5

Secrets From Within

> "For there is nothing covered, that shall not be revealed; Neither hid, that shall not be known."   Luke 12:2

> "These !*?%!&* God-botherers mention the Devil more than we do. They're just trying to scare people."
>   Brian Johnson of *AC-DC*[1]

Outright blatant nods to the Devil and decadence aren't the only way not-so-dumb Rockers spread their satanic message. While watching the CBS Evening News on April 28, 1982, I saw a report which literally knocked me out of my chair. Anchorman Dan Rather, in his laid-back style, started the story by reporting that thirty teenagers in Huntersville, North Carolina, had organized a mass Rock record and tape burning through their church. They were led by a reformed Rock musician turned minister.

Dan Rather than stated that many prominent Rock &

Roll stars are reported to be practicing satanists, spreading their demented messages to an unwary listening public by hiding subliminal satanic communications in reverse in their records and songs. When played backwards, the messages can clearly be heard, so clearly, in fact, that CBS News played three of them over the air. *Led Zeppelin, E.L.O.* and *Styx* were exposed in their hidden backmasks of satanic praise.

A week after the CBS telecast I was invited by some Christian friends who knew of my interest in backmasking, to attend a Rock & Roll seminar at their church. I received news of several more Rock tunes containing backwards and subliminal communications. Using my own records and a friend's reel-to-reel tape deck, I made tapes of the songs mentioned in the seminar, forwards and backwards.

What a confirmation the Lord gave me!

We've already examined the backmasks on *Led Zep's* "Stairway To Heaven," and the *Beatles'* "White Album" in the previous two chapters. *Black Oak Arkansas'* live "Raunch & Roll" LP was next. *Black Oak* was quite popular during the mid-Seventies. They literally dripped evil in their lewd, disturbing stage shows and songs. They met each other in prison and after parole formed a Rock group. On the live cut "When Electricity Came To Arkansas," the song breaks down midway into a flurry of drum beats as Jim Dandy Mangrum howls (literally!) and grunts. His voice sinks to a nerve shredding guttural bass. He yelps like a dog while the band members behind him wail like damned souls burning in hellfire. Jim Dandy screams and hiccups, then begins hissing, "Natass! Natass!" mingled with many other chattering syllables. Before the gibberish begins, Mangrum screams out the name of his personal Demon, "HECATE!"

In reverse, "When Electricity Came To Arkansas" spits out this spine freezing burst of satanic praise: "SATAN! SATAN! SATAN!! HE IS GOD! HE IS GOD! HE IS GOD!"

Technically, the tape I have of this song is impossible. It

can't happen. On a live recording, without the benefit of any studio overdubbing, the odds against speaking certain words so that they will spell out some kind of meaning when played in reverse are astronomical. It's obvious when listening to this cut that no overdubs have been added. These are simply the raw live tracks. How could it happen?

At the Christian Rock & Roll seminar I attended, the minister there maintained that the voices we hear on these songs in reverse are actually the sounds of the demons themselves! As you will see in the Appendix, we have the testimony of an ex-satanist who was of a very high rank at one time. She says that is exactly what happened!

Another live cut, this time from Heavy Metal megastars *Rush,* repeats this "impossibility." The song "Anthem" on their "All The World's A Stage" LP reveals these communications with the Devil: "OH SATAN, YOU, YOU ARE THE ONE WHO IS SHINING. WALLS OF SATAN, WALLS OF SACRIFICE. I KNOW IT'S YOU ARE THE ONE I LOVE."

E.L.O.'s "Eldorado" yields this information: "HE IS THE NASTY ONE. CHRIST, YOU'RE INFERNAL."

One of *Queen's* most famous tunes, the favorite of disco night spots everywhere when it first came out, is "Another One Bites The Dust," from their "The Game" LP. During the chorus in the middle of the song, singer Freddie Mercury's voice slides in and out between the swishing, shooting phase effects the group is so fond of using. Now I know why. THIS is where they hide their secret messages — behind the flanged cymbals and ripping, zapping electronic noises. Played backwards, Mercury's voice yells, "START TO SMOKE MARIJUANA, START TO SMOKE MARIJUANA!"

The devilish *Blue Oyster Cult* also have their own version of subliminal suggestion, but at high speed. On their song "You're Not The One," from their "Mirrors" album, a high pitched, squeaking chatter can clearly be heard above the instruments early in the tune. When slowed down, an eerie voice, muffled by the thudding drums and crashing guitars is spouting whole paragraphs of words and phrases, the clearest of which says, "OUR FATHER, WHO ART IN HEAVEN, SATAN!"

Heavy Metal monsters *Styx* use a backmask in the song, "Snowblind," from the "Paradise Theater" album. The hidden message is, "OH SATAN, MOVE IN OUR VOICES." (In Greek mythology, Styx was the name of the underground river of the dead leading to Hades.)

Those satanic messages literally SCREAM out their meaning clearly enough for anyone to hear, provided they have a reel-to-reel tape deck. More and more backmasked Rock abominations are being discovered every week by dedicated Christian groups and outreach ministries throughout the country. I pray that God will continue to bless them in their work, allowing us all to benefit from their discoveries. It took ten years to find out that *Led Zeppelin's* "Stairway To Heaven" was really a passageway to hell. What a backlog of Devil-Rock songs and albums there must be out there just waiting to be discovered!

What concerned Christian in his right mind can now deny the fact that demons and satanic bands are controlling the sounds our children hear through Rock & Roll songs?

On the "Face The Music" LP, *E.L.O.* repeat their reversal technique in what is the best planned example of backmasking I have ever heard. On the song "Fire On High," no attempt was made to hide the message at all. It's obvious as soon as the needle hits the record that a backwards tape is playing. When reversed, we hear a crystal clear voice booming out the words, "THE MUSIC IS REVERSIBLE. TIME IS NOT. TURN BACK. TURN BACK. TURN BACK."

California's own *Eagles,* (who are no longer together as a group) also have a backmasked Satan-call on the song that made them millions: "Hotel California." The deciphered message is, "SATAN HAD HELP. HE ORGANIZED HIS OWN RELIGION." The song as a whole is tied in with the establishment of San Francisco's First Church Of Satan and inspired by its founder, Anton LaVey. Lyrics like, "They just can't kill the beast," "This could be Heaven or this could be Hell," "We haven't had that spirit here since 1969," and "You can check out any time you like, but you can never leave" are obvious ties to Satanism.

1969 was the year LaVey's "satanic Bible" was published, a book which I refuse to read, even for research purposes. I have seen the cover, though, and surprise of surprises, there's evil bald-headed Anton himself glaring out from the back book jacket. With his left hand he's making the Il Cornuto Devil sign!

Take note parents and young people: I really don't think the founder of the First Church Of Satan is going to use an occult sign that some Rockers say means "Long Live Rock & Roll." This is a lie and they know it! I believe it's the other way around; the Rock stars were given the Cornuto as a sign of allegiance to their lord and master — SATAN!

There's one other tie-in between "Hotel California" and the First Church of Satan for all you skeptics out there: the original satanic church founded by LaVey and his followers in San Francisco was located on California Street!

On the *Cars'* "Candy-O" record, the chorus of "Shooby Doo" reversed very clearly and chillingly reveals many voices chanting in unison, "SATAN, SATAN, SATAN, SATAN..."

Those evil jerks the *Rolling Stones* are guilty of back-masking as well. On the song "Tops" from the "Tattoo You" record, "I LOVE YOU SAID THE DEVIL" is the reversed message.

Long after the *Beatles* broke up, John Lennon was still up to his old tricks in record reversal. On "Meat City" from his "Mind Games" album, Lennon inserted a backmask which says, "CAN'T LET YOU SHOOT MY KIDS." Contained on the last record he ever made, "Double Fantasy," there is a creepy Yoko Ono tune called "Kiss Kiss Kiss," When reversed it perfectly justifies Lennon assassin Mark Chapman's claim that demons gave him the strength and opportunity to kill the former *Beatle*. From within the midst of the swirling, eerie crunches and unearthly whines we hear the reversed voice of something resembling Yoko Ono saying, "SATAN IS COMING . . . SIX SIX SIX . . ." and then, "WE SHOT JOHN LENNON!"

The "Double Fantasy" album was completed and already in the stores when John Lennon died in December of 1980. No one went back and changed or added anything to "Kiss Kiss Kiss" afterwards. Mark Chapman IS telling the truth! Demons DID decree Lennon's death, and then bragged about it before it happened on his own record! This should be a sobering example to all Christians everywhere: If you mess with witchcraft, like the Lennons did, someday you'll pay the price. That price is your life and soul.

The Plasmatics use a backmask on their "Coup d'Etat" record. When translated, it says, "CONCENSUS PRO- GRAMMING IS DANGEROUS TO YOUR HEALTH. THE BRAINWASHED DO NOT KNOW THEY ARE BRAIN- WASHED."

Pink Floyd, the English band that pioneered LSD abuse, have a song on their blockbuster "The Wall" album called "Goodbye Blue Sky," (about nuclear war). When deciphered, a slyly snickering, shivery voice of a cultured Briton declares: "CONGRATULATIONS. YOU'VE JUST DISCOVERED THE SECRET MESSAGE. PLEASE SEND YOUR ANSWER TO OLD PINK, CARE OF THE FUNNY FARM, CHELFORD . . . "

The *Floyd* also use an unreversed, straightforward ap- proach to a blasphemy of the 23rd Psalm in the song, "Sheep," from their "Animals" LP. A metallic robotic voice buried in the right channel of the mix states: "THE LORD IS MY SHEPHERD, I SHALL NOT WANT. HE MAKETH ME TO LIE DOWN THROUGH PASTURES GREEN. HE LEADETH ME THE SILENT WATERS BY; WITH BRIGHT KNIVES HE RELEASETH MY SOUL. HE MAKES ME TO HANG ON HOOKS IN HIGH PLACES. HE CONVERTETH ME TO LAMB CUTLETS. FOR LO, HE

HATH GREAT POWER AND GREAT HUNGER. WHEN COMETH THE DAY WE LOWLY ONES THROUGH QUIET REFLECTION AND GREAT DEDICATION MASTER THE ART OF KARATE, WE SHALL RAISE UP AND THEN WE SHALL MAKE THE BUGGER'S EYES WATER."

On *Cheap Trick's* "Heaven Tonight" album the song "How Are You" has a high speed track chattering away over the lines:

> "I heard your voice
> I couldn't stand it
> You know you talk too much
> You even scare my friends
> The words you said
> I know you're lying
> You lie, you lie, you lie . . . "

When slowed down, that frontmask proved to be the Lord's Prayer! *Cheap Trick* is trying to subliminally create the illusion of godliness. What a deception!

Led Zeppelin's backmask "SATAN IS REALLY LORD" (from the song "Over The Hills And Far Away") is hidden through these lyrics:

> "Many is the word that only leaves you guessin'
> Guess about a thing
> You really outta know . . ."

Those old Acid-heads the *Jefferson Starship* have a song on their 1970 "Blows Against The Empire" album called "A Child Is Coming," about a new world order on its way. Toward the end of the song, a reversal of the chorus reveals a voice singing over and over, "SON OF SATAN."

Just before the song "Still Life," on *Iron Maiden's* "Piece Of Mind" LP, a backmask says, "MESSIN' WITH THINGS YOU DON'T UNDERSTAND."

AC-DC's "Hell's Bells" from their "Back In Black" LP contains lyrics which say:

"I'll give you black sensations
Up and down your spine
You get into evil
You're a friend of mine
See the white light flashin as I split the night
Cause if God's on the left
Then I'm stickin to the right."

Reverse those horrible words and you'll hear what I heard: "I WILL MESMERIZE YOU/ BUT HE IS SATAN/ LET ME OUT/ SATAN HAS ME PRISONER."

The earliest example of a Rock & Roll backmask I have been able to find is the *Beatles'* song "Rain" (written by John Lennon, naturally). The chorus, "When the rain comes/ they run and hide their heads" is reversed at the end of the tune. The chorus continued is "THEY MIGHT AS WELL BE DEAD/ CAN YOU HEAR ME/ CAN YOU HEAR ME . . ." This is only further proof that Lennon was the instigator of this whole backmasked mess we find ourselves in today.

Motley Crue's "Shout At The Devil" LP includes a cover version of the *Beatles'* song "Helter Skelter." The role "Helter Skelter" played in the 1969 Manson killings is well known. This was one of the songs from the *Beatles'* "White Album" that Manson claimed to hear voices on. Those voices told him to start killing in order to begin "Helter Skelter," a new world order. Reverse the words as sung by *Motley's* Vince Neil, and you'll hear: "I'M STILL THE MASTER." Satan's shouting with glee that after all these years, he's STILL the master of Rock & Roll!

On the *Venom* LP "Welcome To Hell," the song "In League With Satan" contains a very audible backmask. When reversed it says, "SATAN! RAISED IN HELL. RAISED IN HELL. I'M GONNA BURN YOUR SOUL. CRUSH YOUR BONES. I'M GONNA MAKE YOU BLEED. YOU'RE GONNA BLEED FOR ME."

Another *Venom* LP "Black Metal" has a short backmask

finishing off one side, which, when reversed, says, "I WILL RETURN."

Grim Reaper has an LP called "Fear No Evil." A backmask is found very plainly at the end of the song, "Final Scream." When reversed it says, "SEE YOU IN HELL."

On *Cheap Trick's* "Dream Police" album the song "Gonna Raise Hell" has a backmask. When reversed it says, "SATAN HOLDS THE KEYS."

For all the recording industry bigwigs who swear that front and backmasking has never been done, here are 29 examples, 99% of which I have on tape, stretching over the last 20 years through every conceivable group, producer, arranger, label, engineer, studio, country and continent. This phenomenon may not be able to be explained, but it certainly cannot be denied any longer.

A debate has been started which will probably outlast us all about exactly who or what these voices and messages are and how and where they came from. I don't know the answer to those questions, but, as in everything, I believe the Bible may give us wisdom on the matter. In Revelation 13:5-6 we read, "The beast was given a mouth to utter proud words and blasphemies and to exercise his authority for forty-two months. He opened his mouth to blaspheme God, and to slander His name and His dwelling place and those who live in Heaven."

That is my contribution to the debate. I believe that even now Satan and his demons are blaspheming and insulting God and the Lamb with their horrible Rock record covers and backmasked broadcasts from hell. What was supposed to be a joke by John Lennon has become a very real and very frightening proof of Bible prophecy, in my opinion.

We're just touching the tip of the iceberg, dear friends in Jesus. If you want to do your own research into this Devilish phenomenon, a reel-to-reel tape deck is a must. A record turntable that spins either way like the kind used at radio stations can also be used.

In a normal listening of a suspected Satan-Rock record,

you usually won't be able to hear anything wrong. It's the regular song lyrics played forward that are the clues to the hidden messages buried beneath. It's usually that verse or line that strikes you as odd when you first hear it, or perhaps has a weird double meaning to it as well that almost always is the backmask. This means, of course, that you'll have to decipher the words when played FORWARDS before you can dig any deeper. That's not always an easy task given the drug and drink slurred singing styles of current Rock & Rollers.

As for all you skeptics reading this, one thing's for sure: hearing is believing, and there's plenty more out there to hear! For those who want to make your own tapes and decide for yourself what you hear, pray about it. Ask God for guidance and the Holy Spirit for understanding. Keep one thing in mind, though. We need to be aware that this is happening, but we shouldn't get so hung up on backmasks that we forget about the tons of FORWARD Devil praise contained in Rock lyrics.

Never forget that Rock records contain incredible demonic power just waiting to break out against the listener. Never, ever listen to such records for research purposes without prayers for protection and the power to bind those demon spirits!

It is impossible for dozens of records from different groups with different managers, record companies, and production people spread across several continents with a span of many years between them to mount a conspiracy of this magnitude. Only Satan or God could do such a thing, and the Living God does NOT blaspheme Himself!

Some skeptics have said, "Maybe all these bands have the same producer."

They do, indeed . . . Satan himself!

CHAPTER 6

Public Enemies

"Woe unto the wicked! It shall be ill with him: for the reward of his hands shall be given him."   Isaiah 3:11 — KJV

"And I laughed to myself at the men and the ladies who never could conceive of us billion dollar babies."   Alice Cooper[1]

The following pages of this chapter contain photographs of various Rock music albums on sale in your local music store today. Parents, do you and your children have these works of Satan in YOUR home today? ? ?

Figure 22

ABOMINOG, by Uriah Heep, 1982. What kind of madness produces covers like this one? Uriah Heep was one of the first of the Glitter-Rock bands of the 70's. Faces like this are just a foretaste of Rock & Roll Hell.

Figure 23

SHOW NO MERCY, by Slayer, 1983. California-based Slayer have inscribed a message and a curse to their fans along the clear band of vinyl on side one of this record. It says: SATAN LAUGHS AS YOU ETERNALLY ROT.

Figure 24

AGENTS OF FORTUNE, by Blue Oyster Cult, 1976. The Tarot
cards in the man's hand spell out this message: "HE WHO
COMES AGAINST THE FORCE FACES DEATH." Praise God
for telling it like it is in Luke 12:4-5!

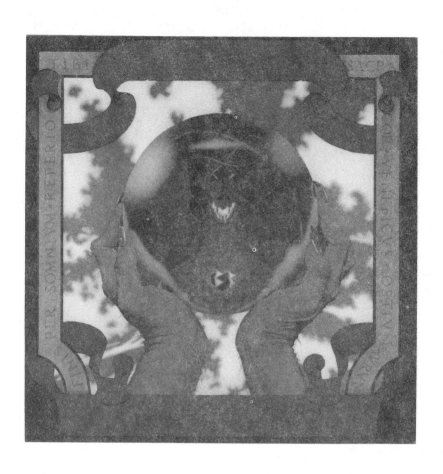

Figure 25

SACRED HEART, by Dio, 1985. This album cover is just loaded with subliminals. Engineering the concept was probably a breeze for Ronnie James Padavana and wife Wendy since he frequently brags in print that he is thoroughly familiar with the occult.

Figure 26

DON'T BREAK THE OATH, by Mercyful Fate, 1984. Have you
ever heard anyone actually deny Jesus Christ point-blank?
You'll hear it on this record. This band/coven is hard core,
dyed-in-the-wool Devil worshipers, dangerous and deadly.

Figure 27

DON'T BREAK THE OATH (Inner sleeve), by Mercyful Fate,
1984. I John 2:22 says that anyone who denies Jesus is an
Antichrist. That makes this band much more than
blasphemers. They are active agents of the Devil. Read "The
Oath." *(See opposite page.)*

164

The Oath

By the Symbol of the Creator, I swear
        henceforth to be
A faithful Servant of his most puissant
        Arch-Angel
The Prince Lucifer
Whom the Creator designated as His
        Regent
And Lord of this World. Amen.

I deny Jesus Christ, the Deceiver
And I abjure the Christian Faith
Holding in contempt all of it's Works

Solo: M.D.   Solo: H.S.

As a Being now possessed of a human Body
In this World I swear to give my full
        Allegiance
To it's lawful Master, to worship Him
Our Lord Satan, and no other
In the name of Satan, the ruler of Earth
Open wide the Gates of Hell and come forth
        from the Abyss
By these Names: Satan, Leviathan, Belial,
        Lucifer
I will kiss the Goat

Solo: H.S.   Solo: M.D.

I swear to give my Mind, my Body and
        Soul unreservedly
To the Furtherance of our Lord Satan's
        Designs

Do What Thou Wilt, Shall Be The Whole Of
        The Law

As it was in the Beginning, is now, and
        ever shall be
World without End, Amen.

Solo: H.S. – M.D.

(Music: King Diamond; Lyrics: King Diamond)

Figure 28

FEAR NO EVIL, by Grim Reaper, 1985. What kind of message do you think Grim Reaper is trying to send us here? The power of Satan and death rolling right over the Church? Hebrews 2:14-15 says differently.

Figure 29

LIVE EVIL, by Black Sabbath, 1982. This cover is a window into the demon-possessed soul of Black Sabbath. "LIVE EVIL" is drawn so that it is the same backwards as forwards. An evil live concert can also mean to live an evil life.

Figure 30

THE LAST COMMAND, by W.A.S.P., 1985. We Are Sexual Perverts takes on a whole new meaning after listening to this record. Blood drinking Blackie Lawless holds the apron strings that tie this whole deviate dog pack together.

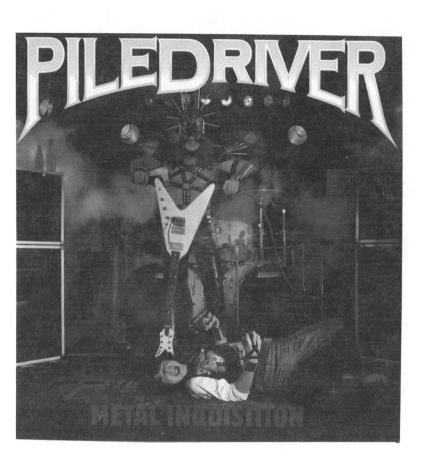

Figure 31

METAL INQUISITION, by Piledriver, 1985. Mr. Piledriver
calls himself "Lord" and "God" on this record, but Revelation
21:8 tells his fate. There'll be no guitars, amps, or microphones
before the Judgment Seat of Almighty God!

Figure 32

NUNSEXMONKROCK, by Nina Hagen, 1982. This high priestess of Hades holds a very special relationship with the Prince
Of Darkness. The baby is making the Il Cornuto Devil sign
with its left hand.

Figure 33

THE RIGHT TO ROCK, by Keel, 1985. This cover is a
blasphemy of the Ark of the Covenant described in detail in
Exodus 25:18-22. The record was produced by KISS bassist
Gene Simmons.

Figure 34

**BLACK METAL, by Venom, 1982. I can't express in words just
how evil this record is. BLACK METAL is not a put-on. It is
music made by real satanists praising their lord.**

Figure 35

STAY HUNGRY, by Twisted Sister, 1984. "I was just like the kids today. I listened to AC-DC and Black Sabbath, and it didn't affect me one bit." — Dee Snider, "Hit Parader," April, 1986, p. 56.

CHAPTER 7

Drugs, Drugs, Drugs

"What? know ye not that your body is the
temple of the Holy Ghost which is in you,
which ye have of God, and ye are not your
own? For ye are bought with a price: therefore glorify God in your body, and in your
spirit, which are God's."
1 Corinthians 6:19 & 20

"I only ever get ill when I give up drugs."[1]
Keith Richards

As everyone knows, drugs are a standard part of the
Rock & Roll lifestyle. "Sex, Drugs, and Rock & Roll" was a
favorite catch-phrase of the Sixties.

The Rock stars won't admit it, but these are the facts:

(1) Liquor and drugs, (often in combination with each
other), have killed a staggering number of prominent Rock
stars at the height of their careers.

(2) Rock songs and Rock lyrics promote drug use.

(3) Young people look up to Rock stars.

(4) Young people listen to Rock songs.

Young people are smarter and more sophisticated today than ever before. They're getting the message loud and clear. You can count on that.

Never before in the thirty-two year history of Rock & Roll have the rules of common decency and respect for one's body been so relaxed. As if the mental damage were not enough, some Rock stars actually wallow in the physical destruction of their own bodies, building whole careers on this pathetic facet of the big time Rock nightmare.

It would be too easy to become bogged down in the thousands of details regarding drug references, busts and arrests, overdoses, and Rock superstar addicts, but that's really not necessary. The evidence is a close as your neighborhood record store or Rock music magazine rack.

Rock & Roll promotes illicit drug use and abuse. We all know that.

Pop stars used to deny that their songs were about drugs. Now they don't even bother. They just keep grinding out the same old tried and true song formulas guaranteed to make them millionaires. "Do dope. It won't hurt you. We do it. Do dope and be like us." That's what their songs are saying.

The drugs marijuana, amphetamine, "downers," LSD, cocaine, and yes, even heroin are frequently mentioned in the lyrics of literally thousands of Rock songs, past and present. Often times these lyrics are buried in the song's "mix" so that F.C.C. watchdogs and other persons in positions of authority such as parents and church and school administrators cannot recognize them for what they are. Sometimes a kind of "street code" language is used to mask the drug references. One thing is certain. To the average high school kid sitting in his or her room listening to Rock music with headphones on, the hidden drug messages of a *Black Sabbath* or *Rolling Stones* tune are as plain as day. *Black Sabbath's* "SWEET LEAF," from their third LP,

"Master Of Reality," glorifies marijuana:

> "You introduced me to my mind
> And left me wanting you and your kind
> Oh yeah . . . "

The Rolling Stones' "SISTER MORPHINE," on their blockbuster "Sticky Fingers" album, includes these lines:

> "Sweet cousin cocaine
> Lay a cool, cool hand on my head
> Tell me, Sister Morphine
> When are you
> Comin' round again . . . "

Some other classic *Stones'* tunes that mention and promote drugs either by title or lyric, are as follows:

"STONED" — "Where am I . . . Outta my mind . . . "

"19TH NERVOUS BREAKDOWN" — "On our first trip I tried so hard/ To rearrange your mind . . . "

"LADY JANE" — In drug jargon, heroin is known as "The Lady In White," and marijuana is often called "Mary Jane."

"MOTHER'S LITTLE HELPER" — "She goes running for that little yellow pill . . . "

"BROWN SUGAR" — Another term for Mexican heroin.

"RIP THIS JOINT" — Self explanatory.

"COMING DOWN AGAIN" — Self explanatory.

The first American hard Rock band of the Sixties, *Steppenwolf,* (still touring in the 1980's), took a fierce, anti-establishment, pro-drug stance with many of their songs, most notably "The Pusher," and "Don't Step On The

Grass, Sam." They helped set the stage for today's Drug-Rock bands. The San Francisco based *Jefferson Airplane,* (now the wildly popular *Jefferson Starship,* with a long string of hit singles and LP's), penned one of the first LSD songs, "White Rabbit."

As a matter of fact, the devilish, mind-bending drug LSD is the single most important reason why we are witnessing the runaway Satanism so rampant in all Rock songs today. LSD was the thread that bound all the Sixties superstars together, from the *Beatles* to Jimi Hendrix, and, indirectly, the second generation of modern Rockers who were to follow, treading on that legacy. From 1967 to 1970, ALL the major Rock groups had experimented with "Acid." Some were so in love with the drug that they plunged head-long into its' unplumbed depths of darkness, never to emerge again. *(Pink Floyd, Donavan, The Doors.)*

The drug LSD can best be summed up in one word: "Intensity." Even after years of study, scientists still don't know much about it, and are completely ignorant of why it acts as it does once inside the human body. LSD reacts differently with every user. It is so dependant on each individual's complexities of personality that NO ONE really knows at the outset whether their "Trip" will be a blissful excursion, or a horrible black nightmare of fearful, paranoid, devilish torture.

When under extremely heavy doses of the drug, (another variable, since the user has no way of knowing the microgram content before ingestion), the typical tripper may become comatose, his short circuiting brain shooting like a meteor into the uncharted regions of his own personality.

As soon as psychic control is lost, the real danger, both to body and soul, begins. LSD is in reality a bridge between the spirit world and our own. Once this doorway has been opened, Satan and his demons come and go as they please. The tripper has given the Devil the key to his soul! In this electrically charged atmosphere, the presence of spirits can clearly be felt. Voices and thoughts buried deep in the person's subconscious begin coming to the surface — the communications of demons! It is at this point that the "Bad Trip" freakouts we have all read about happen. People have burned themselves, jumped from second story windows, and flung themselves headlong into traffic to escape the living nightmares LSD has created within them. When the powerful drug finally begins to wear off, the exhausted user slips into an uneasy, half-conscious doze. Bizarre, technicolor dreams of pulsing, crawling THINGS often invade his God-given sanctity of sleep.

Once having tripped, the person in question will never be the same again.

Ask Charles Manson and members of his demonic "Family," who tripped frequently in their desert commune in California's Death Valley. The night of the grisly Sharon Tate butcherings, which Manson ordered, at least one of his zombie killers admitted to having been "coming off a Trip" while hacking away at her screaming, innocent victims.

LSD is the Devil's drug. Much of the music of the 1960's was created while under its influence. All of the major Rock acts of the Sixties and Seventies not only tried LSD repeatedly, but openly bragged in print of its power in achieving wisdom and spiritual salvation.

What a cruel joke!

It would be a strange coincidence indeed that of the twenty or so stellar Rock stars who have died at the peak of their careers, or became near vegetables from their drug and liquor intake, all were heavily influenced musically by LSD. None could handle it.

Jimi Hendrix, the "Voodoo Child" who often ate Acid before his concerts, is a prime example. He claimed the drug had released his mind from its earthly prison, allowing him to create "Electric Church Music" about cosmic forces and other dimensional planetary gods. In the end, his years of LSD use and abuse had nearly driven Hendrix insane.

Here are some quotes from Jimi Hendrix, taken from his friend Curtis Knight's biographical tribute, *Jimi*.

> "There are so many different beliefs that something must be phony. I used to go to Sunday School, but the only thing I believe in now is music."[2]

> "Well, I haven't been having much of an appetite lately; I've been getting stoned a lot. I just don't seem to remember to eat."[3]

> "Things like witchcraft, which is a form of exploration, and imagination have been banned by the establishment and called evil. It's because people are frightened to find out the full power of the mind."[4]

> "One time on a Trip I saw walls breathing — and the principle feature of the experience is that you and what you are experiencing are inseparable."[5] (Hendrix's debut LP was titled, "Are You Experienced?")

> "On bad Trips sometimes I saw monsters too horrible to explain, and a drug-induced psychic horror is not easy to handle."[6]

Hendrix was indicted in 1969 for attempting to smuggle heroin and hashish across the Canadian border. On September 18, 1970, he died from a barbiturate overdose. He had choked to death on his own vomit.

We have already traced *Rolling Stone* Brian Jones' miserable descent into dissipation and death. He was one of the first English Rockers to take and promote LSD. According to Jones' live-in lover, Anita Pallenberg:

> "The first time he took Acid he saw creatures coming out of the ground, the walls, the floors. He was looking in all the cupboards for people, 'Where are they?' That's when he said to me, 'Dress me up like Francoise Hardy . . .'"[7]

"So I dress him like a chick, you know? It's like he came out of it a haunted man . . . "[8]

No one knows more about corrupting and destroying innocent human beings through drugs than Anita Pallenberg.

Author Tony Sanchez tells of the heavily heroin-addicted Pallenberg forcing the young teenage daughter of her private chef to accept an injection of heroin. The frightened child became violently sick, but what did that matter to Anita? This was one of the evil sorceress' favorite games: corrupting innocent victims. Luckily, the little girl didn't die, but of course she will carry the memory of that horrible experience with her as long as she lives.[9] Later in his book Sanchez relates how Anita's partner in decadence, Keith Richards, plied a young naive journalist visiting in his home with cocaine and heroin as a means of livening up an otherwise dull evening. The fledgling author later became a junkie, so infatuated and impressed was he with the "great" *Rolling Stone,* Keith Richards.[10]

Jim Morrison of *The Doors* was also a manically compulsive tripper during the early years of the group's existence. He would later abandon LSD to become a full fledged alcoholic, but Acid had definitely left its mark on this "mystic shaman" who died mysteriously on July 3, 1971, in Paris. The following Morrison interview, taken from the pages of Circus Magazine, is full of the metaphysical gobbledygook so popular among the "Acid Head" generation of the time.

"We evolved from snakes and I used to see the universe as a mammoth peristaltic snake. I used to see all the people and objects and landscapes as little pictures on the facets of their skins . . . "[11]

When asked about Shock Rock king *Alice Cooper,* Morrison replied:

"I haven't heard them. I've just read a few things about them . . . sounds great. I like people that shake other people up and make them uncomfortable."[12]

Pete Townshend, the nearly deaf guitar bashing bozo behind *The Who,* had his own chilling brush with psychedelics as he was returning to New York by air from the California Monterey Pop Festival in 1967.

George Tremlett's biography, *The Who,* tells the story in Townshend's words:

"I'd also tried the most powerful psychedelic drug available at that time, S.T.P. . . ."[13]

"I felt that if I had cut off my own head the horrible feeling would go on for eternity because I wasn't in my body — I was trying to get away from it . . . "[14]

Even Beatle John Lennon, an Acid dropping friend and contemporary of Brian Jones, was not immune to LSD's deadly effects on the mind. Lennon himself stated that his use of LSD:

"Went on for years. I must have had a thousand trips . . . "[15]

"Lots. I used to just eat it all the time."[16]

When asked if he had suffered many Bad Trips, Lennon replied:

"Oh yeah, I had many, . . . I stopped taking it because of that, you know. I just couldn't stand it."[17]

LSD by far wasn't the last drug Lennon tried, however. Also in the Wenner interviews, he admitted to having used heroin.

"Heroin? It was just not too much fun. I never injected it or anything. We sniffed a little when we were in real pain. I mean we just couldn't . . . people were giving us such a hard time."[18]

In Rolling Stone Magazine, Lennon's widow, Yoko Ono, expanded on their experiments with heroin:

"We were not drug addicts; we were not as drug oriented as people think. When John took drugs, he took them in extremes, and that was true of me too . . . "[19]

"I wasn't frightened, maybe because we were together . . . But we were taking it in celebration, not out of depression. We were artists. We were celebrating ourselves. It was beautiful to be on a high. And then, after we took drugs for a while, we would stop and go through the withdrawal, which is terrible . . . "[20]

Celebrating art by destroying one's body? What sense does that make?

The late Sixties popstar Acid boom seems to have given way in the mid Eighties to an even more sinister and chilling trend: the heroin craze. A jumble of Rock's biggest stars are, or have been, heroin addicts. These people flaunt their thousand dollar a day habits for all to see, creating an exclusive mystique, an aura of "hipness" tragic in its implication for fans following blindly in their wake. Heroin overdoses have also killed more Rock stars than any other drug-related disaster.

A partial listing of some of the premier Rockers who have been involved with heroin at one time or another include:

FRANK BEARD — Drummer for *ZZ Top*.

JIMMY PAGE — guitarist for *Led Zeppelin*.

DEBBIE HARRY — of the Punk-New Wave group *Blondie.*

LOU REED — Punk pioneer.

JOHNNY THUNDERS — guitarist for the band that most influenced *KISS:* the *New York Dolls.*

JOHN PHILLIPS — of the legendary *Mamas & Papas.*

ERIC CLAPTON — guitar superstar.

DICKY BETTS — of the *Allman Brothers Band,* who invented the much copied style of "Southern Rock."

JAMES TAYLOR — soft rock crooner.

DAVID BOWIE — first of the bisexual "glitter rockers."

JOHNNY WINTER — Albino Blues-Rock megastar and former band mate RICK DERRINGER.

KEITH RICHARDS — *Rolling Stone,* his former lover ANITA PALLENBERG, and former girlfriend of singer Mick Jagger, MARIANNE FAITHFULL.

NEIL YOUNG — millionaire singing idol.

JOHN LENNON, former *Beatle* and wife YOKO ONO.

And last, but not least, the demented IGGY POP.

Iggy, (born James Jewel Osterberg), is an obviously disturbed performer in Rock's destructionist school. His reputation for doing physical harm to himself in a live concert situation simply boggles the mind. Only a deeply deranged person, (or a satanically motivated one), could roll around on a stage full of broken glass, as Pop has done, or jam pencils into his flesh, or jump without warning into his audience, heedless of who or what he is jumping into. Pop's most recent exploit was to expose his private parts in Detroit to several elated photographers and thousands of his fans at the same time.

In Biblical times this kind of behavior would have been called demonic possession. Today it is described as showmanship.

The Bible describes demonic possession in great detail, especially in Matthew 8:28-33, and 17:14-19, and also in Mark 9:17-28. Some of the Biblical descriptions of the demon possessed could just as easily apply to the screaming, drugged out, wild eyed Rock stars jumping and falling about on today's stages and TV screens. (See figure 36.)

Figure 36

The thrill of performance — or demonic possession?

Soul-destroying drugs such as speed and heroin also played their part in Iggy Pop's death-Rocking stage act. With his group, *The Stooges,* he became a legendary Rock & Roll cult hero until his heroin addiction blotted out the commercial progress the band was making. As part of his 1979 comeback, Iggy gave an interview in Creem magazine, from which the following quotes were taken.

When asked how he and the rest of *The Stooges* had prepared themselves for a typical frenzied concert performance, Pop replied:

> "Two grams of biker Speed, five trips of LSD and as much grass as could be inhaled before the gig. I found this concoction effective enough to completely lose my senses, and then before a gig we'd gather like a football team and hype ourselves up to the point where we'd scream 'O.K. guys, whadda we gonna do? KILL! KILL! KILL!' Then we'd take the stage."[21]

> "I am totally into corruption."[22]

> "I am exactly the man who Friedrich Nietzsche could only write about. I believe that statement is incredibly healthy and that every human being has the capacity to achieve it."[23]

(Nietzsche was the German philosopher who first started the "God is dead" movement.)

> "See, I play hard, and . . . I love my revenge . . . "[24]

> "Well, I HATE women. I mean, why do I even have to have a reason for that? It's like, why are people reviled by insects? I use em because they are lying, dirty, treacherous, and their ambitions all too often involve using me . . . "[25]

> "What produces a 'Dork?' Usually a kind and loving household. Plus the fact that he's usually a decent, bright guy with a distinct lack of aggression."[26]

Iggy claimed he first became involved with heroin through his German girlfriend Nico, a weird humanity-despising acquaintance of Lou Reed, the man whose best known song, "Walk On The Wild Side," was about a transvestite. Nico had told Pop that he was not full of the POISON, (heroin), and that people wanted to see a real performer on stage. In order for him to be one, she said, he needed some "Poison."

Iggy wasted no time in taking her advice.

Things rapidly got out of control. Booking himself into a sanitarium hospital to cure his raging addiction, Pop was visited one day by the homosexual king of "Space Rock," David Bowie. The two became fast friends, with Bowie organizing Pop's comeback album. He even played keyboards on the accompanying tour.

"I SNUB YOU:"

"You are a beast
You are a pig
You've been a pig for long enough now
I'm making my move
I'm making an end to you
My seething hate is driving me nuts
What can I do to obliterate you . . . "

"LOCO MOSQUITO:"

"I got to hit my baby on a Saturday night
You know the Devil made me do it
I know it wasn't right
I'm sick of hanging round with old transvestites
They stare at my rubbers
It makes me uptight . . . "

"DOG FOOD:"

"Dog food is so good for you
It makes you strong and clever too
Dog food is a current craze
Eat some every day . . . "

186

(See figure 37.) All three of these songs came from Iggy's "Soldier" LP, a snarling, anti-social hate-fest filled with tunes mocking the conservative ideals and morality that have made America what it is today. The back of the album has drawings of an angel and a devil beside Pop's photo, a picture of mentally ill paranoia if ever there was one.

Iggy and *The Stooges* were one of the first "Heavy Metal" bands. The term reflected Detroit's titanic automobile industry with its noise, grit, roughness, and shiny

Figure 37

Iggy Pop — A soldier for Satan.

exterior hiding a roaring engine inside. *The Stooges* as well as *Alice Cooper,* got their first big breaks in Detroit.

Iggy's inspiration to pursue a career in Rock & Roll came from attending an Ann Arbor *Doors'* concert where he had become entranced by Jim Morrison's mesmerizing stage presence and antics. What an incestuous brothel the community of Rock & Roll is! Jagger influences Morrison, who in turn initiates Iggy, who influences Bowie, who in return helps Iggy by producing his record. All these people and more must share the blame for what Rock has degenerated into in the last fifteen years.

One final quote from Iggy Pop:

> "I became increasingly aggressive toward others. I learnt a unique and indispensable skill, which is to make Rock & Roll. I stopped my parents dressing me and started becoming a CONNIVING COLD HEARTED SON OF A BITCH, which I've been since the beginning of *The Stooges . . .* "[27]

What a fine slave for Satan Iggy Pop is! Icy, hellish hate seethes from this Rock & Roll demon with every scorching sentence he spits out. His influence on the modern Punk Movement cannot be fully calculated.

A staggering number of the cream of Rock's crop, not to mention those unfortunate enough to be admitted into their immediate circles, have died in the prime of their lives, many from heroin overdoses. Their martyrdom at the top of their careers has ensured the fact that their names will live forever in the hearts and minds of their fanatical followers.

Here is a list of some of those dead performers, plus the drugs that killed them:

JAMES HONEYMAN SCOTT — guitarist for *The Pretenders* — cocaine overdose.

JANIS JOPLIN — The most famous white female Blues singer ever, from a heroin overdose.

GARY THAIN — Bass player for one of the English trailblazers of "Glitter Rock," *Uriah Heep*. He died from a heroin overdose.

TOMMY BOLIN — Famous jazz guitarist who also did a stint with the foremost Heavy Metal band of the Seventies, *Deep Purple,* from a heroin overdose.

CARL RADLE — Long time bassist with Eric Clapton. Heroin overdose.

SID VICIOUS — Bass player for the first Punk band to become famous, the *Sex Pistols.* Vicious was free on bail for murdering his girlfriend when he died, not unexpectedly, from a massive heroin overdose.

BON SCOTT — *AC-DC's* original singer, dead of alcohol poisoning and suffocation.

JOHN BONHAM — *Led Zeppelin's* drummer — "An over-consumption of vodka."

JIMI HENDRIX — Barbiturate overdose. He choked to death on his own vomit.

KEITH MOON — *The Who's* drummer, and a close friend of John Bonham and John Lennon. Moon ingested far too many barbiturates, which, when combined with his usual massive alcohol guzzle, killed him in his sleep.

BRIAN JONES — Barbiturates, alcohol induced drowning.

ELVIS PRESLEY — Barbiturates, other assorted "Downers," and a possible heart attack.

JIM MORRISON — Alcohol and drug induced heart attack. At least that's what authorities THINK happened. No one seems to know for sure.

BOB MARLEY — Marijuana induced brain cancer. Reportedly smoking up to a pound of prime Jamaican Ganja a week for many years, Marley's cancer spread swiftly from his lungs to his brain.

BRIAN EPSTEIN — *The Svengali* like *Beatles'* manager and mentor was found dead in his bed of a Carbitol overdose.

There have been many near-fatal misses by several Rock performers indulging in their favorite addictions. Among them are:

PAUL KANTNER — One of the founding members of the *Jefferson Airplane/Starship,* this man suffered a deadly stroke before his 40th birthday. The LSD he has consumed in the course of his career would probably fill a government stockpile for a year.

ALICE COOPER — A hopeless alcoholic, Alice committed himself into a sanitarium and later made a record based on the ordeal.

JERRY LEE LEWIS — One of Elvis Presley's closest friends and downer buddies, Jerry Lee was hospitalized, fighting for his life against a chest wall filled with abscesses. Dismissed, he would later appear on Tom Snyder's syndicated "Coast To Coast" TV show, a hollow, thin shadow of his former hell-raising self, his voice cracked and weak.

GREGG ALLMAN — Leader of the *Allman Brothers Band,* Gregg was the object of a Federal investigation regarding his substantial cocaine habit.

RON WOOD — The newest member of the *Rolling Stones* was arrested with 260 grams of cocaine on the island of St. Maarten, in the Caribbean. He and his girlfriend served five days in jail, and were deported. (One gram of pharmaceutical cocaine would be worth $500 on the street.)

SYD BARRETT — The founding father of *Pink Floyd* and the resulting psychedelic movement, quickly became a near vegetable from LSD abuse in his short career, preferring to putter about in his garden rather than make music or meet other humans.

After reading the information just presented, who in their right mind can claim that Rock & Roll and the use of mind-decaying, death-dealing drugs aren't one and the same thing? Still, there are those skeptics who would say, "Sure, there's probably a lot of drugs to be had in the inner circles of Rock's royalty, but that doesn't mean that there's a conspiracy to make our kids take em."

Don't be so sure.

Frequent scandals pop up from time to time in the newspapers regarding what is known in the recording industry as "Payola," (Record company reps allegedly give radio station managers and disc jockeys gifts of drugs like marijuana and cocaine. In return the DJs play specified records over the air to the point of saturation.) Similar disgraceful exposes have been made public since the 1950's, since Rock began.

Ever wonder why record prices keep going up while the quality of the product has plummeted in recent years? The price of cocaine, a drug that fuels the industry, isn't getting any cheaper. Witness the following excerpts from several letters to the California music newspaper, "Bam:"

> "Corporate executives were once identified in my favorite music publication as cocaine junkies in designer jeans . . ."[28]

191

"Nationalize the cocaine industry. If record producers had free cocaine they wouldn't need so much money . . . "[29]

"It's everybody's fault. Ninety per cent of the musicians I've met in the last five years have been arrogant, self-aggrandizing and somehow convinced that their ability to write within a framework of 20 chords makes them "Artists" and heirs to instant fame and fortune . . . "[30]

The record company executives, the album producers, the engineers at the recording sessions, and the musicians themselves many times are ALL stoned on various drugs such as cocaine, LSD and marijuana when they make and record their music. In the hyped-up, glitter-star world of Rock & Roll, 100% energy must be expended in maintaining that precious "image" 24 hours a day. The spastic, rocket-fuel burst of many snorts of Coke gives that badly needed push to sagging musicians and studio personnel. LSD used to be the drug of choice among these same addicts, but has now been overshadowed by cocaine. The records the Rockers made while tripping are still around, though. Take these remarks by John Lennon about how his supergroup the *Beatles* used to make records:

"I mean like 'Rubber Soul' was Pot, or the one before with the white drawing on it. You know, it was like pills influenced us in Hamburg, drink influenced us in so and so and, I don't know, there are no specific things . . . "[31]

" . . . I thought I was taking some uppers, and I was not in the state of handling it. And I can't remember what album it was, but I took it and I just noticed . . . I suddenly got so scared on the mike, I said what is it, I feel ill. I thought I felt ill and I thought I was going cracked. I said I must get some air. They all took me upstairs on the roof and George Martin (producer at many *Beatle* sessions) was looking at me funny, and then it dawned on me I must have taken Acid . . . "[32]

Lennon also added,

"'Help' was made on Pot. 'A Hard Day's Night' I was on pills. That's drugs, that's bigger drugs than Pot. I've been on pills since I was 15, no, since I was 17 or 19 . . . Since I became a musician . . . I've always needed a drug to survive . . . "[33]

Numerous people claim that LSD has a far reaching potential for good, as it opens up its users to psychic stimulation and the total reality of recognizing overlooked spiritual forces for what they are. If that's true, then those same users are just as apt to be influenced by dark, evil forces.

One thing's for sure — soon after the Acid craze firmly took hold in 1967, the civilized world saw a return to superstitious paganism, witchcraft, cults, astrology, and the study of Eastern religions such as would have been thought impossible during the no-nonsense, (and no drug), days of the 1950's, a mere decade earlier. This hunger for the supernatural, nurtured by LSD, took root in the Sixties, and grew strong in the Seventies. We are now watching it bloom in full flower, spawning groups like *Iggy Pop,* the *Plasmatics, Ozzy Osbourne,* and *Iron Maiden.*

The Bible speaks often about evil, demonic spirits contacting and possessing humans in order to further their own devilish ends, such as in the book of Mark, chapter 5, verses 1-13. What possessed the John Lennons of the Rock world to make music while tripping on LSD?

The Beatles and LSD started the drug ball rolling, and it has now become an avalanche. Once millions of minds have been blown on Acid, which direction do they wander off in? The occult has always been a haven for thrill seekers jaded by an oversupply of drugs and too much money, and rich Rock & Rollers are no exception. Where they lead, our young people follow.

All evidence is increasingly pointing to the fact that today, in the 1980's, those youngsters are heading straight for heroin. What else can await them once they start envying their precious "Stars." Are we seeing a direct connection between the phonograph needle and the hypodermic needle?

The whole of today's music and recording industries, top to bottom, is rotten, eaten away by the decaying side effects of the drugs it consumes in such gargantuan quantities.

It will consume us too someday soon, if we let it.

CHAPTER 8

The Sins of Sodom

"Know ye not that the unrighteous shall not inherit the kingdom of God? Be not deceived: neither fornicators, nor idolaters, nor adulterers, nor effeminate, nor abusers of themselves with mankind, nor thieves, nor covetous, nor drunkards, nor revilers, nor extortioners, shall inherit the kingdom of God."

1 Corinthians 6:9 & 10

"I may not go down in history, but I will go down on your little daughter."　　　　David Lee Roth[1]

"There's nothing wrong with going to bed with somebody of your own sex. I just think people should be very free with sex — they should draw the line at goats."　　　　Elton John[2]

One of THE biggest Rock idols of the Seventies at the time of the above interview, every new Elton John LP was a guaranteed chart buster. His concerts were Standing Room Only. He even coaxed the reclusive John Lennon out of semi-retirement in 1974. They shared the stage

Thanksgiving Day at a concert in New York's Madison Square Garden.

Besides being one of Rock's biggest draws, and a fine pianist, Elton John is also a practicing homosexual, according to the interview quoted above. In the smutty world of Rock & Roll, where sexual identities blur amidst the mascara, freaky costumes, and hip wiggling concert shows, Elton certainly is not alone in his perversion.

Another powerful Rock name is that of David Bowie. His sway over his own masses of totally devoted fans cannot be fully described in just a few short paragraphs. Bowie founded "Glitter Rock" in 1972 with the release of his "Ziggy Stardust & The Spiders From Mars" LP, and gave the movement a leader: himself. A year earlier he had announced his bisexuality to the world on the covers of British Pop magazines. He began wearing dresses, earrings and bracelets, hose and garters, lipstick, and rouge in concert and on album covers. He dyed his hair orange, then streaked it with purple.

There is a word which aptly describes such behavior: Transvestite.

Bowie's basic weirdness is enhanced by his eyes; they are two different colors, (the result of a childhood accident in which a playmate poked him in the eye with a stick). One iris is green, the other a silvery blue. His mismatched eyes, emaciated face and body, orange hair, womens' clothes, and self avowed homosexuality have made this man (?) the idol of millions. During the early Seventies, he grew rich by exploiting his outcast image to a thrill-seeking public breathlessly awaiting the newest in sexual shocks.

David Bowie did not disappoint them. One of his favorite, (and most photographed), tricks when performing live in concert was to drop to his knees facing guitarist Mick Ronson. He then would clutch the man's hips, thrust his face forward, and proceed to simulate homosexual acts. Instead of turning fans off with such sick displays, swarms of fresh converts to Glitter Rock flocked under Bowie's banner of black self-debasement.

Trying to hide his sick abnormality under the guise of being an "artiste," Bowie never fails to make self-serving, pseudo-intellectual comments in interviews. He claims that what he does on stage and record really has nothing to do with Rock & Roll. He regards himself as more of an actor, having studied mime earlier in his career. He claims his records and concerts are really just free-form experiments in intellectual exploration. In order to see the obvious lie behind all this, one has only to examine a picture of David Bowie on his knees before Mick Ronson, as appeared in "Circus Rock Immortals, Volume I" (page 72).

Gays worship Bowie, mainly for his "courage" in coming out of the closet, and also for writing a song which has become the Rock & Roll Gay Liberation Anthem, "All The Young Dudes." At the end of his own version of the tune, Bowie can be heard laughing to his homosexual lover as the chorus begins fading, shouting uproariously, "How do ya feel?!," and proclaiming, "I can do this for years!!"

Bowie's ex-wife Angie made some revealing comments about the weird homosexual-lesbian world she and David enjoyed in a 1979 interview in "High Society Magazine," (a soft core pornographic smut-book that specializes in pictures of naked movie stars):

> "David and I used to have a lot of scenes with other girls. We were twenty minutes late for our own wedding, though, because we were having a scene with another girl. We had gotten up early that morning and decided to have another chick; she was a beautiful girl — an actress . . . "

> "I don't think there is any difference between being good in bed with a girl and being good in bed with a man . . . "

> "There's four or five guys and me and all we do is pick up chicks and have a laugh and see who can poke them first. We've been doing this for many years . . . "

197

Like her famous husband, Angie Bowie's emaciated face and fishbelly white toothpick frame is topped by a bird's nest of hair which periodically changes from neon orange to industrial green. *The Rolling Stones'* huge worldwide hit "Angie," from their Jamaican voodoo "Goat's Head Soup" LP was written about Mrs. Bowie.

There is a present (and steadily growing) connection between the twin smut worlds of Rock & Roll and Pornography. A self-proclaimed lesbian, Angie Bowie gave an exclusive interview to a pornographic magazine on the shocking, anything-goes sex world she and David inhabited. Is it because these Rock scum, the very dregs of society, feel more comfortable around debased, amoral creatures like themselves, or is it because no other reputable magazine would even consider publishing such filthy memoirs? Whatever the case may be, each new sordid scandal and controversy only serves to increase the wealth and fame of degraded Rock Stars like David Bowie.

The "Grand Old Man" of the Gays, Bowie's career has now reached the point where no amount of bad publicity can hurt him. He thrives on it. Busted for marijuana possession with Iggy Pop, Bowie wore flashy gangster clothes when appearing in court to answer the charges. A mere slap on the wrist, and he was free to go.

Nothing seems to be able to stand in Bowie's way as he makes ever bigger strides in the enlargement of his own already legendary career. Attaining artistic credibility came with his starring role as John Merrick, the "Elephant Man," on the Broadway stage. His performance won rave reviews. Overnight, he became the darling of the ultra-posh New York Theater District crowd.

In May of 1982, an album adaptation of Bertold Brecht's "Baal" featuring David Bowie in a key role appeared at record stores all over the country as this limp-wristed king of the abnormal world of Homo Rock solidified his stand in the Theater. (Baal was the heathen god mentioned in the Bible who demanded human sacrifice to quench his fiery thirst.)

From a common pervert looking for action on the street, David Bowie has become the undisputed Drag King of Rock & Roll Homosexuality. His leaps into records, movies and the stage have made him acceptable to a section of society that would never have embraced him before. Like a blood-sucking parasite, he has wormed himself into the very fabric of the straight society he despises so much.

"David Bowie? Oh, he's not so bad. A little weird, maybe. Didn't he star in that Broadway play that was such a success?" This is probably the image Bowie would like most to present to the "Establishment," that of the consummate "artiste," even as he picks their pockets and corrupts their youth with his weird ideas about love and human sexual relationships.

The real problem here lies in not considering David Bowie and those like him to be especially dangerous. This man blazed the trail of perverted Homo Rock. His legacy should not be taken lightly, and here's why. Let David Bowie tell you his philosophy in his own words, taken from an interview in Rolling Stone Magazine, 1972.

> " . . . I hate weak things. I can't stand weakness. I wanted to hit everybody that came along wearing love beads . . . "[3]

> "I guess drugs have been a part of my life for the past ten years, but nothing very heavy . . . I've had short flirtations with Smack (heroin) and things, but it was only for the mystery and the enigma. I like fast drugs. I hate anything that slows me down . . . "[4]

> "I've never been in love, thank God. Love is a disease that breeds jealousy, anxiety, and brute anger . . . It's a bit like Christianity . . . "[5]

"I think I might have been a bloody good Hitler. I'd be an excellent dictator . . . "[6]

"I have this dream. I'd like to host a satellite television show and invite all the biggest bands onto one stage. Then I'd come out with a great big wheelbarrow of machine guns and ask them, 'Now how many of you are gonna do anything? How many are going to pick up a gun and how many of you are going to cling to your guitars?'"[7]

"I believe that Rock & Roll is dangerous. It could well bring about a very evil feeling in the West . . . It's got to go the other way now. And that's where I see it heading, bringing about the dark era . . . "[8]

"I feel that we're only heralding something even darker than ourselves . . . "[9]

"(Rock & Roll) lets in lower elements and shadows that I don't think are necessary. Rock has always been the Devil's music. You can't convince me that it isn't."[10]

During this interview, Bowie said he saw a body fall outside the plate glass window of his room. He leaped from his chair, startling the interviewer, and whipped down the window shade. A star had been drawn on the shade, and beneath it the word "AUM." Bowie lit a black candle, blew it out, and told the frightened reporter that his bizarre behavior was for protection from "the neighbors." In reality, he was casting Black Magic spells, calling upon the demon Aum for protection.

The Bible talks very clearly about homosexuality and lesbianism. These perverted acts are an abomination of God's plan for human sexuality. There is no room for dissent on this subject, according to Scripture. Man is not to lie with man, nor woman with woman. It's that simple. Homosexuality is absolutely forbidden, for it is an enormous sin.

> "Thou shalt not lie with mankind, as with womankind: it is abomination."   Leviticus 18:22.

> "For this cause God gave them up unto vile affections: for even their women did change the natural use into that which is against nature: and likewise also the men, leaving the natural use of the woman, burned in their lust one toward another; men with men working that which is unseemly, and receiving in themselves that recompense of their error which was meet." (AIDS?)
> Romans 1:26 & 27

Unfortunately, religious principles and the sordid world of Rock & Roll are light years apart. It's not enough that prominent Rockers pick pockets, trash morals, offer our children drugs, and spew out a never ending stream of obscenities, now they even want to erase the God-given line between the sexes! "Do your own thing, baby," is their message to millions of disillusioned young people looking for a leader; "If it feels good, do it."

Without fundamental principles and laws regarding sexual behavior, mankind itself would have become extinct centuries ago. Never forget that the twin cities of Sodom and Gomorrah were utterly destroyed by God for their homosexual wickedness. (See Genesis 19:1-30.)

With the mass potential Rock has for infecting uncounted numbers of youngsters with this dangerous homosexual trash, as spouted by the David Bowies and Elton Johns, a very real threat exists for coming generations. Indeed, unless the problem is quickly brought under control, there may be no proper sexual legacy left for them to inherit.

There couldn't have been a David Bowie as we know him without a Mick Jagger. The modern age of sexual confusion was born many years ago when Jagger and drug buddy Keith Richards started wearing makeup and lacy, frilly costumes in concerts and interviews with the press. Were they boys trying to be girls? No one knew for sure. Jagger's girlfriend, Marianne Faithfull, was bi-sexual, as was Keith Richards' lover, Anita Pallenberg, but this was more of a joke than anything else to the two "Glimmer Twins." They could both have their pick of any number of women when their girlfriends were busy with their own female sex slaves.

The Rolling Stones' music, old and new, is a far cry from the Gay anthems of David Bowie. The *Stones* have always preached the degradation of women, not male homosexuality. The *Stones* were the first musical sado-masochists in Rock. A case in point: to promote their 1975 "Black & Blue" LP, the *Stones* launched an ad campaign with pictures of a bruised and battered woman tied bondage style over the group's album. These graphics appeared on billboards coast to coast, and in every major American music magazine.

This example uncovers another sick issue: the sado-masochistic element so prevalent in today's Rock songs, (and indeed, in every facet of the entertainment industry, movies and television included). The S&M phenomenon has grown to gigantic proportions during the last decade. We hear songs like "Whip It" by *Devo*. We see photos of Rock groups like *KISS* and *Judas Priest* draped in leather and chains, carrying riding crops. (In the case of *Judas Priest,* this aura of sexual perversion may not be entirely an act, since lead singer Rob Halford allegedly appeared in an English porno film before joining the band.)

As usual, *The Rolling Stones* started all this back in the early Sixties by playing at being homosexuals and sadistic women-haters. The banner was picked up by David Bowie and *Alice Cooper* at the beginning of the Seventies. They advanced the concept much further, loudly declaring their total independence from society's sexual laws and taboos.

With all the safeguards and guidelines solidly trampled into the dirt, we are now observing a no-holds-barred era of Rock & Roll smut like never before. Somewhere along the way sex has become equated with violence, the more powerful the better. Sado-Masochism is the order of the day, and Rock & Roll, (as well as the underground porno industry), happily promotes this sickness.

One very disturbing factor in many of today's top tunes is the sound of whips cracking at strategic points in the songs. Songs by Kim Carnes, *ZZ Top,* Billy Squier, Joan Jett, *Prince, Devo,* and *Alice Cooper* are full of such noises. The title of a *Rolling Stones'* tune, "When The Whip Comes Down," reveals the depth of the abnormality eating away at the very foundations of our society right now.

All these tunes and many more, cruise hypnotically along until CRACK! the whip noise startles the unprepared listener out of his or her trance. CRACK! CRACK! Lest there by any misunderstanding about the motives behind such music, these lines from "Whip It" make things perfectly clear: "Crack that whip/ Break your mama's back ... "

Another good example is on Prince's 1981 "Controversy" album. One of the songs is titled, "Sexuality." The whips crack, and Prince whines and whimpers, as if being flogged bondage-style. His howls of pain soon turn into moans of delight as he is whipped into sublime sexual submission. These are some of the lyrics to "Sexuality:"

> "Stand up and be counted
> This is your life
> Second Coming
> Anything goes
> Sexuality is all you'll ever need
> Sexuality, let your body be free
> I'm talking bout a revolution
> We've gotta organize
> Reproduction of the New Breed
> Leaders stand up!
> Organize ... "

Another of Prince's records is called "Dirty Mind." More of his filthy song titles include: "Sister," (about incest), "Head" (a sexually descriptive term), "Jack U Off," and "Soft & Wet."

Whip cracking isn't the only evidence of homosexual S&M domination being crammed down young people's throats via their ears. If you've ever heard a hard core Rock & Roll song on the radio, TV, or stereo, you may have noticed how often the singer SCREAMS between verses and choruses. Have you ever wondered WHY all that screaming is necessary?

Over the years many musical hacks have half-heartedly explained away the phenomenon of Rock screaming as being a release of pent up sexual frustration, or perhaps a triumphant jungle yell left over from our primeval ancestors, unlocked by Rock's liberating forces. In the course of my own research, I have found a shocking answer that makes much more sense.

While interviewing members of the Gay community about this subject, I was told that the frequent screams punctuating most Rock tunes ALL come from the homosexual penetration of the male. This seems to be a matter of common knowledge among informed Gays, and an object of no little humor.

How ironic that a bragging, swaggering, macho, virgin-ravaging Rocker like *Van Halen's* former singer David Lee Roth, for example, is really warbling a Gay mating call when he screams during songs. (He usually does this at least ten times per album, long ago making it his trademark.)

Let us backtrack a little. When did all this screaming begin? Today's Rockers are simply recycling old tried and true formulas; they didn't originate the device. Anyone listening to old *Beatles'* songs, and even their later albums for that matter, cannot help but notice that a lot of screaming was going on. THEY were the first Rock band to scream themselves silly. On some songs, John Lennon would scream until his voice broke, then scream some more. Often, he and Paul McCartney would screech in unison during instrumental breaks in the various songs. Now, no one is accusing the *Beatles* of being homosexuals. All the available public evidence seems to indicate that they liked girls just fine.

" . . . they didn't call them groupies then, they called it something else. If we couldn't get groupies, we would have whores and everything, whatever was going . . . "
— John Lennon[11]

If that's the case, then who influenced THE BEATLES to scream like banshees? Did they simply introduce such behavior out of nowhere? Of course not. All artists are influenced by their predecessors, and the *Beatles* were no exception. On their first few LP's, they covered many songs written by Richard Penniman, (also known as "Little Richard.") HE was the first of the Fifties Rock & Rollers to scream, scream, scream. He was also a flaming homosexual.

Little Richard was well known as the most flamboyant Rocker of his era. With his penciled eyebrows, exquisitely coiffed hairdo, lipstick, silks, satins, and heavy jewelry, he astounded audiences everywhere, and got rich doing it. At one time, guitar superstar Jimi Hendrix got his start in Little Richard's backing band.

Little Richard was best recognized in performance as pounding on a grand piano while he shouted his way through dirty songs like "Good Golly Miss Molly," "Rip It Up," and "Long Tall Sally," screaming till his voice gave out. Paul McCartney learned to ape Little Richard's style perfectly.

Little Richard turned his back on Rock & Roll in 1957, and became a preacher. He also made several Gospel records. Ashamed of his homosexual past, he was quoted as saying, "You can't drink from God's cup and the Devil's cup at the same time." (A paraphrase of I Corinthians 10:21.)

THIS is where all the screaming in Rock got its start: from a homosexual. *The Beatles,* the world's biggest Rock act, stole it, and turned it into a phenomenon copied by every Rock band since 1964.

Screaming was the "in" thing to do at concerts in the early Sixties, especially for *The Beatles* and *The Rolling Stones. The Beatles* would scream, and so would their audiences of thousands, (mostly pre-teen girls). In fact, the resulting roar was so overwhelming that both the *Beatles* and the *Stones* rarely could hear themselves playing.

In the "Musician Player" magazine, *Beatle* drummer Ringo Starr had this to say,

> "I used to lean over and try to read Paul's lips to keep track of where we were at, because I simply couldn't hear anything. I was actually lip reading the songs to see where we were!"[12]

What was REALLY happening there, in the midst of all that frenzy? Little Richard screams, *The Beatles* scream, the audience screams, everybody screams.

The Bible tells of demon possessed persons healed by Christ who had terrified the surrounding populace with their screams. (Mark 5: 1-9) That blasphemous work of infernal evil, "The Exorcist," graphically depicted the little girl's possession by demons with horrifying screams and yells. This would seem to imply that screaming is a part of demonic possession. When the tremendous power of the Devil washed over those performers and that audience, they screamed their guts out.

One of the more recent Rock groups known for their screaming was the first of the Punk bands, England's blasphemous *Sex Pistols.* They were the epitome of amoral anarchists, headed by a foul-mouthed ghetto urchin with vaseline in his hair named Johnny Rotten, and a bass-playing heroin addict, Sid Vicious. (Vicious first popularized the self-mutilation with the safety pins craze which swept England and Europe in the mid Seventies. Punk fans shoved the pins through their cheeks and lips, creating a grotesque new fashion fad.)

In the course of their brief career, the *Sex Pistols* became famous because of three things: (1) Johnny Rotten's screaming, (2) Unleashing a string of foul gutter language, oaths, and curses while on a British TV talk show watched by most of England, and (3) Vomiting on passersby at London's Heathrow Airport. Oddly enough, "The Exorcist," (and the case histories which inspired it), used those same three themes prominently in their representations of demonic possession: Screams, Curses, and Vomit.

From the *Beatles* to the *Sex Pistols*. The music has changed, but the Devil-directed screams remain the same, screams that recall the mass baptisms by Hell-Fire begun in 1964 by the *Beatles* and the *Rolling Stones*. The manic hysteria generated in those early concerts of the Sixties has quite simply changed the face of the Earth.

Fans no longer go to such deafening screaming lengths as they used to at Rock concerts, but that initial seed of demonic possession was sown in 1964-65, over twenty years ago. Today we are reaping the harvest of that horrible planting.

After all the screaming was over, the Sexual Revolution began. After releasing all that pent up sexual tension at those Rock concerts, the Devil had his hand firmly on the rudder of an entire generation's voyage into darkness and hell. First came the screaming Rock concerts. Then came the Pill. Then came abortions on a massive scale, then the current VD and Herpes epidemics — a satanic conspiracy which has nearly eroded the very moral foundations our society is based upon. The newest curse, of course, is AIDS.

Rock & Roll is about sex. Head *Rolling Stone* Mick Jagger readily admits it. He said,

> "Rock Music is sex and you have to hit them in the face with it . . . " [13]

Even the term Rock & Roll itself has a sexual connotation. It was first coined in 1954 by Cleveland disc jockey Alan Freed. Originally, "Rock & Roll" was gutter slang for having illicit sex in the back of parked cars at drive-in movies, i.e., "Rocking & Rolling."

The screaming that started Satan's Sexual Revolution is still going on. Today's Rock stars may not even know why they're doing it, but they couldn't care less.

It's become a tradition.

One of the newest and youngest screamers making the music scene in a big way is Joan Jett, formerly of the *Runaways,* now with her own backup band, the *Blackhearts.* With their dopey, tuneless, Heavy Metal mishmash, "I Love Rock & Roll," the *Blackhearts'* debut album and single smashed its way into the "Billboard" Top 10, quickly reaching the #1 spot and sticking there like glue for many weeks. Other cuts from the LP erupted from radios for months on end. (It seemed more like years.)

Joan has had quite a Rock & Roll career for someone barely out of her teens.

An L.A. hustler named Kim Fowley put together the *Runaways* in the mid-Seventies as a way to make some quick cash. No one in the 5-girl group was over seventeen, and their debut album made much of that fact, the back cover photos also listing the girls' ages. Cheap sensationalism aimed at a thick skulled, lusting male audience with allowance money to burn was what the *Runaways* were about. Manager Fowley bought the band's equipment, then taught the girls how to play their instruments. He also wrote many of their songs, negotiated their contracts, and produced their albums. When he felt they were ready to begin fleecing the public, he put the group on the road, parading them onstage in revealing outfits.

Seventeen year old lead singer Cherie Currie, (an angelic faced blonde), wore a corset-garter belt affair with black lace panties and fishnet stockings when she sang. There are pictures of her leaning over to give her panting audiences a clear view of her blossoming cleavage, as well as one particular photo in a November, 1976 issue of Creem Magazine which showed her poised with a hand microphone shoved between her legs. For a grisly finale to this vulgar peep show, Currie would spit up artificial blood from her mouth in concert until the front of her shirt and pants were soaked, an obvious imitation of demented Devil Rockers *KISS*.

Kiddie Porn had met Rock & Roll, thanks to a greedy cradle robber out to make a fast buck. One of the *Runaways'* best known songs was "Cherry Bomb." (Cherry is street slang for a person who is a virgin.) Joan Jett resurrected the tune on her "Glorious Results Of A Misspent Youth" LP.

When it became obvious that the group had no real talent, the *Runaways* folded. Soon after, Joan Jett started her solo career, and is now the idol of countless thousands of adoring teenyboppers, as her best selling albums attest.

Whips, screams, S&M bondage, Kiddie Porn-Rock, incest and homosexuality. Things have come a long way since Elvis Presley! Magazines like "Playboy," "Hustler," "Oui," and "Penthouse" that do features and articles on prominent Rockers feel right at home in the depraved atmosphere of Homo Rock. They sponsor year-end Music Polls, and foster the image of the Rock Star as an admirable role model for the upwardly mobile, (or those who would like to be). As a matter of fact, the worlds of Pornography and Rock & Roll are not too far apart at all. Both have bright lights, big bucks, sick displays and greedy men and women behind the scenes; both feature EXPLOITATION as an indispensable tool to dredge up the millions from the pockets of perverts and outcasts everywhere. One dirty hand washes the other, with Rock and Pornography feeding off each other in a disgusting, mutually dependent relationship of deviated lust.

A case in point: Author Tony Sanchez tells of head *Stones* Mick Jagger and Keith Richards being invited for an extended stay at Playboy magnate Hugh Hefner's palatial Chicago estate. They readily agreed. In the presence of swarms of voluptuous women, the decadent Rockers had sex with many of the young "Bunnies," and smashed Hefner's furniture in their spare time. A smiling Hugh Hefner basked in the reflected glare of so much superstar-struck status.[14]

Today Rock & Roll and Pornography have married, creating an entirely new and ravenous monster. It is uncontrollable. It's no use trying to "nip it in the bud," as it were. That time is long past. "Porno Rock" is here to stay. Here and now.

And it can only get worse.

We're all to blame to a certain extent for having allowed "Porno Rock" to happen. From the beginning, shocking sexual exposes about prominent Rockers have oozed into the public eye. As far back as 1959, Rock & Roller Chuck Berry, (the *Stones'* biggest musical influence), was embroiled in a two year court trial for violating the Mann Act, (transporting an underaged female across state lines for immoral purposes). Berry's contemporary, piano pounding hell raiser Jerry Lee Lewis, was literally hounded out of Rock & Roll in 1958 for marrying his thirteen year old cousin.

If only we and our parents had heeded the early warnings about Rock & Roll leading to sexual immorality! We've made second rate clods like Mick Jagger, *Van Halen,* Rod Stewart, Pat Benatar, and *KISS* into cultural gods. Their faces and stories have appeared very frequently indeed on the covers of the "National Enquirer" and "People" and "US" magazines, periodicals with a combined circulation of many millions. They're not just Rockers anymore. They've become something larger than life. We read avidly about their divorces, salaries, paternity suits and sex lives. We see them on TV talk shows. *The Rolling Stones* even made it onto the CBS Evening News during their record breaking 1981 U.S. tour, as well as garnering a center spread in Life Magazine.

Can it be possible that a band of 40-year-old drug-decayed Black Magicians selling out a concert hall is news? Can we really be that starved for entertainment?

Rock & Roll superstars don't just dominate our stereos and radios anymore. They have slithered into our TV's, and onto our coffee tables. They've invaded every aspect of our homes, and from all appearances, it looks like the great untapped well of motion pictures may be the site of their next attack.

The Beatles, The Rolling Stones, The Who, The Clash, The Ramones, the *Sex Pistols,* David Bowie, *AC-DC,* and *Led Zeppelin* have all made their own movies, as have countless other groups. Most of them tested the water in the Sixties with various experimental celluloid sagas. Now they're producing sick epics for the silver screen in earnest.

Unless someone stops them.

Something very strange and evil is happening in our society. With albums like *Iron Maiden's* "Number Of The Beast," Ozzy Osbourne's "Diary Of A Madman," and the *Plasmatics'* "Metal Priestess," the music industry is beginning to parallel Hollywood's movie monopoly in terms of gory, satanic works of sickening despair. Every other movie that comes out is a horror picture — not the old Frankenstein-Dracula suspense melodramas of the Forties, but a hacking, butchering, senseless spray of bloody intestines and mindless maniacs.

Picks to the brain, needles in the eyeball, chainsaws tearing through torsos — THIS is what Hollywood has become. With freaks like Ozzy Osbourne and *W.A.S.P.* already at work spreading their own sicknesses, Rock & Roll is not far behind.

One common theme binding all the "Gore Flicks" and "Splatter Films" together is sex. Time after time, the young teen age victims are caught having sex. Immediately after this the chopping, stabbing butchering begins. Sex and violence. Violent sex. We are being systematically DESENSITIZED by such movies and records. We are being made CALLOUS and indifferent to pain, love, and suffering. We are being taught to develop a ghoulish taste for the obscene, the blasphemous, and the demonic.

211

What has Rock & Roll got to do with horror films? Well, what about the "Rocky Horror Picture Show," a movie so popular that thousands of theaters across the country show it again and again to packed houses until their prints wear out?

Huge cult audiences have claimed "Rocky Horror" as their own. They dress like the characters in the movie, and wait in long lines outside the box office for hours. Once inside, they know every line of dialogue by heart, screaming obscenities along with the actors on the screen.

One of the main stars of "Rocky Horror" was an Englishman named Tim Curry, who played the part of — what else, a transvestite. He wore lipstick, pearls, black garters, stockings, and panties in the film. Curry has several solo records to his credit besides the "Rocky Horror" soundtrack.

What kind of a movie is "Rocky Horror?" Well, let's just say that, for a crash course in the smutty marriage of Rock & Roll and the gritty abyss of homosexuality, there is nothing quite like "The Rocky Horror Picture Show." The movie seethes with violence, nudity, profanity, homosexual encounters, lesbianism, transvestites, Sado-Masochism, cannibalism, and other perversions, all set to a rollicking Rock & Roll beat. The majority of the scenes are shot at crotch level, allowing the audience to join in the vicarious thrills of eyeballing the well-proportioned men and women dancing on the screen in their underwear and jockey shorts. For at least half the film, star Susan Sarandon is clad only in bra and panties.

Tim Curry, glowing in heavy mascara and lipstick, struts and wiggles his lacy bottom at the audience while he sings. He is wearing black fishnet stockings and high heels, a shimmery black girdle, and a string of pearls. Later, he changes into a sparkly green evening gown.

"The Rocky Horror Picture Show" is literally crammed with scenes of wicked perversions. In a fit of rage, Tim Curry flogs his groveling servant Riff Raff with a cracking bullwhip. As the hunchback crawls on the floor, his face a mask of agony, Curry whips him again and again and again, a hellish light of indescribable excitement in his eyes. He is breathing heavily, SAVORING each slap of the whip. This is Sado-Masochism at its grisliest, an utter abomination of God's holy plan for our sexuality. Tenderness and love have been replaced by pain and evil domination. This scene can only be described as satanic.

Gory violence and murderous mayhem play their part in "Rocky Horror" too.

When 300-pound singing star Meat Loaf makes his entrance astride a revving mammoth motorcycle, dressed as a California Hell's Angel, Curry reacts with psychopathic hysteria. Grasping a short handled pick, Curry follows the biker into a frozen food locker, and hacks him to death, emerging later from the frosty fumes with his weapon and gloved hands dripping blood.

Later on, "Meat Loaf" is served at the evening meal. Curry and the other cannibals are eating his dead flesh on plates.

The degradation doesn't stop there. In one particularly sickening scene, Tim Curry seduces both Susan Sarandon AND her husband in different beds. Having totally degraded both the unfortunate travelers, Curry pulls out all the stops as "Rocky Horror's" final scenes play themselves out. All the previous hints of wicked degeneration fly full tilt in the film's perverse climax, all of which cannot be printed.

"The Rocky Horror Picture Show" was one of the first "Rock Operas," the commercially successful blending of Rock & Roll with motion pictures of a conceptual nature. It became a cult phenomenon, and there is where the real danger to its' fanatical followers began. In some theaters, "Rocky Horror" has played nonstop for several YEARS. Audiences took this depraved mass of celluloid so seriously that they literally brainwashed themselves with it, watching it over and over until every scene, every character, EVERY

BIT OF DIALOGUE was completely memorized. Then they began dressing as individuals from the movie, mimicking the action on the screen by rising from their theater seats like zombies to dance, yell, and repeat the smutty lines in perfect synchronization.

Even in a small town in the heart of the Midwest, on a freezing February night, where I saw "Rocky Horror" almost ten years after its first opening, the audience in the theater I attended was dressed to the teeth and well prepared for the evening's entertainment. Half of the people in the crowded cinema were costumed and made up as their favorite character, complete with stockings, bras, and underwear. It was immediately obvious that they RELISHED their roles, and took the whole affair very seriously indeed.

When the transvestites on the screen danced, the people around me jumped to their feet and rushed down the aisles. In their luminous face makeup, sequined jackets, and black underwear, they looked like refugees from a mental ward let loose in a costume shop. It was obvious that "Rocky Horror" is MUCH more than a movie to its trained, hardcore devotees. It had become an important part of their sordid lives.

"The Rocky Horror Picture Show" is in reality Satan's Show. Many of the most perverse scenes are played out amidst backdrops of crosses, stained glass, churches, and religious paintings and sculpture. All the most vile elements of the freaked out, amoral, anything-goes, L.A. cult mentality are vividly displayed: Bikers, Nudity, profanity, sado-masochism, homosexuality, transvestites, and alien beings, all glossed over with the well known stamp of Hollywood lewdness.

What has kept audiences coming to see this show for years on end? It has no plot. The actors were unknown at the time the movie was made. It has no well-known songs in its soundtrack, (except to hard core fans). It is not a comedy, nor a farce. In fact, it takes itself very seriously indeed.

"Rocky Horror" DOES have shock value galore. It also has given audiences across the country a chance to go to the theater and use freely all the foul language at their command. They can come practically naked and dance and sing to lewd Rock songs. It is a special windfall to homosexuals, since it allows them to be their own sinful selves without pretending to be normal. It is THEIR movie, filled with THEIR heroes.

"Rocky Horror" is nothing less than a satanic experiment in audience manipulation and crowd control. Here is what the Bible says about transvestites:

> "The woman shall not wear that which pertaineth unto a man, neither shall a man put on a woman's garment: for all that do so are abomination unto the Lord thy God."   Deuteronomy 22:5

"Rocky Horror's" makers and backers, guided by the Devil, set out to see to what extent young people could be conditioned to respond to certain satanic stimuli, and the entire operation has proven to be a resounding success.

The major ingredient here is Rock & Roll.

When millions of dollars start cash registers smoking, and millions of people begin worshiping a bisexual drag queen like Tim Curry, you can be sure the Devil is laughing, toting up the number of fresh souls being corrupted.

"Rocky Horror" is an abomination. It is not rated X. It does not play in the run down, decrepit porno houses of New York and Los Angeles, as one might expect. Instead, it's as close as your neighborhood theater, the one where your friends and children go.

Thanks to Rocky Horror's example, visions of a self-perpetuating, uncontrollable tidal wave of Smut-Trash-Rock films seems inevitable: Corruption for corruption's sake.

The Bible tells us to keep our minds on Godly things, not to wallow again and again in evil excrement like "The

Rocky Horror Picture Show." Some relevant words from Scripture include:

> "Finally, brethren, whatsoever things are true, whatsoever things are honest, whatsoever things are just, whatsoever things are pure, whatsoever things are lovely, whatsoever things are of good report; if there be any virtue, and if there be any praise, think on these things." Philippians 4:8, KJV.

Well, what's next? Just when honest, God-fearing people think they've seen it all, something even more obscene comes along to break more records and make more millions.

One of the most recent examples is the incredibly successful film "Purple Rain" starring black Rocker *Prince*. "Purple Rain" is THE Rock movie of the Eighties. It's a slick and street-wise glimpse into the life of an up and coming Rocker still stuck in the clubs of some grey metropolis (Minneapolis) as he yearns for the big time. It is the stuff of which all Rock dreams (or nightmares) are made. The Rocker is played by *Prince* (also known as Rogers Nelson). *Prince* has perfected a patented look about him throughout the film: his unblinking eyes gape insanely; his tight lipped mouth opens only to sneer; his hollow face reflects a spiritual nothingness no amount of crowd pleasing can restore. The word is "zombie."

Prince only comes alive when rolling on the floor of the spotlighted stage as he mimics sexual gyrations, or when seducing Appolonia Kotero (his girlfriend). In the standard sex scene, the accurate descriptive word is "smut." Music is played during the scene which is composed entirely of earth thudding crunches and a female voice wailing like one of the damned. "It's backwards," *Prince* explains to his eager sex partner.

After listening to many hours of backmasked messages on records, this section of the movie chilled me. No longer are evil broadcasts in reverse confined to Rock recordings, now they're booming out at unsuspecting audiences in movie theaters as well! (The soundtrack album of "Purple Rain" also contains a backmask section.)

"Purple Rain" is about suicide, wife beating, utter hopelessness, and the soul saving effect good Rock & Roll has on the mindless masses of morons who populate the movie. At the end, Prince sings/screams at the club crowd, "I'll die for you . . .," a lyric inspired by his father's aborted attempt to blow his brains out.

The critics simply gushed over "Purple Rain." It's held over engagements at movie theaters across the country were proof of its unqualified success. As a result, *Prince's* dazed features have (dis)graced the covers of every one of the major and not so major Rock fanzines. The soundtrack LP was a whopping "monster" as they say in the industry, and everyone called *Prince* Rogers Nelson "THE star of the 80's."

Well, here's one person that doesn't share that view. "Purple Rain" is not a work of genius; it's common garbage. Here's why: *Prince's* "dynamic" stage show, isn't anything new and improved. Jimi Hendrix did the same things on stage fifteen years ago with a lot more finesse, AND played the guitar at the same time better than *Prince* ever could. Nelson's sloppy imitation of Rock legend Hendrix is just warmed over rehash minus the flavoring. As far as his ACTING ability goes, *Prince* doesn't act, he sneers and gawks. Most of the movie he seems to be trying to hypnotize himself and everyone he meets. Too much time spent in front of the mirror, I guess.

As for Appolonia Kotero, anyone can put their girlfriend in a movie and call her a star; the casting couches of Hollywood are filled with those kinds of women. The music in this film, though popular, is also nothing special. We must not forget that *Prince* began his recording career with songs about masturbation, homosexuality, and incest. In the movie he shoves his hips into the face of his female band mate as she kneels before him, then pretends to masturbate. It's obvious that *Prince* is just updating his musical perversions. It's also interesting to note that "THE star and musical genius of the 80's" was thrown off the *Rolling Stones'* 1981 tour because the audiences were disgusted by his performances. They threw shoes, bottles, and anything handy at "His Highness." It's a good thing tomatoes were out of season.

Perhaps *Prince* should realize that his perversions are the cause of his difficulties, not just the symptoms. We should pray for *Prince* as we do for all who are outside Christ, but we should also recognize garbage for what it is: garbage.

"Purple Rain," I'm sorry to say, is just that.

Perhaps if we can understand the past and present, we can see what the future may bring in regards to the rancid world of Rock & Roll. To recognize the enemy and take him by surprise is half the battle.

What new debasements are waiting on Rock's horizon? What fresh forms will such experiments in blasphemy take?

The next chapter may help us find out.

CHAPTER 9

Video Madness

> "After this I looked, and, behold, a door was opened in heaven: and the first voice which I heard was as it were of a trumpet talking with me; which said, Come up hither, and I will shew thee things which must be hereafter."   Revelation 4:1

> "Turn on your receiver . . . "   *Nazareth*[1]

Today, in the 1980's, Rock & Roll has moved out of the concert hall and into the TV set.

When it took its brand new position in the marketplace during the early Fifties, television's ideal was to "bring the family together." Just the opposite has happened, but the important thing to note is the fact that television today reaches over 80 million American homes. There are a lot of people out there glued to the tube! If some greedy opportunists have their way, Rock & Roll will be the most watched program on those TV sets, and we're not talking about some hazy number of years in the future; we're talking about right now.

Today and tomorrow.

In the past few years, a video boom has come upon us. Video games, satellite dishes, cable TV multi-channels and "superstations," home computers, video cassettes, video disks, and even video mens' magazines equivalent to living, breathing Playboy "Playmates" have come into mass acceptance, not to mention the hard core pornographic video industry's amazing leaps forward.

Rock & Roll has not been left behind.

The "in" thing these days is for Rock groups to stage and film their own videotaped sessions of their most popular songs for public distribution. The Rolling Stones have been doing it for years. The finished videocassettes are then sold, rented, or used as promotional advertising on late night music shows, and even on the widely syndicated "Billboard Top 10" TV spot hosted by Casey Kasem. The Home Box Office cable channel has a special series devoted exclusively to Rock & Roll videos — "Video Jukebox," as well as shows like "Solid Gold" and the 24 hour "Rock Around The Clock" of MTV. As more and more groups discover the unlimited potential to be had in spreading their messages via these mini-movies, the weird and the violent become commonplace.

For example, Kim Carnes' "Bette Davis Eyes" video promotion had hands slapping faces in synchronization with the crack of a whip. Her follow up, "Draw Of The Cards," found Carnes prowling through a misty haunted mansion, groups of zombies done up like rejects from a Mardi Gras nightmare following her. One of the monsters grabs Carnes, lifts her high above his head, and shoots out a snaky, foot long tongue from his distended mouth. Michael Jackson's famous "Thriller" video featured the dead coming back to life in all their rotting, blue-skinned splendor.

This is the stuff of which nightmares are made, Rock

nightmares put to film for our children to watch and absorb.

Gratuitous, smutty sex has its place in the new breed of Rock videos, too.

To boost their hot #1 single, "Centerfold," the *J. Geils Band* opened their promo film with lanky, zapped-out singer Peter Wolf dancing around desks in a deserted high school classroom as he lipped the suggestive lyrics about taking his "centerfold's" clothes off in a motel room. Suddenly, in march a long line of buxom, fresh faced girls who look to be barely out of their teens. They are all wearing different varieties of lacy "baby doll" negligees. They dance and surround the drooling Wolf, pouting their wet lips and rolling their eyes at him with a perverse mock innocence.

Even a supposedly "G-rated" artist like Olivia Newton-John is not above wallowing in sex to rake in a few more million dollars. Her #1 album and single "Physical" smashed all kinds of Billboard records in 1982. She performed and appeared at various awards shows, made a videotape of the album, and even starred in her own TV special to support the record.

Olivia Newton-John has talent, of course, and her songs have appealed to a wide audience of all ages, but what made "Physical" such a whopping success on both sides of the Atlantic was the generous view of Liv's legs and backside on the album cover, promo photos, single sleeves, and personal appearances.

Many radio stations banned playing "Physical" outright because the lyrics were too suggestive. Newton-John's follow up hit, "Make A Move On Me," was even more so. On the first run sleeve of the single, she is seen perched on a seaside tree branch, her filmy white dress billowing in the breeze. It is billowing because she has it hiked far past her knees, even past her thighs and hips. The photo is so revealing, in fact, that it is obvious Olivia Newton-John is not wearing any underwear.

This "flasher" image spilled over into her smash TV special and appearance at the American Music Awards' "Top Songs Of '81" telecast. Her "Physical" video and television spectacular both presented Newton-John as a sweaty, sexy piece of meat ready to be grabbed by the highest bidder.

A lot of good, conservative, God-fearing Christians LOVE Olivia, and would probably rather not dwell on the fact that, by throwing away her pride and shamelessly undressing in public, she has finally achieved the much coveted, gold plated title of Superstar.

But ignoring the problem won't make it go away.

The simple fact of the matter is that artists on the fringe of Rock & Roll, like Newton-John, are all influenced by whatever direction Rock & Roll takes. As the moral safeguards loosen up in one field, they unravel in others as well. It's a confusing problem with no easy answers, but Christians concerned about what they and their children see on TV should be aware that outright blatant Rock & Roll groups are not the only culprits in the ever increasing decay of our society's moral fabric; it is also these other, supposedly more wholesome performers, who are at fault.

Rock's devilish dominance of the entire communications industry has filled every inch of the field. Nearly every musical performer in the related fringes owes his allegiance in one way or another. What is truly frightening about all this is the way Rock has slid so comfortably into the video drivers' seat, barely missing a beat in the transition from vinyl to cable. The definition of greedy hucksterism, Rock & Roll now has its foot in the very door of our homes via the TV set. Revolting groups with their tasteless, insipid songs, and whacked out, drug dripping impressions are found on a whole variety of cable channels, MTV being the most notorious.

Rock is not just for listening any more; it's for watching, too. And that can be dangerous.

With the universal notion of television as a NECESSITY rather than one of life's luxuries, Rock & Roll is gaining the attention of tens of millions of people it would not otherwise have reached. It is playing with our childrens' minds and molding their future goals. Its message is offensive to many. So why do we continue to put up with it? Because our kids like it? Just because we like something, that doesn't mean it's good for our mental and spiritual well being!

With television safely under his thumb, Satan is busy covering other bases as well. For example:

The "Picture Disc" is sort of a cross between records and video. A color photograph of the group or singer is etched into the record vinyl by sophisticated laser techniques. As the teenage listener "gets into" the music, he can also stare at his favorite group as it goes around and around on the record turntable, 33 and a third times every minute. This is self hypnotism aimed at gullible, unwary music buyers, plain and simple! Some groups who use picture discs include: *The Beatles, AC-DC, Venom, Slayer, The Rolling Stones,* Ozzy Osbourne, *Blondie, The Runaways, The Sex Pistols,* Elton John, and *Iron Maiden.*

The Devil is also merging radio and television into a new and powerful tool. In some cities, thanks to the technology behind satellite transmission, a "simulcast" concert can be watched on TV and listened to on the local F.M. radio station at the same time. Rock & Roll is making huge strides, using the F.C.C. and cable TV as its footstool. With the mad rush landslide expansion of video recorders, video players, video disks, blank tape sales, 24-hour, 50-channel cable superstations, video games, and Rock video promos, there is nowhere to go but up.

Rock & Roll has finally invaded the privacy and sanctity of our homes like never before. It used to be that if Dad vetoed Junior's latest obnoxious Rock record, the stereo could be turned off, or the record banished to another room to be listened to in private.

The TV is an entirely different story. It is the centerpiece of most American homes, and is avidly, habitually watched by family members of all ages, from toddlers to grandparents. THIS is where the next crest of Rock's slimy wave is surfacing. They WANT that vast untapped reservoir of audience, and video promotions are only the first step in reaching that goal.

Think about it from the teenager's point of view: what with the time, expense, gasoline, and other assorted wear and tear hassles involved in going to see Rock groups "live," what could be better than having the same concert in your own living room?

A sagging world economy and skyrocketing travel costs have forced all but the biggest and most outrageous Rock acts from touring at all. They're beginning to put the money they're saving by staying off the road into their video projects.

The sky's the limit in this exploding industry, as wide as a million dollars, and as high as the imagination. What if the hard core Satan Rockers like *Venom* and *Mercyful Fate* begin booking video airtime?

There are two gigantic cable networks which specialize in Rock-only programming. One is called MTV, (Music Television). Using "Veejays" to introduce their 24-hour-a-day, 7-days-a-week Rock & Roll videos, concerts, commentary and interviews, MTV has a multi-million dollar budget with which it plans to perpetuate the Rock industry for at least another decade. MTV has been on the air since August of 1981.

As MTV programming head Bob Pittman put it:

> " . . . The best we can do is encourage these people, support them, and when they create this art, give it exposure . . . "[2]

Rock & Roll as art? He's got to be kidding! How can sexploitation, Satan worship and sadistic violence possibly be described as art?

The second giant in the field is the USA Network's "Nightflight," which broadcasts Rock & Roll for twelve straight hours on the weekends. One of its most popular segments is "New Wave Theater," a showcase of L.A.'s most obnoxious and disgusting Punk bands. Nightflight is no fly-by-night organization. Its sponsors include Pepsi-Cola, the Wrigley Corporation, and Chevrolet.

MTV and Nightflight. Add to these two pioneers the dozens of independent producers scattered across the country, and it should become painfully obvious that we are going to be seeing a lot more Rock & Roll on our TV sets than ever before. These independent producers with a burning vision are rushing to make sure Rock & Roll saturates this new cable industry from the largest East Coast metropolis to the smallest Midwestern farm community. What does this mean for our children, and our families? Seeing insane Rock scum do their depraved thing in concert is one thing. Watching them jump around on the family TV screen is quite another matter entirely.

In the early Sixties only 6% of American homes had cable TV. By 1982, that number was five times higher and rising astronomically by the month. The whole industry is just getting off the ground, and Rock & Roll has joyously hitched a ride.

Rockers are certainly no strangers to television. ABC's "In Concert" series started the trend of presenting big name Rock acts on the tube over a decade ago with the deranged *Alice Cooper* band. *Cooper's* performance was so vile that the Dayton, Ohio station I was watching at the time stopped the telecast after fifteen minutes and substituted an old movie in its place. Officials at the station later claimed a massive wave of consumer phone calls radiating outrage and disgust had triggered the cancellation. Apparently, most Midwestern viewers felt they could survive the night without watching *Alice Cooper* play with snakes and hang himself in front of hundreds of frothing fans.

"In Concert" spawned a whole slew of imitators, and it wasn't long before every weekend found teenagers across

America glued to their TV sets, watching the latest in Rock Glitter groups.

The second wave of this well-planned invasion of the American home followed a few years later with popular, youth-oriented comedy shows like "Saturday Night Live," "Fridays," and "Tom Snyder's Coast To Coast," all of which featured stellar Rock acts as their focal points. When the jokes got stale, the music took up the slack.

I'll never forget watching the *Rolling Stones* when they hosted "Saturday Night Live," as singer Mick Jagger extended his tongue and licked rhythm guitarist Ron Wood's lips in an insultingly offensive "French Kiss." The homosexual overtones displayed made me gag.

"Saturday Night Live" and Tom Snyder's "Coast To Coast" have showcased at one time or another virtually every famous (and infamous) Rock group and solo artist currently blasting away. The *Plasmatics* appeared on the Snyder show and blew up a car. The ratings soared. *KISS* were Snyder's guests, and we were treated to the loud mouth of drunken member Ace Frehley as he guzzled liquor on the air.

Rockers know where the money is, and like mongrel dogs sniffing out a bone, they always dig it up. Today, the big money is in TV and video promotion and it won't be long until we all find ourselves drowning in a never ending, polluted ocean of sewer sludge oozing out from our TV tubes to the tune of Heavy Metal guitars.

THIS is the wave of the future.

And it's not just in the planning stages, it's happening right before our eyes. Satan's henchmen, *The Rolling Stones,* have already made video history and set the precedent all lesser bands will inevitably follow. They capped their record-busting 1981 American tour with a special video performance carried on the Viacom cable network which was seen by millions. One day after the *Stones'* broadcast, drunken British superstar Rod Stewart did the same thing.

The January 29, 1982 edition of the California music

paper "Bam" describes the scene in detail:

> "On December 18 and 19, America saw and heard the most important Rock videos produced to date. On those evenings, *The Rolling Stones* and Rod Stewart presented LIVE televised and stereo-simulcast concerts (from Hampton, Virginia and the L.A. Forum, respectively) which together reached more people than years of touring could do. With tour costs rising every day, don't be surprised if video concerts such as these take on more and more importance . . . "[3]

About the *Stones'* video performance in particular, "Bam" had this to say:

> " . . . I had not seen what the band could do with good lighting. The colors were truly magnificent, occasionally taking on an almost animated quality. Two moments near the end were positively surrealistic: while the crowd was cheering for the encore after "Jumpin' Jack Flash," searchlights cut through the Hampton venue like futuristic laser beams; and when the band came out to begin their final tune, "Satisfaction," thousands of balloons dropped from the ceiling, looking like, with the quick edits and multiple angles, a journey into the center of some strange molecule. The effect was like something straight out of Fantasia."[4]

> "Director Ashby employed numerous moving crane shots to give the viewer a sense of the scope of the concert: the constantly moving sea of bodies dancing to every song, the communal celebration in the hall. There was one long, graceful shot near the end that took us from the back of the auditorium to a close up onstage in a sweeping, sensual movement just over the heads of the crowd that in just a few seconds seemed to capture the enormity of the event . . . "[5]

So there it is in black and white from one of Rock's respected publications: these videos aren't a simple ego trip to the bands that produce them; they're expensive to make, and painstaking in detail. These groups are deadly serious about the work they're doing, and they wouldn't be doing them at all if they weren't sure of getting a massive return on their initial investment.

Some of the *Stones'* early video attempts and concert clips, (their "Jumpin' Jack Flash" promo in particular), set standards in evil pictoral debauchery still unrivaled today. Who could forget seeing Mick Jagger's wild, LSD-popped eyes caked in mascara as he held the open mouthed audience in the palm of his sweaty hands, or the tattoo of Satan on his chest when being filmed for 1969's "Rock & Roll Circus?" *The Rolling Stones* were intensely serious about their video projects then, and they're every bit as dedicated to them now. The technology has just caught up with their hellish ideas, bringing them more hordes of fresh fans than ever before.

The *Stones* may have been the pioneers in the Rock Video field, but the number of bands following their lead by making videos of their own today simply can't be counted. The scene has changed so incredibly in such a short time that a group's video is now at least as important as the record it promotes. For example, in 1985, old *Rolling Stone* Mick Jagger made an MTV video titled, "Just Another Night" from his first solo album, "She's The Boss." (By the way, the *Rolling Stones* have not broken up, though plenty of people wish they would.) Mick has wanted to be an actor almost since he got too famous to be just a Rock star, and finally, after fifteen years, he gets his chance! Unfortunately, he's just as terrible as he was in his earlier flops. The video begins with Mick and his date exchanging a few pleasant words. No amount of make-up and bad lighting can disguise Mick's mummy face or the cocaine sparkle in his sunken, burning eyes. While he thickly chews over his simple lines, Mick's eyebrows shoot up and down like grasshoppers. The guy has all the charisma of a department store dummy. The high point of the video, (at least from Mick's viewpoint), comes when he is lying in bed with his dark skinned female partner, his slithery tongue licking all over her neck and face. Without this MTV exposure, would Jagger's solo album have broken the records it did? MTV, after a short but deadly struggle with its competitors, has emerged as the undisputed leader of the Cable-Rock-Video networks. To strengthen their lead and cement their position forever, they attempted in 1984 to strong-arm the entire recording industry into guaranteeing MTV exclusive rights to all new Rock videos as soon as they're made in return for tons of cash.

When I began researching Cable-Rock in general and MTV in particular, I found out something both horrible and yet logical, knowing what we do about Satan's hand in modern Rock & Roll. Some mental institutions refuse to show Rock videos on the TV sets watched by their patients. Why? Because the mentally ill and psychotic get even more disturbed when they see those videos. It sends them into fits, rages, and deep depressions. For those that are demon possessed or otherwise afflicted in mind and spirit by Satan, the sight of those Devilish videos just increases their torment. It reinforces the fact that the presence of Lucifer rules over their lives, even down to what they watch on TV!

Now, I'm not pretending to be a psychologist, but you don't have to BE a psychologist to see the sly and wicked stamp of Satan in most of today's Rock videos. Here are some things I saw after just one evening of watching MTV: (Remember, this stuff runs 24 hours a day)

In his popular "EYES WITHOUT A FACE" video, Billy Idol drops to his knees within the lines of a pentagram chalked on the floor. Burning candles are set at the five points of the Satan-symbol. Raising his arms defiantly to Heaven, he sings the line about "saying your prayers . . ."

In Ronnie James Dio's mini-film "ROCK & ROLL CHILDREN," Ronnie is a black magician complete with cape and crystal ball, his lair a dusty old occult shop. Two punked-up kids, a boy and a girl, seek refuge from a storm inside his devils' den. Manipulated by Dio's spells, they are transported to another dimension. The place where they find themselves is a horrible world of the "straight" society. They don't fit in. The girl can't get a job because of the way she looks. Her "goody-two-shoes" classmates torment her, and her suburban Middle America family with their plastic smiles and money-worshiping attitude disgust her. As for the boy, his brutish, sweating father beats him with a belt for playing the guitar, and rips Rock posters from his son's bedroom wall. These children would rather do anything than stay in this world, so they run away — right into Ronnie James Dio's arms.

Dio's message should be very, very clear to everyone, both parents and young people. When families turn into hateful power game units and homes become battlegrounds, the Ronnie James Dios of this world will take up the slack. The Rock stars will fill the void left by mean spirited and misguided parents. Dio and his kind will be glad to shelter young outcasts and misfits, molding them into the kind of person Satan wants them to be. Parents, take note! Ronnie James Dio is giving you fair warning before he snatches your children right out from under your nose!

Motley Crue's 1985 "SMOKIN' IN THE BOY'S ROOM" video continues the authority/alienation themes so increasingly seen in today's MTV Heavy Metal. A high school student loses his homework through no fault of his own, then must face the principal's wrath. As usual with this type of video, the authority figure is painted as a mean spirited, one-dimensional clod gleefully administering punishment on the poor helpless victim — the innocent student. It is only by escaping to "The Other Side" where *Motley Crue* lives, that the boy receives the courage to rip up his paper and throw it in the principal's face. As the video ends, the kid mutters, "Maybe now they'll listen to my side."

A band called *Aztec Camera* was next, with a song titled, "OBLIVIOUS." The group consisted of skinny young men that looked more like boys. They all had unhealthy pale white complexions, and wore strange lop-sided "I've got a secret" grins that stayed frozen on their faces. They looked like they belonged in David Bowie's bedroom, not the forest where they were singing. One boy with a guitar sat in the forks of a tree, a weird Hansel & Gretel house behind him.

A black man dressed like some kind of primitive witch doctor climbs a ladder up the tree. He wears an inverted cross around his neck. When he is within touching distance, the boy pushes him off the ladder so that he falls back to the ground. Different Tarot cards flash for a couple of seconds at regular, subliminal intervals. The whole effect of this video was very, very disturbing and off-key. In fact, if you look closely at many Rock videos you will see the band members casting spells with quick hand movements and weird gestures.

"UNDERCOVER OF THE NIGHT" featured the *Rolling Stones* as terrorists who kidnap a frightened Mick Jagger. Keith Richards holds a pistol to Mick's head, and later, after throwing a hood over him, blows his brains out.

Twisted Sister's "WE'RE NOT GONNA TAKE IT" is well worth watching, because it shows us exactly HOW Rock bands reach kids with their sick messages. A father screams and rages at his teenage son, trying to break his spirit while thundering out the question, "What are you going to do with your life?"

The boy's reply? "I wanna Rock." He strums a tremendous crashing guitar chord, and burly, hairy-chested transvestite Dee Snider drags the father down the stairs by his hair, then repeatedly smashes a door in his face.

After *Twisted Sister's* "inspired" performance came some MTV commercials, which is something the cable channel originally swore it would never do. Apparently, like most people and organizations associated with Rock & Roll, they care a lot more about making money than pleasing their viewers. Rock fans complain loudly about being forced to sit through commercials while they wait for their favorite video, but they keep watching anyway as they roll more joints and open more beers.

The ultimate extension of this frightening video trend is "Wolf Rock TV," a Saturday morning cartoon show with a Rock & Roll format that also shows the newest videos! Such an abomination didn't happen by accident. Evil, exploitative plans like this are meant to brainwash young children and groom them into being the potential record buyers of the future. It's an ad man's fondest dream come true, and let me tell you friends, it makes me plenty mad! Throwing such trash at impressionable teenagers is bad enough, but little kids!

Another example of Video-Rock brainwashing of children is the fact that at some video arcades where youngsters hang out a new "Video Jukebox" is appearing. By using the same tokens they feed into "Space Invaders" and "Tempest," they can see the latest Rock videos on a big TV screen while the music blasts out of the speakers below. The kids literally flock around to get a good look whenever someone starts one of the videos. The machine I saw was made by an Amityville, New York company.

Satan has left nothing to chance. Teenagers, little kids, pre-teens. Who's left? Believe it or not, "Christian" Rock videos at times play on MTV side-by-side with the secular garbage. On June 12, 1985, the CBS Evening News featured a report on Christian Rock videos. Following in the secular music world's wake, so-called "Christian Contemporary" groups are making their own videos. The only trouble is that aside from the words, they look just like the worst MTV has to offer. As a matter of fact, one Christian Rock video by *DeGarmo & Key* was turned down by MTV as being too violent and disturbing in its unedited form. Some of the scenes from the mini-film were shown. They included a skeletal human face with rays blasting out of its eyes, and several men sitting in chairs as their roasted flesh disintegrated from their bones. The number 666 also received prominent attention. The band *Stryper* was also interviewed. They looked just like a dry-cleaned *Motley Crue.*

It was extremely interesting to note the reaction of Dave Marsh, a Rock writer and critic from way back. He is often quoted on camera by CBS whenever a piece of music-related news is featured. When questioned about Christian Rock videos, Marsh said that in his opinion they had no effect on non-Fundamentalists. In other words, he didn't think that they were really evangelizing anyone. Since the bulk of their audience was already saved, their message was falling on deaf ears.

I believe that such efforts are just polluting and confusing us in a storm of compromise and hypocrisy. What will the world think of such nonsense? God's Word, the Bible, couldn't be any plainer:

> "And be not conformed to this world: but be ye transformed by the renewing of your mind, that ye may prove what is that good, and acceptable, and perfect, will of God."   Romans 12:2, KJV.

When the commercials and rotated videos on MTV have run their course, a "Veejay" comes out and spouts off the latest Rock & Roll trivia such as who's playing where, how to get tickets, and other gossipy tidbits about the big name stars' latest escapades. Occasionally on late night MTV whole concerts are presented in their entirety. As usual, Heavy Metal is the favorite subject. The night I watched MTV, *AC-DC* was on live from St. Louis. Having never seen these satanic skull bashers myself, I was very interested in seeing just what kind of a show they would put on.

If one word could describe their two hour set it would be: "Devilish." Both the singer and Angus Young were possessed by an electrifying energy so powerful it literally threw them across the stage. I just don't see how it's humanly possible for one pitiful skinny little man like Angus Young, (even with a head full of cocaine), to run, jump, crawl, sprawl, and violently shake himself to pieces all that time without even stopping for breath.

When Angus jumped into the crowd to play, his ten burly security guards went with him, brutally shoving kids out of the way. One fan grabbed Young by the elbow as he passed, and it was then that the REAL power behind Angus Young's performance revealed itself.

The face that snarled back at that clutching fan was not human. There was nothing about it that even remotely resembled a human being. With his ragged broken teeth, and his eyes popping out of his head, he opened his distended mouth and slavered like some kind of wild animal before jerking his arm free and rushing back to the stage. Drool ran from the corners of his mouth and mucous hung in streams from his nose.

Ever wonder what all those contorted faces are all about that Rock stars always make on stage? You know, when they grind their teeth and gnash their tongues just before they let out some ungodly scream? I think at that time they are in the grip of forces powerful enough to crush their bodies in an instant. They call it adrenalin, or the "buzz" of the crowd.

I call it demonic possession!

Watching MTV for any length of time is a draining and hypnotizing experience. Satan's power is masterfully displayed through these Rock videos. I urge all Christian families to keep your homes entirely free from such filth.

Long before MTV came along, Rock movies were paving the way for today's videos. People that have little knowledge of Rock & Roll may not realize that virtually every big name group has made its own movie at one time or another. Some have made several. These projects have ranged from feature length cartoons, ("Yellow Submarine"), to in-concert documentaries, ("Gimme Shelter"), to musical "Rock Operas," ("Tommy"), and ("Jesus Christ Superstar"). How did this phenomenon get its start, and what are its implications for the youth of today?

Hollywood and Rock & Roll have been partners in crime from the beginning. Once firmly established musically on records, Rock stars of the Fifties naturally began moving towards film as the next logical step in their careers. Elvis Presley did more to popularize this transition between platter and camera than any other performer in Rock's roster, at least in the beginning. Once Elvis had clearly blazed the trail, (not one of his dozens of movies lost money), his contemporaries ran for the cameras like rats following the Pied Piper. Rock movies began to attain an air of respectability, though they were still regarded for the most part as strictly teenage fare.

The Beatles changed all that.

Their 1964 debut film, "A Hard Day's Night," appealed to theater goers of all ages with its wacky, breakneck pacing and innovative script and photography. At the heart of the music was the freshness of *The Beatles* themselves as they were just beginning their world conquest. They had single-handedly shaped the style of future Rock movies for the next decade with the commercial and critical triumph of "A Hard Day's Night." Another fringe benefit to this newly created type of teen film was the soundtrack album which always followed every movie's release. Thus, with movie and record together, the dollars doubled, and the millions multiplied.

With a bang and a lurch, Rock & Roll movies took off into the Hollywood stratosphere.

1967's "Yellow Submarine" ushered in the age of Psychedelia to movie screens across the world as well as unveiling the concept of "Cartoon Rock." At one time, *The Beatles* even had their own Saturday morning cartoon series. People simply could not get enough of them, and quickly elevated the Liverpool quartet to the status of cultural gods. Having one's very own cartoon surely must be the ultimate in status symbols! Imagine how these four working-class punks from English slums must have felt watching their own caricatures on the TV screen. What immense power to mold the destiny of a generation lay in their greedy grasp!

Paul McCartney has said,

"I remember many times just sitting outside concert

235

With the legendary *Beatles* paving the way down that
yellow brick road to movie megabucks, Rock groups from
Pink Floyd to the *Grateful Dead* lined up behind their
leaders, anxious to dig their own gold in the Hollywood
hills.

One of the earliest of the new breed of Rock "concert
movies" was "Jesus Christ Superstar," based on the incredibly popular double album of the same name, released
in 1970. Its cast included some of the biggest Rock names
of the time.

Andrew Lloyd Webber and Tim Rice were two agnostics
intent on debunking what they felt was the myth of Jesus
Christ's deity. Their production of "Superstar" portrayed
Jesus in a strictly humanist sense, a wise philosopher con-
fused by the peoples' wish to elevate him to the status of a
god.The part of Christ was vocally portrayed on record by
Ian Gillan, lead singer for the famous Heavy Metal band,
Deep Purple.

In "Jesus Christ Superstar," Mary Magdalene hints of a
secret love affair with Jesus, a mere man in the grip of
political forces beyond his control. He agonizes over his
own helplessness and the futility of trying to affect change
in the face of so much corruption and mistrust. He has
become a pawn in a game he cannot win. Finally, he is
tortured, and dies on the cross, a pitiful wretch, an enemy
of the State, his utopian dreams blasted forever and scattered to the winds with his own miserable death.

Here is what the Bible says about those who would seek
to demystify Christ into human terms:

"For I testify unto every man that heareth the words
of the prophecy of this book. If any man shall add unto
these things, God shall add unto him the plagues that
are written in this book. And if any man shall take

away from the words of the book of this prophecy, God shall take away his part out of the book of life, and out of the holy city, and from the things which are written to this book."   Revelation 22:18-19

"Jesus Christ Superstar" had a far reaching impact on Christians everywhere as their children gobbled up copies of the record and played it at every opportunity. A whole host of famous and lesser known Rock stars appeared on the album — Rock & Roll meets religion. The two are about as far apart from each other as can be, but that tiny detail didn't worry Webber and Rice. They married the two concepts and made millions. Even in the most conservative Christian homes it was suddenly O.K. to listen to Rock & Roll as long as it talked about Jesus. Christ had become a trendy addition to everyone's household, conceived, sold, and marketed just like Ivory Soap or Gainesburgers.

Some pastors, led by the Holy Spirit, preached from the pulpit about the terrible blasphemy of explaining away God's divine plan for our salvation as a mere cosmic accident. Few people listened.

Satan had snared untold thousands of new souls.

Once "Superstar's" songs had been ground into millions of brains, it was time for even more mass media exposure. "Jesus Christ Superstar" became a movie. (And also a Broadway production.) Both young and old alike could now go to the theater and bop to those rollicking Rock & Roll tunes Judas and Jesus were singing. It was "far out, man" — Christ up there on the silver screen in Technicolor and Cinemascope, with tanks rolling across the Judean desert. It was a real feast for the eyes as well as the mind. Finally, Jesus was brought down to a level we all could understand.

He had become human.

Well, no one wants to admit it at this late date, but we were all taken in by the slickness, (and sickness), of that ad campaign. We were so busy appreciating the merits of making Christ accessible to more souls that we missed a few vital points: Jesus Christ was not a mere mortal; He was God become flesh. His plan for our salvation didn't end with His death; it began there. It is not for us to decide what Christ's full purpose was here on this Earth; our primitive brains could not hold the revelation even if it were given to us in all its glory. We are as a very small animal when compared to the life force that is God, our pitiful minds are so weak. How dare Andrew Webber and Tim Rice pretend to speak for all of us when baring their own addled doubts and half-baked blasphemies!

Why did we listen?

Rock & Roll has nothing to do with Christianity. One is about licentious excess in the extreme, the other with controlling our baser natures so as to attain a higher and better form of existence through obedience to Christ. "Jesus Christ Superstar" O.K.'d the union between Rock and religion. Many other Rock movies since then have greedily milked that same concept.

Take the 1974 film of the Rock opera "Tommy" for example. *Who* lead singer Roger Daltrey starred, and the rest of the band made cameo appearances. The remainder of the cast included some of the biggest names in both Rock and Hollywood — Ann-Margaret, Eric Clapton, Oliver Reed, Elton John, and Tina Turner. Those good old Rock standbys — sex, drugs, and lots of violence, were the backbone of the movie, as they were in the original double album.

Tommy is homosexually raped by his uncle, (played by dead *Who* drummer Keith Moon). He is injected with massive doses of LSD by the Acid Queen, (Tina Turner), until he transcends his human form and becomes a leader of the masses, a deity complete with a crown of thorns. Killings, riots, brutal beatings — all have their place in the film which director Ken Russell called "One of the greatest works of art of the 20th Century."

Right!

So much for the traditional Rock draws. The truly disturbing aspect here is the way Russell has incorporated religious themes into all this violent wickedness. Crowds of cripples and deformed worshipers flock to be healed inside a blasphemous church. Pete Townshend *Who* guitarist), John Entwhistle (Bass), and Eric Clapton lead the processional between the pews as the afflicted reach out their hands to be healed. Townshend and company are dressed in "holy vestments" — cassocks and stoles; they are playing electric guitars as they walk down the aisle. The processional, you see, is to the tune of raucous Rock & Roll. The congregation takes communion before a huge towering statue of Marilyn Monroe, her plaster dress flying high above her thighs. The people below can easily look up and see her underwear.

The idea for "Tommy" was originally conceived by Pete Townshend as he was flying to New York from *The Who's* appearance at the 1967 Monterey Pop Festival. It was during this flight that he willingly ingested the extremely powerful psychedelic drug STP, and experienced psychic death.

From the ashes of a bad Trip the world's first Rock Opera was born. It catapulted the sinking *Who* back into the limelight and made them millionaires for the first time in their career. "Tommy" even became a stage smash. What a triumph for *The Who!* From drug-induced nightmare to record to film to stage, this violent band of drunken pill poppers suddenly were spokesmen for a generation. Their records were instantly and eagerly devoured by millions of fans worldwide.

The Who, of course, played at the Cincinnati, Ohio concert on December 3, 1979, where eleven young people were trampled to death fighting to get inside Riverfront Coliseum where their Rock gods were performing.

Townshend had these compassionate thoughts to share with his fans about the Cincinnati tragedy:

> "We're a Rock & Roll band. You know, we don't
> !*?%!&* around, worrying about eleven people dying."[7]

> "We did all the things we thought were right to do at the time: sent flowers to the funerals. ALL . . . WASTED. I think when people are dead they're dead . . . "[8]

Even as they played out their savage roles as destructive anarchists on stage, eleven young people outside the Coliseum lost their lives, trampled to death by a maddened mob of 6,000 stomping teens infected by *The Who's* visions of violence. That mob didn't know the difference between play-acting and Rock & Roll reality.

The Who are no longer touring and making records, but Pete Townshend is still considered to be the spokesman for a generation's ideals long since dead and buried. Such is the nature of Rock & Roll that a group like *The Who,* (who built their career out of thumbing their noses at anyone over thirty and demolishing thousands of dollars worth of musical equipment), can influence their audience, incite them to riot, actually KILL them indirectly, then ride a new wave of immense popularity, their heads held high above the stink of their fans' dead bodies. How many more people must die before someone has the courage to put a stop to this insanity?

Satan has sent his troops into all the major fields of cultural entertainment. Rockers collaborate with film makers in their devilish projects, and the directors pay back the favors in turn with tailor-made star vehicles. In February 1985, even Walt Disney featured a two hour Valentine's Day television special cartoon — all set to hard Rock music such as *Madonna, Prince* and *The Rolling Stones!* Satan is working on an all-new, ever-younger generation today, hardening their senses with the combination of blaring Rock & Roll and sexy, violent, science fiction fantasies in the form of Rock movies and videos.

We're facing a crossroads.

Our homes center around our television sets. What we see and learn there is becoming increasingly complex every day. Because we don't know what's coming next, it gets harder and harder to filter the bad from the good, the educational from the trash.

As far as Rock groups are concerned, we're only going to get more of the same sexy, smutty, self-serving garbage they've already been shoving down our radio-controlled throats for fifteen years.

More of the same.

From a staggering variety of seemingly uncontrollable factors, from the state of the American economy to home computers, our attention today is being focused intensely RIGHT ON THAT TELEVISION SCREEN. Through the rest of this decade and in the future, experts tell us that we're going to be using our TV's for a lot more than watching reruns.

Already, technology permits us to pay our bills via the TV, work at home instead of the office, vote on topical issues to selected survey groups, plan the family budget, help the kids with their homework, and play video games, all with our television sets.

We have to realize that Rock groups are buying more and more airtime, producing more and more videos, making more and more movies. They're grabbing up big chunks of our childrens' future unless we put a stop to it right now. These Rock movies and videos are dumping millions of dollars into the laps of Rock scum, giving them another shot in the arm, and a few more debauched years of bilking and ravaging the public until the next change in the wind comes along.

Magic, makeup, homosexuals, science fiction, sado-masochism, men in dresses, demons, and drugs; it's all been tried successfully at one time or another. What we are looking at now, today, is the climax of all those things and more. It's more popular than ever. And Rock & Roll has never been more evil. Satan's no fool; he knows how to use the system!

The TV screen is next.

YOUR TV screen!

CHAPTER 10

Punks, Peace, and Politics

"They that forsake the law praise the
wicked: but such as keep the law contend
with them."   Proverbs 28:4

"I am an Anti-Christ
I am an anarchist
I wanna be
Anarchy..."
The Sex Pistols[1]

Punk Rock is music made to worship death.

At one time this horrible march music of Satan spanned
the entire globe. It has helped destroy the value systems of
ᵣuropean and American youth everywhere. It has left an
ugly, running-sore brand on the minds and morals of a
generation. In Europe and on both American coasts, the
Punk look, attitude, music and mentality is here to stay.

Where did the word "Punk" come from, anyway? A Punk originally was prison jargon for the homosexual "boy" used and abused by the hardened convict sharing his cell. In the movie "Jailhouse Rock," the unspoken implication was that Elvis Presley had become a "Punk" in prison.

We remember too well what the Punks and their music were like in the Seventies — a screaming, cursing, insane mob of monsters. Let's take a look at Punk today.

Another simmering, steam-bath night is descending on Los Angeles in the sweltering summer of 1986, the 10th anniversary of Punk Rock's beginnings. In defoliated, bombed out suburbs like West Hollywood, the Punks, or "Street Survivors," as they are also called, mass on the trashy sidewalks outside their favorite Rock & Roll clubs. California Punks come from far and wide to join in Fascist sprees of Nazish violence and blood letting, a feast of "slam dancing" that leaves many with broken bones, slashed faces, and busted heads. What the *Sex Pistols* sang about, these people ARE.

Some sections of Los Angeles have been completely taken over by Punks. Santa Monica Boulevard is one good example. The place is a nightmare in 3D, a living, breathing abomination, a riveting and horrible example of what thirty years of Rock & Roll has mutated and produced in our young people and our culture. If you ever drive through this area, keep your doors locked and your windows up.

Many Punk clubs here resemble fortresses with barred windows, heavy doors with peepholes, and walls thick enough to repel any enemy invasion. People stand in the street, threatening passersby and harassing traffic. Others lounge on upturned garbage cans, or squat on the sidewalks, bored, waiting for some "action."

Many Punks can be seen ducking quickly into the stinking alleys to do up their "loads," mixtures of codeine and bootleg barbiturates washed down with lots of beer. Heroin is sometimes included in the package — the lunch box of the Punk crowd. The ones that aren't indulging in the barbiturate breakfast (Punks sleep all day), are snorting or injecting Speed. With the shortage of high quality methedrine, and the constant dealer ripoffs, most Punks make their own amphetamine concoctions out of Vicks inhalers and muriatic acid. Like the amyl nitrate "Poppers" so adored by homosexuals everywhere, this mixture is not only lethal, but often fatal. The Punks don't care. They just want to "get off man."

When darkness falls and the drugs hit home the slam dancing begins. It's Rome's Circus Maximus in reverse: the common people assembling of their own free will in an arena of death, offering their bodies to be cut, stomped, kicked, slashed, and trampled. Sometimes they sew razor blades into their shirts before bashing into each other. The Rock music that accompanies this bloodbath is churned out by bands like the *Clash, Black Flag, X, The Dead Kennedys,* the *Castration Squad, Agent Orange,* and *Raw Meat.*

The first thing frighteningly evident when looking at this seething mass of Punks is the fact that, for them, the Sixties' Sexual Revolution is over. These people HAVE no sex. They dress alike, look alike, talk alike, smell alike, and do the same sadistic things to each other. They see no need to wear their God-given sexuality as a badge of individuality. They would rather look like tattered, rag tag remnants from some kind of inter-galactic Hell-A-Thon.

Only the insane and demon possessed practice self-mutilation. It's hard to believe, but in the early days of the Punk Movement in England, it became extremely popular for these outcasts from society to pierce their lips, cheeks, and even noses with needles and safety pins. Sometimes the pins were attached to their ears with a chain. Rival gangs found it easy to show their displeasure with newcomers while slam dancing by grabbing these chains and ripping the pins from their bleeding faces. It was all great fun, of course.

Here is the standard uniform of the "Street Survivor:" blue, green, orange or purple streaked head stubble, (shaved heads are the norm), ripped and stinking rags replacing T-shirts and jeans, skull necklaces, chains, padlocks, nail studded wristbands, thick leather belts, spiked gauntlets and throat collars, German W.W. II helmets, leather jackets, and steel toed jackboots, all decorated with swastikas. Hidden under the jackets are knives, needles, machetes, guns, and lengths of pipe.

These young people have formed an army in the largest cities of America. They have a philosophy. They have a uniform. They have their march music. And they have the undisputed strength of WILL to accomplish their goals.

As LSD drenched English megastars *Pink Floyd* put it so well in their multi-platinum record "The Wall:"

> "We don't need no education
> We don't need no thought control
> No dark sarcasm in the classroom
> Teacher leave those kids alone . . ."

Punks have been the subject of glossy magazine articles and glowing interviews in music trade publications for years. Specialty shops and boutiques are scattered all over England, Europe, New York, Chicago, and Los Angeles which cater exclusively to the stereotyped Punk image and moronic mentality.

Who would have believed it? Death worshiping suicide has become trendy and chic! What exactly has happened here? An entire generation raised on Rock & Roll and drenched with two decades of drugs and demons have turned into animals. They've degenerated into a lower form of life. We are now seeing exactly what parents, pastors, and principals were warning us about when Rock began back in the Fifties.

The Punks were the ultimate extension of Rock & Roll, the last in a long line of mutations, from Elvis to *The Beatles* to *The Stones* to the *Sex Pistols.* Today's Heavy Metal monsters have carried on the tradition. "There Is No Future" is their creed. They have nothing, are nothing, believe in nothing. They are barren, empty vessels for Satan to possess and work through, and he does it in an awesome and frightening fashion.

Violence. Beatings. Blood. Anarchy. This is what Punk is all about.

How did this suicidal, and above all, extremely POLITICAL movement get started? Outrageous as the *Rolling Stones* are, Punk's pranksters make even that vile warhorse pale by comparison. What legacy was entrusted to the thousands of young people who worshiped Punk Rock for 10 years? What evil, rubble-strewn world of insane nightmares will they leave their children? Or was this perhaps the beginning of Rock's final chapter? Where did it start, and where does it leave us today?

The Punk Rock, New Wave and Post Punk periods which began in 1976 and continued into the 80's are all a direct result of decades of Socialism. In a system of government where individual ambition is stifled because the entire populace is invited to partake of the welfare bounty, a terrible cost to society can be the only result, as is the case with England's many problems and struggles today.

Can it be possible that we are seeing America's future reflection in that British mirror?

Loafing under the government dole produced the street Punks on the highways of Wolverhampton and Brixton. A pseudo-military organization in itself, Punk Rock was hatched, ugly and screaming, and immediately began exporting its diseased campaign of chaos to Europe and the United States.

Years ago the phrase "British Invasion" was used to describe *The Beatles'* triumphant spearhead of Rock acts landing on our shores. After the Fab Four's initial assault on America in 1964, we fell in love with those marvelous Moptops and their English ways. Suddenly, anything British was "in." Clothing, hair styles, speech, drugs, groups and music: *The Beatles* shoved it all down our willing throats.

London's tourism industry doubled, then tripled. Everyone wanted to see the country those wonderful boys had come from. Americans loved them especially because they were so "honest, warm, intelligent, and wholesome."

> "And when we got here you were all walkin' around in Bermuda shorts with Boston crew cuts and stuff on your teeth . . . The chicks looked like 1940's horses. There was no conception of dress, or any of that jazz. We just thought what an ugly race, what an ugly race. It looked just disgusting and we thought how hip we were . . . Us and the *Stones* were really the hip ones . . . "[2]
>
> John Lennon.

More and more British bands from *The Animals* to *The Who* to the *Rolling Stones* to the *Moody Blues,* landed in America until our airwaves (and earwaves) were flooded with the "Merseybeat" sound. American attention was firmly fixed on England as the ultimate in musical tastes and trends, a condition which still persists today, more than 20 years later. The hysteria is long gone, of course, but the fascination is still alive and well. It was this musical obsession with the British that allowed the demon-seed of Punk to spread and grow so easily in the fertile American soil.

Long before Punk arrived in full force, America had already been softened up, beaten and dazed by its very own *Alice Cooper,* (from Phoenix, Arizona). After *Cooper* got through shocking and sickening audiences from coast to coast, teens across the land were more than ready for the bludgeoning death blows of Punk Rock. The group chose its name while playing with a Ouija board one stormy night. A demon claiming to be the spirit of a 13th Century witch burned at the stake contacted them and told lead singer Vincent Furnier, (a minister's son) that if he would change his name to Alice Cooper he would become rich and famous, one of the biggest Rock stars of all time. The rest, as they say, is history.

Alice's concerts were experiments in sadistic cruelty. He

would appear to have himself hung, guillotined, and electrocuted. The other band members held knives, and attacked him, punching and kicking. During their 1973 "Billion Dollar Babies" Christmas tour, *Alice* and the boys assaulted one of their road crew dressed as Santa Claus, and pretended to beat him to death onstage before rioting mobs of 30,000+ bellowing young people screaming for St. Nick's blood.

Alice was known to spit on his audience, kick garbage cans off the lip of the stage, and on at least one occasion "accidentally" threw a trick cane into the midst of the frantic, milling, concert crowd as his band played on. The deadly, razor-sharp, compressed-steel-spring blade within the prop sliced a young fan's hands to ribbons as he struggled to hold onto his souvenir. Cooper's manager later invited the boy backstage to meet the members of the band, not as a profound expression of regret for the accident, but to make sure the teenager wouldn't sue *Alice* or the arena.

Alice Cooper's best known trick was to hatchet and decapitate baby dolls while singing his hit, "Dead Babies." Synthetic blood poured out of the dolls' severed necks. Immediately after being guillotined, *Alice's* chopped off "head," (another realistic prop) was pulled from a bucket of blood and raised on high for all to see and delight in. His headless torso, (a mannequin dummy) was then drug around the stage, trailing a bloody stream behind it.

Alice stole many of his shocking stage tricks from the late Jim Morrison, (*Doors'* lead singer) a fellow alcoholic and pioneer in madness.

> "In the early days the act's main draw was its aggressive, bizarre behavior. . . In those days I was hanging out a lot with Jim Morrison. I really liked the guy but he had a negative effect on me. He believed that you had to live the role at all times, and I began to pick that up . . . I began to be *Alice* 24 hours a day . . ."[3]
>
> — *Alice Cooper.*

Alice has the following to say about his audiences:

> "I go out and take them by the throat. It's like raping them. And I don't let them go. They have no chance."[4]

> "I have American ideals. I love money. The idea all along was to make one million dollars."[5]

Alice's albums and song titles clearly show the psychotic, sick blasphemies he turned into a multi-million dollar career during the early Seventies. Some examples: "Love It To Death," "Killer," "Hallowed Be My Name," "Under My Wheels," "Halo Of Flies," "School's Out," "Sick Things," "I Love The Dead," "Second Coming," and "Only Women Bleed."

On "HALLOWED BE MY NAME," some lyrics are:

> "Screaming at mothers
> Cursing the Bible
> Hallowed be my name . . . "

On "SECOND COMING," he speaks of walking on the water,

> " . . . with angels by my side
> So have no gods before me
> I'm the light . . . "
> "The Devil's getting smarter all the time . . . "

He certainly is. If there were any doubt in our minds, we have only to look at the career of *Alice Cooper,* a Devil-worshiping, alcoholic death Rocker, a forerunner of Punk, and a by-product of a demonic seance with an Ouiji board.

Alice himself declared:

> "Someone the other day called me the grandfather of Punk . . . I'm still the best around and that's why I keep going . . . every time I'm about to put my leathers away, there's always some Punk band that thinks

they're better. I love the challenge ... I've got a reputation to keep. Our last tour was a #1 box office draw. We're one of the few bands around that can tour without an album to promote. We're more like a traveling carnival, an event."[6]

Even though *Alice Cooper* was the most outrageous act of his time, most people consider the *Sex Pistols* to be the first of the modern Punk bands. With members named Sid Vicious and Johnny Rotten, they wrote sick anthems like "I'm A Lazy Sod," "Pretty Vacant," "God Save The Queen," and "Anarchy In The U.K." Johnny Rotten, (his real name is John Lydon) received his nickname from *Sex Pistols'* manager Malcolm McLaren, due to the singer's unbrushed, rotting teeth.

McLaren formed the *Sex Pistols* shortly after meeting Lydon. McLaren and his wife owned a London boutique called "Sex." The shop specialized in S&M bondage clothes and pornographic T-shirts (which the police confiscated). The McLarens were prosecuted for the offense. When Malcolm McLaren first met Lydon at "Sex," he asked the grubby ghetto urchin if he could sing. Receiving a mumbled affirmative, he put Lydon in front of a huge stereo speaker and played a tape of *Alice Cooper's* "I'm Eighteen." Lydon knew the words by heart. On the basis of this "audition," the *Sex Pistols* were created.

> "Rock & Roll is not just music. You're selling an attitude too ... The kids need a sense of adventure and Rock & Roll needs to find a way to give it to them, wham out the hardest and cruelest lyrics as propaganda ... "[7]
> — Malcolm McLaren.

When the *Sex Pistols* started playing publicly to promote their first single, "Anarchy In The U.K." in late 1976, they found themselves banned in Britain. After insulting respected T.V. talk show host Bill Grundy on the British airwaves with a torrent of venomous profanity and gutter oaths, many thought the *Sex Pistols* had gone too far. Instead of crawling back under the rocks they came from, they became more popular than ever! Even with no radio airplay from the conservative, State-run BBC Network, safety-pinned teens throughout the land bought their records and propelled them upward into the charts.

In January of 1977, guitarist Steve Jones was reported to have vomited on a woman at Heathrow Airport. This was the last straw. Their record company dropped the *Pistols* like a hot potato.

During the Queen Of England's Silver Jubilee anniversary celebration, the *Sex Pistols* released "God Save The Queen, She Ain't No Human Being" as an insult to Her Majesty. The single sleeve bore a picture of Queen Elizabeth with a safety pin stuck through her lips. The record rocketed to #1 in the New Musical Express charts.

> "One night nobody was payin' any attention to me, so I thought I'd commit suicide. So I went in the bathroom, broke a glass, and slashed my chest with it. It's a really good way to get attention. I'm going to do it again."[8]

> "Before I started playing with the *Sex Pistols,* I never really noticed the bass — couldn't tell it from a piano. I heard records as just a wall of sound . . . "[9]
>
> — Sid Vicious.

> "This band hates you. It hates your culture. Why can't you lethargic, complacent hippies understand that? You need to be smashed . . . "[10] — Malcolm McLaren, referring to the *Pistols* and American society.

When the *Sex Pistols* began their first tour of America, something was noticeably wrong. The demented, destructionist, suicidal trash Rotten was peddling didn't ignite U.S. audiences as it had their English counterparts. The economic status of the country wasn't as bad here then; millions weren't out of work, and the majority of

American teens didn't roam the streets looking for sadistic thrills as young people did throughout Great Britain. The *Sex Pistols'* message just didn't sell to kids used to the likes of rich Heavy Metal megastars like *Led Zeppelin* and *Rush.*

Today, of course, all that has changed. The economic picture in the U.S. is a grim one, indeed. The conditions Punk music thrives on — high unemployment, hatred of government, political corruption in high places, and a paranoid fear of a nuclear Armageddon swiftly approaching — are all firmly in place in the social fabric of 1980s America.

It would not take very many years before the demon seed planted in American brains by Johnny Rotten and Sid Vicious would bloom in all its terrible glory. Today we are beginning to see the awful results of that transplantation. We'll soon be paying the price, the same as England has, unless we get a firm handle on the situation right now.

> "Love is two minutes and fifty seconds of squelching
> noises. It shows your mind isn't clicking right . . . "[11]
> — Johnny Rotten.

After that disastrous 1978 tour, the *Sex Pistols* fell apart and broke up, ending Punk Rock's first grisly chapter. The movement they started was doing just fine though and would continue to grow to monstrous proportions through the Seventies and early Eighties. Eventually it replaced and then merged with Heavy Metal as the noise of choice for most teens.

After the total disintegration of Malcolm McLaren's brainchild, Johnny Rotten and Sid Vicious hurtled down two totally different paths, one to instant artistic credibility, the other to death and Hell.

Sid Vicious was arrested for the senseless, brutal stabbing murder of his girlfriend, heroin addict Nancy Spungen, in New York's seedy Chelsea Hotel. The two had spent the night in a long orgy of heroin injections. Deeply into the Twilight Zone, Vicious had no memory of what happened the night Nancy died. Jailed and then released on bail, Vicious ended his own sordid, wasted excuse for a life with a massive heroin overdose.

Johnny Rotten went on to form another New Wave band, *Public Image,* which received mass critical acclaim from the Rock trades. *Image's* music wasn't the roaring, snarling, chainsaw mess that the *Sex Pistols* were so well known for producing. Instead, it used a hypnotic blend of weird jungle chants, arcane rhythms, and voodoo influences. Johnny and his new band became so popular, in fact, that they appeared on Dick Clark's "American Bandstand," that respected yardstick of conservative Rock & Roll success.

Quite a change, isn't it? From blasphemous street Punk-turned-anarchist to American Bandstand star. Just another example of how Rock's demons are integrating themselves into the so called "straight society."

In doing extensive research on the *Sex Pistols* and Punk Rock in general, ALL the descriptions of Johnny Rotten I read had one common theme: his beady, piercing eyes, burning with insane, fanatical mania for his cause. Even though Rotten was called a "misshapen hunchback" with orange, spiky, vaseline-smeared hair, and a greasy, pale, pimply face full of yellow-green rotting wolf's teeth, his eyes stood out in his wasted flesh, commanding, DEMANDING the undivided attention of all those around him.

As writer Charles M. Young said,

> "Rotten glares with demonic self-righteousness that threatens to reduce me to incoherence ... "[12]

> "It's the eyes that kill you. They don't pierce, they bludgeon ... "[13]

> "His voice could turn the Lord's Prayer into brutal sarcasm ... "[14]

253

The monster the *Sex Pistols* created soon burst society's bounds and began raging out of control around the world. The infection spread like wildfire to Europe and both American coasts, as contagious as smallpox, and as deadly as the Plague. This is how the respected newspaper "Village Voice" described L.A.'s Punk scene: "Thriving on self-pity, racism, hippie-baiting, and the abhorrence of sex and the cheesiest sort of nihilism, L.A. Punk is the 'scene that will not die.'"

Today's American Punk Rock Scene got its start on the West Coast on Friday, August 12, 1977, in a Hollywood ballroom called "Myron's." There, for the first time, the "Street Survivors" came out in droves to slam dance to the electronic "music" of Punk pioneers *Devo* and *The Weirdo's,* a local group with songs like "Destroy All Music," and "Why Do You Exist."

Devo was an early pathfinder in the bridge between Old Punk, New Wave and Heavy Metal. Originally from Akron, Ohio, the quintet quickly changed their base of operations to Los Angeles after the release of their debut L.P., "Are We Not Men? We Are Devo!" The name *Devo* itself is short for de-evolution. (The group believes mankind is moving backwards down the evolutionary ladder from apes.) Intensely political, *Devo's* goal is to remake society, (especially American society) in their own image. They consider themselves to be so much more intelligent than the rest of the human race; that their blueprint for the future is mankind's only hope for survival.

Isn't it ironic that these Punks, most of whom aren't smart enough to play a guitar properly, all fancy themselves to be the intellectual saviors of the human race?

One song which gave *Devo* much attention in their early days was called "Jocko Homo," followed by the chart-busting "Whip It," a tune widely interpreted as an anthem to masturbation and S & M lashing. "Whip It" was also the first of the "whip crack" songs so common today. As group member Jerry Casale explained:

"That whip noise was created by a synthesizer on a percussive setting with real fast attack on it, run backwards on a tape . . ."[15]

Machines are making our music! 20th century technology combined with the Satanic principle of reversal to create an entirely new sound, one which was quickly adopted by every Rock act around. It is essential that we realize that the single most important part of Satanism is the principle of reversal. Indeed, this very concept is both the heart and soul of Devil worship. Those lost souls who practice the hideous Black Mass in their mad pursuit of the Prince Of Darkness recite whole anti-Christian passages of verse backwards during the ceremony itself. The cross above the devil worshipers' black altar is hung upside down, (as on Ozzy Osbourne's "Diary Of A Madman" album).

According to demonologist Montague Summers, witch covens attending Black Sabbaths, (also the name of Ozzy Osbourne's first Rock group!) would greet the appearance of Lucifer in the flames they had set by kissing his backside. Early Christians were often crucified on INVERTED crosses by the braying, bloodthirsty Roman soldiers assigned to execute them. Even the name "Anti-Christ" signifies direct, diametric opposition to our Blessed Savior, Jesus Christ.

Have you ever wondered why Heaven is always thought of as being "up," and Hell "down?" Or why Godliness is described in terms of blinding light, and Evil in terms of utter blackness? The answer is simple: Satan, though a created being, is the reversal of God. Every demonic, despairing, fearful, hateful, hellish thing he stands for is exactly the opposite of our Lord's loving bounty of blessings. It simply CANNOT be mere coincidence that these kinds of concepts decorating so many Heavy Metal Rock album's covers and songs are accidents. There's a method behind all this madness, make no mistake; and the Lord God, in His infinite wisdom and mercy, is revealing the reason to us all if we will only take the time to look closely.

In Revelation 9:20 & 21, the Bible tells us that in the Last Days of this planet we will see a return to occultism, witchcraft, and Devil worship such as never before witnessed in the history of mankind. This is already happening, and is continuing today, growing faster and more deadly with the passage of every single year. The decade of the Sixties started the ball rolling, (thanks to the *Beatles* and the *Rolling Stones*)the Heavy Metal-Punk decade of the Seventies honed it to razor sharpness, and now, well into the Eighties, the wildfire is burning totally out of control. As the flames of Punk died out, Heavy Metal poured on the gas.

In the sturdy, no-nonsense, super-scientific 1950's who would have believed in demonic possessions, Indian transcendental gurus, Black Masses, and LSD trips into the cosmos? It would simply have been written off as a script to a bad horror movie. No one then could possibly have foreseen the gigantic leaps ahead the Devil was to make during the next twenty-five years.

The nightmare has now come true.

It's time to choose sides, and our Blessed Lord is making the choice very easy for all Christian believers. In His wonderful mercy He is allowing the forces of Satan through Rock & Roll to become so blatant in their advertising for human converts that true Christians everywhere cannot help but see the Devil's plan for what it is. Satan is marshalling his forces for the end this very moment.

How many thousands of souls did he snare in the Acid-dropping Sixties? How many millions more turned from God to become callous, brutal fans of Punk Rock during the Seventies? There's still time to enslave another generation out there. Unless we firmly make up our minds and hearts that this WILL NOT HAPPEN AGAIN. Don't be afraid to choose sides. The Bible says in Luke 11:23 that those who are not for God are against him. It says the converse in Mark 9:40. There is no middle ground. Let us not be afraid to draw the line now before more of our precious friends and children are lost.

With a two-pronged assault, Satan is appealing to the post-Punk masses of drug-slugged "Headbangers" through groups like *Krokus, Scorpions, Judas Priest, KISS* and *Iron Maiden.* At the same time he is winning over the rest of today's teens with the perverted likes of *Prince* and Madonna.

Of the first category, *Krokus* is the sickest. With fan clubs in their native Switzerland as well as the United States, Germany, England, and around the world, this group is truly disturbing in their slick professional delivery and "no future" attitude of total brainless despair. There is one other thing about *Krokus* that marks them as being from the Satanic Twilight Zone:

They sound EXACTLY like *AC-DC.*

Krokus' singer, Marc Storace, has a voice and singing style identical to that of the late Bon Scott. The two are vocal twins. *Krokus* is also one more link in the chain of Satan-Rockers given the power to spread the Devil's message throughout the entire world. The group's logo features a slanted version of the "Satanic S" on all its records, something that *KISS, AC-DC,* and *Black Sabbath* all share. These jagged symbols were also used by the Nazi S.S. as their sign of Satanic terror. The sign represents the power of Lucifer falling to earth from Grace as a lightning bolt. (Luke 10:18.)

Let *Krokus* tell you their philosophy in their own words, taken from their 1982 release, "One Vice At A Time:"

"DOWN THE DRAIN" —

"My mother was a B-girl
My old man was a tramp
Some folks say they conceived me
On a loading ramp
I was only 14
Took to petty crime
Stole from supermarkets with this girl of mine
Now I'm nearly 20
Sick in heart and brain

Haven't got the courage
My life is . . .
Down the drain
No roots
No home
No country
No hope
No faith
No luck
If there's a God in Heaven
He doesn't give me bucks
No self respect
No honor
No family
No cash
No church and no religion
I'm only human trash . . . "

Can we take such lyrics as these at anything but face value? These people ARE human trash! They prove it with every song they write, and every verse they sing. Each new album they produce is more disgusting than the last. How long can this go on?

Rock stars like *Krokus'* Marc Storace appear to be downright ridiculous at first glance. When a Christian friend of mine saw Storace's picture in a Rock magazine, the first comment out of his mouth was, "I'd like to see that guy in the Army givin' the Sarge fifty push-ups. He'd last about five minutes." (Storace was wearing women's leotards, his hair stuck straight up about eight inches, and a bear claw necklace was hanging from his throat.)

Like most of Satan's tricks, looks can be deceiving.

In interviews, this Swiss ding-dong usually has trouble stringing three words together, and when he does, his message is always about how *Krokus* just wants to be "The best Rock & Roll band in the world," and how "Rock & Roll is all about having a good time. It's not to be taken seriously." These demons in human form almost never drop their mask, but it happened in Creem Magazine. Praise God for forcing some words of truth from the lips of these liars! When asked why

Heavy Metal music was so appealing to kids, Storace replied,

> "To me it's tribal. And primal — old jungle rhythms, that boom-boom-boom. It's a ritual and has — believe it or not — a spiritual context to it . . . "[16]

When asked if good and evil powers were at his command, the *Krokus* vocalist said,

> "If you bring them in, if you allow them entrance. If you allow yourself to meditate with the dark powers and, through yourself, let them be seen, they will be seen and people will react to them . . . "[17]

The dark powers Storace is speaking about are demons. Here is confirmation straight from the horse's mouth, young people! If you don't want to believe me and all the others who are standing up against Satan's Rock, then listen to your Heavy Metal heroes and don't say you haven't been warned!

These Punk Metal bands could care less about the fans who made them famous. *Devo* is the most notorious in their hate for humanity. For example:

> "We have an attitude towards humanity. It just so happens that 95% of people seem to be a—holes and 50% of those are women . . . "[18]

On the current state of Rock & Roll, *Devo* had this to say:

> " . . . everybody's into demons, witches, devils, ghosts, goblins, Gothic sex. It's always songs about big consequences for screwing or some Christian guilt-ridden double standard macho sex where they're gonna lay a girl . . . "[19]

Christianity, of course, is a sizeable stumbling block to *Devo's* unique worldly vision. Here are some of their comments regarding religion:

"The evil spuds are the ninnies and the twits, the guys in the polyester suits beating the Bibles . . . "[20]

"Are we subversive? That would depend on who's using the word. I'm sure Jerry Falwell would see us as subversive, and that's good . . . "[21]

What place does love hold in the world according to *Devo*?

" . . . Men and women promulgate hideous modes of interaction, hideous mythology. That has no place, as much as nationalism and war has no place. What is called love is a hideous blasphemy of the idea. We'd prefer people to be more like Spock on 'Star Trek' . . . "[22]

"You needn't go very far to tap into people's cynicism. They all know what they pretend to believe in is wrong and bad for them, but no one can seem to stop it. Everybody knows the smile face really has fangs and horns, and that 'Have a nice day' really means 'I hope you die' . . . "[23]

There it is in their own words: love of one's country, patriotism, (or "nationalism," as they prefer to call it) has no place in their world. They would like people to be empty, emotionless machines like Mr. Spock. It's interesting that they use the "fangs and horns" analogy in describing their goals. Satan sneaks through once again, barely hidden under the surface of their deceiving words. Above all, and we must not lose sight of this, *Devo's* message is political in nature. They blame our government, our morals, our entire society's guidelines and safeguards for what they see as the disintegration of civilized humanity. These are good, thought-provoking points, but what kind of alternatives do they have to offer?

Here is their alternative:

" . . . I mean, scolding a pig won't stop him. You have to whack him on the head with a shovel. We have to get out the old cattle prod. And if people aren't willing to do that because they're afraid they might lose their quanset (status quo) hut, then forget them . . . "[24]

"Life as we know it is going down the tubes . . . Let's get on with it . . . "[25]

"What we need now is real aliens to come down and threaten us . . . Why don't they blow up the Capitol and then come on everybody's T.V. sets? Looks like we're going to have to do it. We could have been put here for that reason."[26]

These lines from "Thru Being Cool" on their 1981 L.P. "New Traditionalists" sum things up pretty well:

"We're through being cool
Eliminate the ninnies and the twits
Going to bang some heads
Going to beat some butts
Time to show those evil spuds what's what . . . "

("Evil spuds" refers to Christians — see quote on previous page.)

What *Devo* is suggesting is revolution, plain and simple! We've heard this line before, during the radical Rock & Rolling Sixties. We may even now be poised on a seething cesspool of Punk/Metal revolutionary hatred that could make the Sixties anti-war protests look like a kid's birthday party. All that's lacking is the right spark to set off the bonfire. This time Africa or South America could be the match to light that fuse instead of Vietnam.

Surely no one alive today can fail to remember the role Rock played in the vicious Vietnam youth peace protests of the Sixties. The half a million plus Woodstock Festival held in August, 1969, was organized as a protest against the War.

Groups and performers like *The Doors,* Bob Dylan, *The Rolling Stones, Jefferson Airplane, The Grateful Dead, Steppenwolf, Jimi Hendrix, Janis Joplin,* Arlo Guthrie, and

John Lennon all wrote and screamed out their protest songs to fuel the raging fire. Lennon's "Give Peace A Chance" became an official anti-war anthem sung by a quarter of a million protestors marching on Washington, D.C. after the invasion of Cambodia. Hendrix's "Star Spangled Banner," (the song that closed Woodstock) was the ultimate slap in America's face.

These performers and many others like them marshalled millions of young people to their side with their Rock & Roll bugle call. They played benefit concerts for subversive Leftist organizations like the Yippies, (organizers of the bloody Chicago riots during the 1969 Democratic convention) and the S.D.S. (Students for a Democratic Society).

So many years have gone by since the flag burning, draft dodging, peace marching, bomb dropping days of 1969 that some people don't remember clearly what a turbulent and uncertain time it was for America.

Rock & Roll helped make it that way.

Rolling Stone Mick Jagger planned to run for Parliament during the Vietnam era under the Labour Party. His natural laziness killed the project. In 1969 the *Stones'* song, "Street Fighting Man" became THE power anthem of violence for disgruntled youth everywhere, proclaiming in its lyrics:

> "Hey! Think the time is right for a palace revolution
> I'll shout and scream
> I'll kill the King
> I'll rail at all his servants . . .
> Everywhere I hear the sound of marching, charging feet, boy
> Cause summer's here and the time is right for fighting in the street, boy . . . "

Jagger himself joined a massive Vietnam anti-war demonstration outside the American Embassy in London's Grosvenor Square in the late Sixties. He linked arms with the other members of the crazed mob as they battled police, spurred on by the presence of the High Priest of Anarchy.

> "War stems from power-mad politicians and patriots . . .
> There shouldn't be any Prime Minister at all . . .
> There should be no such thing as private property . . .
> Anarchy is the only slight glimmer of hope . . . "
>
> — Mick Jagger[27]

Mick Jagger's Rock & Roll voice wasn't the only one being heard by the hordes of young rioting malcontents worldwide. During the late Sixties John Lennon in particular had a rapt audience of untold millions sitting at his feet, intently listening to his every word as if it was a Biblical pronouncement. When he held "bed-ins," "peace festivals," and "bagisms," the eyes of the world were glued upon him. Isn't it amazing? A common working class petty thief from Liverpool could control the thoughts of half the globe with an off-hand remark! (Lennon made a statement in a 1966 interview that the *Beatles* were "bigger than Jesus, now . . . " and that "Christianity is doomed to pass away . . . ") A slew of *Beatle* record burnings throughout the Bible Belt showed Lennon what God-fearing Americans thought of his sarcastic blasphemies.

What were Lennon's intentions — as international peace monger or Communist sympathizer? His fierce anti-war stance, anarchic Rock records, and loud-mouthed public protests brought him to the attention of President Richard Nixon, who personally ordered that he be kicked out of the United States. It was feared that Lennon might appear at several benefit concerts for various subversive radical groups, thus quadrupling their audiences and donations. Shortly after establishing residence in New York City, Lennon had been approached by radicals Jerry Rubin and Abbie Hoffman for just such a purpose.

Some people think that the whole idea of Jagger and Lennon as political forces to be reckoned with, holding a constituency of millions, has been blown out of proportion.

Not true! These revolutionaries nearly toppled their respective governments with their political activism!

After years of legal wrangling and maneuvering, the case against John Lennon was dropped, and he became a legal resident alien. Proudly holding his "green card," he continued to live in New York City until his death. Lennon and wife Yoko Ono are also widely regarded as the forerunners of the Punk Movement with their openly political songs and weird musical meanderings. Their enormous influence on modern day Punks is evident when listening to one of the most popular Punk bands — *The B-52s*. One member of the group likes to mimic Yoko Ono's nerve-shattering caterwaul to spine-chilling perfection.

> "**Ono:** 'We were doing a lot of the Punk stuff a long time ago.' **Playboy:** 'Lennon and Ono, the original Punks.' **Ono:** 'You're right.'"[28]

What Lennon and his contemporaries did politically in the Sixties could easily happen again in the Eighties, but this time the protest signs won't be carried by long-haired, cowardly Pot-smoking hippies wearing love beads and Indian feathers. This time the young people behind those bricks, bottles, and swastikas are apt to be leather jacketed street Punks with shaved heads and glue sniffed brains. Instead of flowers they'll carry knives. Their skin is hard and their scars are red from the rehearsed combat of endless nights of slam dancing.

This is an enemy from within the very core of our society. With the end of American involvement in the Vietnam conflict, the entire Rock & Roll fueled protest movement died down overnight and went underground. It remains there today, waiting like a festering wound to explode at the earliest opportunity into a new wave of radical violence. Punk Rock was the dress rehearsal, the second "British Invasion" of our cities, homes, minds and morality.

Today we find ourselves in the "Post-Punk" era, a time when Rock & Roll music has never been more brutal and disgusting, its followers never more callous, violent, and empty-headed. Heavy Metal rules.

Britain's huge Fascist National Front, for example, is a hate filled organization flocked to by thousands of English "skinhead" Punks. They ENJOY playing at being Nazis. Only it's not playing anymore. Things are becoming deadly serious on both sides of the Atlantic.

And what about those kids on Santa Monica Boulevard in West Hollywood, U.S.A., slam dancing to the songs of *Devo* and *Christian Death?* Do they realize they're being systematically and simultaneously desensitized and re-programmed as violent Fascist robots by their beloved Rock & Roll? Of course not! These people believe in nothing, exist as nothing, and see no future of any kind on the world horizon.

"No sense makes sense."[29] — Charles Manson

All they know is "skanking;" when the music begins, kick and stab those around you. Punch the closest face and slice the nearest neck. All they know is "The Worm;" get down on the dance floor and roll around like an epileptic. If someone kicks you in the teeth, or smashes your fingers, welcome the next blow. If you roll on broken glass, enjoy the pain; watch the blood.

The Rock heroes they worship have names like *Black Flag, The Germs, Suicidal Tendencies, Fear, Flesheaters,* and *The Damned.* The songs they so eagerly ingest have titles like "Let's Have A War (So You All Can Die)," and "I Was So Wasted."

As a spokesman for *Black Flag,* a Southern California Punk/Metal band known for attracting thousands of savage fans who bloody each other to the tune of blitzkrieg Rock & Roll, puts it:

> "Violence — I shouldn't even call it violence — physical contact, getting hurt, doesn't bother me . . . "[30]

> " . . . I've experienced the violence myself. I was at a gig once and six Huntington Beach Punks jumped me and started trying to beat the crap out of me. One of them got me down on the ground and tried to kick my face in. My feeling about the whole thing was, 'Well, !*?%!&*, I'm here to have a good time. I just kept dancing.'"[31]

This raging mob of senseless, degraded, hyped up street Punks and Metal maniacs, their noses bloody and their razors sharp, are ready to march. If someone would only give them a target, they'd be glad to obliterate it. Are we going to sit idly by and watch our young people, the hope for America's future, turn into a mindless mob of Rock & Roll killers? Are we going to allow our cities to go up in flames once again when their Rock-induced rage runs riot?

I sincerely hope not.

Punk Rock, Heavy Metal and anarchy are the same thing. No one's in charge. No one gives orders. The rules are simple: there are no rules. If you see any orderliness and decency about you, destroy it. That's the political side of Punk/Metal. The way outright paganism has crept into the picture is an even scarier development. Now the Punks don't just dance together, they kill together. It's a movement born in ghettoes, but over the years it has spread into every conceivable social and economic strata.

There aren't many rapes at Post-Punk concerts, because the people have become asexual. Violence has taken the place of lust as a prime behavioral motivator. Even rich kids like the California "Surf Punks" from Hermosa and Huntington Beaches have adopted the look and made it their own. The amoral attitudes behind the trend begin to creep in later. The 1960's hippie generation's wanton sexual hi-jinks were bad enough, but at least they were preaching the merits of peace and love, not death and

266

destruction. Today's Punks, spoon fed on hair-raising Rock & Roll, could care less about having sex with strangers. They would much rather watch someone's blood flow. If they can't find anyone else, their own will do.

Thanks to groups like the *Plasmatics, Black Flag,* and the *Sex Pistols,* (who promote the Punk philosophy to the tune of Heavy Metal), the boundary line between the two huge audiences has been erased, allowing them all to come together in one gigantic mass orgy of Satanic destruction.

Religious elements pertaining to Armageddon, the Book of Revelation, the Judgement Day, and the Devil's demons have saturated modern Rock & Roll to the point where its audiences have just plain gone crazy. It has driven them nuts. We've already documented in grisly detail *AC-DC's* satanic flirtations. Legions of other groups like *Iron Maiden, Plasmatics, Blue Oyster Cult, Dio, Krokus, W.A.S.P., Black Sabbath, Led Zeppelin, The Rolling Stones, Ozzy Osbourne,* and the *Sex Pistols* have clearly shown by their actions that the Devil is their master. They and their imitators have all heaped tons of smoldering Armageddonist and occult trash into Rock's bubbling cauldron. It's sulpherous fumes have blown clear around the world, igniting young people everywhere.

If indeed, we are living in the Last Days as foretold in Biblical prophecy, then how can we as Christians afford to ignore the tell-tale signs of satanic manipulation of the medium of Rock & Roll? As the Bible tells us:

> "And have no fellowship with the unfruitful works of darkness, but rather reprove them." Ephesians 5:11.

Think about it: what could be better for the Devil than a tailor-made audience of millions of young people, YOUNG people who in a scant few years will produce yet another generation to be seduced by Satan's songs? What easy marks the prominent Rock groups, producers, executives, and performers are for the Devil with their titanic lusts for wealth, fame, power, drugs and sex!

The brutal, bludgeoning blast of the modern Punk/New Wave/Heavy Metal trends is the latest example of the classic Luciferian principles of audience possession and manipulation: hate, violence, disfigurement and ugliness are in control. To Satan, pain is ecstasy; hideousness is beauty.

All these Punk types are so possessed by the demons of Rock & Roll that they stick safety pins through their lips, dye their hair purple, and have fun at teen dances by clubbing, stabbing, and kicking weaker human beings than themselves. They slice themselves in blood sacrifice just like the priests of Baal did in I Kings 18:25-29. If that's not satanism, (and Nazism), what is?

A small group of select people who control the record industry, (as well as many top bands) motivated by demons and drugs, have completely saturated the U.S. and European markets with Heavy Metal and Punk Rock. Now they are turning their attention to the rest of the world, South America in particular.

A few years back Heavy Metal megastars *Queen* completed a mammoth tour of South America where tremendous audiences packed sport stadiums from Brazil to Argentina. Those kids where introduced to Rock & Roll for the first time. (*Queen's* lead singer, Freddie Mercury, refuses to deny reports that he is a homosexual.)

The Rolling Stones also have their eyes on the vast continental well of Latinos who are blissfully unaware of Rock music. In a Victor Bockris interview, Keith Richards made these remarks:

> " . . . There's audiences in South America, nobody goes there. Behind the Iron Curtain they're screaming for somebody to come and see them . . . "[32]

> " . . . The audiences are there and they're crying out to see people that they keep reading about. I mean they buy thousands of magazines just to see some crappy

pictures of Mick and Bianca on the middle page spread
. . ."[33]

(Bianca Jagger, Mick's ex-wife, was a Nicaraguan.)

Rock & Roll is gradually rotting away the stability of the entire Western Hemisphere from beneath our very feet, and Heavy Metal Rock & Roll is spreading like a plague all over the world. The latest country going under: Brazil. An incredibly huge 10-day long Rock concert/festival/extravaganza was held in Rio De Janeiro in late winter, 1985. Nightly crowds of 200,000 South Americans saw groups like *Queen, AC-DC, Nina Hagen, Ozzy Osbourne, Rod Stewart, Iron Maiden,* and the *Scorpions.*

These Devil-mongering groups, having blasted and burned out the minds, ears, and souls of the youth of Europe and America, are now turning their attention to greener pastures. They're finding plenty of new converts in the masses of South America. Just how seriously the fans take Heavy Metal Rock & Roll down there can be seen by the following conversation between a teenage Brazilian festival goer and a Rock magazine correspondent:

> "I'm here because I want to see my gods. My friends and I traveled here from six hours away, and some of us sleep on the beach at night. It is a dream-come-true for us to actually see our gods. In life, you have much pain. But Metal lets us feel power in our veins. When you see a band go BAM, POW, you go crazy."[34]

It's happening right now. The one-two punch of Punk Rock and Heavy Metal is trying to knock out democracy at every turn while presenting an image of uncompromising honesty and incredible power. Heavy Metal hypnotizes, and the Punk Rock brutalizes. One numbs the brain, the other burns the soul. Together these two incindiary trends could set the Third World afire, not to mention England, Europe, and America, where they're already wreaking havoc.

Simply put, today we have American and English Rock bands exporting Communism and Satanism to the rest of the world, and that's un-American.

We must not permit this here. There is already a very vocal anti-Rock movement growing in the grassroots of America. It needs to be strengthened.

This really is a simple case of survival of the things generations of Americans have broken their backs and lost their lives for: decency, freedom to enjoy culture and things of lasting beauty, love of God and one's country. What the Nazis did in Germany the street Punks could do in America and England, if they're allowed to get stronger and stronger, even more violent and destructive. We need to cut the problem off at the source.

The source is Rock & Roll.

CHAPTER 11

Rocking for Jesus

"Be not deceived; God is not mocked; for whatsoever a man soweth, that shall he also reap."   Galatians 6:7

"What's puzzlin' you is the nature of my game . . . " "Sympathy For The Devil" by *The Rolling Stones* [1]

One popular substitute for Rock & Roll is a style of music called "Christian-Rock." A controversial debate on the merits of this alternative is building and growing day by day.

Here are some of the questions being asked: What exactly is "Christian Rock?" Are Gospel and Christian Rock the same thing? Is it possible for Rock and Gospel to co-exist? Is Christian Rock as bad as secular Rock & Roll? If not, why not?

These are confusing questions. Perhaps the most confusing of all is: what exactly is Rock & Roll itself? To someone over thirty years old, Rock & Roll might be Elvis Presley. To the aging hippie generation of the Sixties, Rock might be *The Beatles* and *The Rolling Stones.* For teens today, their idea of Rock might well be *Twisted Sister.* For even younger pre-teens the concept of Rock & Roll may be embodied in the pretty pin-up faces of *Duran Duran.*

Satan is taking evasive action in this area, brothers and sisters. To use a military analogy, how can we take aim on our enemy when we don't even know what he looks like? In the terrible, tragic conflict of the Vietnam War, American troops faced the same kind of dilemma: the enemy might have a uniform — then again, he might not. The enemy could even be a child holding a hidden hand grenade. The same is true of Rock & Roll. Satan doesn't want us to get a fix on his position, that's why so much confusion exists in this area.

Let's zero in on Satan by defining some terms and clearing up some common misconceptions. Everything played on the radio, both AM and FM, is not necessarily Rock & Roll, though it is often called just that. There is another category that much of this music fits into, and it's called "Pop." Many people think Pop Music died in the mid-Seventies with the demise of such "teeny bop" and "bubble gum" artists as *The Archies,* Bobby Sherman, David Cassidy, and *The Osmonds.* Not true. Pop is still very much in evidence in today's music; it's just changed with the times. Generally speaking, Pop music can be described like this: Upbeat, peppy melodies, lots of catchy musical "hooks," a length of about 3 1/2 minutes in order to fit easily into radio formats, fairly inoffensive lyrics about teenage love and rejection, and a major emphasis on the "clean" image of the groups or singers involved, many of whom end up as posters on the bedroom walls of teenage America.

Did you know that when *The Beatles* first made it big in the United States they were classified in record store racks as "Pop Artists?" The music they played was not "Rock & Roll" in the purest sense. (Not their original tunes written solely by themselves, anyway.) *The Rolling Stones,* on the other hand, were bona fide Rockers. Why? Because the *Stones* started out playing the Blues, and the Blues is the base of modern Rock. There were Country & Western influences in early Rock, too, but the Blues was the foundation Rock was built on. First came the Blues, and then the Blues became Rock, and now today, by and large, Rock has become Heavy Metal.

Pop has always been a kind of squeaky-clean, dorky second cousin to the messy, dirty, loudmouthed older brother of Rock & Roll. The point here is this: Pop and Rock are not the same thing; just because a song has drums and guitars in it doesn't make it Rock & Roll.

Another misunderstood and mistitled category, especially by older adults, is so-called "Acid-Rock." This term is often used to describe any music that has the most negative elements of Rock in it: loud, screaming guitars and weirdo lyrics booming out of a wall of noise. Quite simply, "Acid-Rock" is music made to take LSD by. Jimi Hendrix's music was true Acid-Rock. So are songs by the early *Jefferson Airplane* and a whole slew of other Sixties dinosaurs. Specific ALBUMS like "Sergeant Pepper's Lonely Hearts Club Band," by *The Beatles,* and "Their Satanic Majesties Request," by *The Rolling Stones* were meant to be listened to while under the influence of LSD, but those groups were not technically "Acid-Rock" bands. To use a term like "Acid-Rock" to describe a teenagers' favorite music in the Eighties only makes the parent look like a fool in the young person's eyes. To all intents and purposes, "Acid-Rock" is dead; it died with Jimi Hendrix in 1970. (By the way, LSD or "Acid" has not disappeared along with the music it inspired, unfortunately. There are plenty of kids out there still tripping, many times while listening to "Satan-Rock," today's version of yesterday's nightmare.)

Also, parents, don't make the mistake of calling your child's music "Punk" or even "New Wave." Those terms are today almost as obsolete as "Acid-Rock." Things move quickly in the modern musical marketplace; it's hard for teens to keep up with it all, much less parents!

There are a few die-hard groups in England, Chicago, New York and the American West Coast who still play Punk Music, but they are quickly dwindling to cult status. Like all Rock, Punk was an image as well as a musical style. The words "Punk Rock" conjure up a picture of shaved heads, Mohawk hairdos, (in the Fifties they were called "Don Eagles"), safety pins, razor blades, and a screaming, slashing musical mess running 100 miles a minute: that's what Punk was. Where did it go? It moved next door and merged with what is now known as "Heavy Metal."

(As far as "New Wave" is concerned, that faddish, foppish, freakish movement didn't last long, either. New Wave bands wore wrap-around sunglasses, white shirts, skinny ties and pointed shoes. They tried to look like Buddy Holly and sing like early Elvis.)

This brings us to the biggest and most all-pervasive element of contemporary Rock & Roll: Heavy Metal. I call Heavy Metal "Satan-Rock" because that's just exactly what it is. Bare-chested singers wearing leather jackets with socks stuffed down the front of their spandex pants, spikes and studs sticking out of their knuckles and knees while they scream into a microphone until the veins pop out on their heads — THAT'S Heavy Metal! Blood-drinking bass players flashing demon signs with their fingers as they dance around pillars of flame and walk inside giant glowing skulls — THAT'S Heavy Metal! Pentagrams, blasphemy, witchcraft, demonism, lewdness, drugs, and insanity all make up what is the modern phenomenon of Heavy Metal music. Parents, the chances are your children either listen to Heavy Metal or radio-oriented Pop music exclusively. If they listen to neither one, count yourself blessed.

Actually, then, there are only three kinds of Rock &

Roll: (1) the original 1950's variety that started the whole grisly ball rolling via stars like Chuck Berry, Bo Diddley, Bill Haley, Elvis, and Little Richard, (2) the Sixties superstar groups that took drugs and sex out of the porno shops and into the record shops, and (3) today's "Metal music."

Now that we've got a handle on the various types of secular Rock & Roll, we can begin looking at "Christian-Rock." What exactly is it? Christ-Rock seems to me to be first of all a total contradiction in terms. Jesus Christ has nothing to do with Rock & Roll. 2 Corinthians 6:14-16 tells us to have no fellowship with unbelievers, wickedness, darkness, Belial, or idols. How then can Christ be unequally yoked with the perverse paganism of Rock? I wish someone would tell me, because I have no idea how such a thing is possible.

Is Gospel music and Christian-Rock the same thing? My opinion is that they are not. Gospel music is a proclamation in song of the good news about Jesus, showing a wide range of styles and beautiful arrangements; Christ-Rock is slapping a few "Praise Gods" on top of the same old Rock & Roll dinge.

Is it possible for Rock and Gospel to co-exist? You tell me. Is it possible to be saved and lost at the same time? Is it possible to serve both God AND Mammon?

Finally, is Christian-Rock as bad as secular Rock & Roll? If not, why not? In order to try to answer this very complex question, please allow me to give you an example from my own experience.

A few weeks ago I went into a Bible bookstore located within a shopping mall complex in the town where I live. A display of Christian records and tapes caught my eye. Included in this display was a tape deck, headphones, and a rack of demonstration cassettes of the newest artists for customers to listen to. I heard many lovely and moving songs from a wide variety of groups. None of them even remotely resembled secular Rock music. Then I picked up and played a tape by a band called *Stryper*. Believe it or not, they are the forerunners of a new trend in Christian music: Heavy Metal Christian Rock! The music on that tape was no different than *W.A.S.P.* or *AC-DC.* Only the words were positive praise to the King, WHEN you could hear them, that is.

Totally disgusted, I approached the older woman working there and invited her to take a listen. After a few minutes with the headphones on, she flipped off the tape and looked at me as if to say, "So what?" A young Bible salesman was also there at the time. I engaged them both in a friendly debate about the pros and cons of so-called "Christian-Rock." I think their views are typical of many. Here are some of the points they made.

1) Anything is better than Heavy Metal secular Rock, even bands like *Stryper.*

2) Christian-Rock will act as a bridge to get young Rock listeners to something better eventually.

3) The words are different, so the music and message is better and more positive.

4) Kids buying Christian-Rock usually buy other Christian records as well.

5) The BEAT (or percussion), has Biblical relevance in the Old Testament, therefore the beat itself is not the problem.

6) There are many interpretations as to where to draw the line, so who's to decide?

7) Taking the Rock candy from children without giving them something in return will only drive them away and into wherever it is that you don't want them to go.

8) There's no escape from Rock. They'll just get it somewhere else.

The comments of those two well-intentioned people just floored me. I went home that day and thought long and hard about what they had said. After much reflection, prayer, and conversations with many young people, both saved and unsaved, the conclusion I came to was the same as the one I immediately felt in my guts when I listened to that *Stryper* tape: THIS IS WRONG! Rock & Roll and Jesus Christ are completely incompatible, in my view. Why throw pearls before swine, beloved? Now some people reading these words may feel differently; I firmly believe that we all can agree to disagree in the love of Christ — that's one of the most wonderful things about being a Christian. But let's recognize a very simple fact: just because a sign says "Bible Bookstore" or "Christian Music" on it doesn't make it off limits to Satan. (2 Corinthians 11:14-15.)

The best illustration I can think of is that of a heroin addict. To someone who has never been a "junkie," they may know that heroin is dangerous, unhealthy, even deadly; but only a person who has been completely enslaved by the drug with all the de-humanizing horror that involves, can REALLY understand the peril. I think the same is true of Rock & Roll. To someone exposed very little to Rock, (especially someone over the age of 30), "Christian-Rock" may not seem like such a big deal. They know instinctively that Rock by its very nature is unwholesome, at times disgusting, and perhaps even spiritually hazardous. Somehow, they seem to think that Christian-Rock will be different just because Christ's name is tacked onto the front! They don't understand the danger because they've never been totally immersed in the satanic baptism of Rock & Roll!

I've worshiped Satan-Rock, brothers and sisters, that's why I'm here to give you this message! I've never been a heroin addict, but I have been a Rock & Roll junkie, and both drugs lead to death. If Satan is the King of Rock, then what stops him at the door of the Gospel record store? Do you think he just turns his back when a "Praise God" group starts using Rock rhythms to sell records? When we accepted Christ as our Lord of Lords and King of Kings and were buried with Him in baptism, we cast Satan out of our lives and invited the Holy Spirit in; every Christian knows this. But Satan is still waiting outside our bodily temples, just hoping for a chance to find a weak point in our lifestyles so he can throw a zinger or two at us. We should always remember one thing about Satan: HE NEVER GIVES UP! Neither should we. Why do you think Paul tells us to daily put on the Full Armor of God in Ephesians 6:13-17? Paul knew all about the tenacity of the Lord Of This World. "Resist the Devil, and he will flee from you." — James 4:7. Let's do some resisting!

In Luke 13:24-27 we hear from our Lord the warning to make every effort to enter the Kingdom Of Heaven by the narrow door. Rock & Roll, especially Heavy Metal, is not a narrow door, beloved; millions of people are fanatic followers of Rock! Matthew 7:21 tells us that not everyone who proclaims allegiance to Christ will enter Glory; just because a Christian Rock song says "Praise God" doesn't make it real. Let's learn to recognize Satan's latest trick as he tries to infiltrate music meant for our Lord. The best way to do that is to address those eight points made by the people in that Bible bookstore:

1) Anything might be better than Heavy Metal Rock & Roll, that's very true, but if anything might be better, so will nothing at all. If the choice is: listen to secular Rock or listen to Christian-Rock, why not just turn everything off and read the Bible? If the Rock addiction is still being fed, what's being gained?

In Tokyo, Japan, the police have a unique way of dealing with hard core drug addicts. When these people are caught, they're thrown into a cell for three days to go "cold turkey" into withdrawl. Needless to say, it is a horrible ordeal, but so is being mugged and beaten to support someone else's drug habit. In New York City, on the other hand, something called a "Methadone Program" is used instead of the brutal cold turkey approach. In this program, the addict is slowly eased out of his addiction through a series of synthetic heroin injections and treatments in decreasing doses. He has the comfort of hospital beds, sympathetic doctors, and free dope to look forward to. The upshot of all this is that

Tokyo has a handle on its drug addiction problem; New York does not.

Here's the point: if someone's addicted to Rock & Roll, they should take the cold turkey approach and GET OUT OF IT! There's plenty of other music to listen to, if they'll just do it. Playing half-hearted games with the things that enslave us and block our way to Christ is a pathetic answer to a monstrous problem. (Read Revelation 3:15-16.)

2) To the contention that Christian-Rock will serve as a bridge to get young listeners to something better eventually, I have this to say: How do you know? Isn't it just possible that those kids will stick to the Heavy Metal Christian Rock like Stryper exclusively, which will in turn cause that sector to flourish, diluting the entire Gospel-Praise music in general? This is COMPROMISE, plain and simple! Jesus didn't compromise, not with the Jewish leaders, not with people, not with the Father, and not with Scripture. Let's do the same and quit fooling ourselves, because we're sure not fooling Christ.

3) "The words are different, so the music and message is better and more positive." This is a very popular rationalization made by people who just don't understand that Rock & Roll, especially Heavy Metal, is by its very nature evil. I have some Christian friends whom I respect immensely who hold to this view. They are both gifted music majors, and the incredible wealth of knowledge they possess about musical forms and styles throughout history is truly astounding. The only problem here is that Rock & Roll is not just another progression in a long line of ever-changing musical styles; Rock was created by Satan to be used by him over 30 years ago, and we're just now seeing the deadly reality our parents and preachers were warning us about in 1954. How do we know? Because Rock was founded on the principle of rebellion. No one can deny that fact. Rebellion is the crime that caused Satan's fall, yet we say that the rebelliousness of Rock has nothing to do with Satan. That just doesn't make sense! Read I Samuel 15:23

which says:

"For rebellion is as the sin of witchcraft."

There is a famous phrase that goes like this: "The medium is the message," and vice versa. We know Satan controls secular Rock — that's obvious. I maintain that the Heavy Metal "sound" is a message into and unto itself, (not to mention the backmasks that may be contained therein). Heavy Metal is instantly recognizable to a Rock fan; it has been so dissected and fine tuned to the point of total conformity that even though hundreds of groups may play Heavy Metal music, all the songs sound the same. What makes that Heavy Metal "sound?" Basically four things: (1) Lots of screaming, (2) Three chords, (3) Buzz-saw guitar leads that imitate Eddie Van Halen, Randy Rhoads, or the guy from *Black Sabbath,* (Tony Iommi) and (4) Repetition.

Image is critically important to Rock & Roll. To a young Rock fan, that Heavy Metal image, no matter what the words, conjures up a certain feeling and remembrance in his or her mind. They're remembering the old stuff even as they're listening to the newer, so-called "more positive" Christian Metal.

This is not repentance.

Instead it is a nostalgic longing for what you can't have by diluting what you've already got. So the words say, "Praise the Lord," so what? When beautiful harmonies and clear voices of lovingkindness sing "Praise God" in a peaceful and lovely musical arrangement, that's one thing. When snarling, distorted voices yell "Praise God," (like *Stryper*), over the crash and bang of Heavy Metal music, two things happen: (1) that good message is obscured by the medium, (and why should it be, if the words are what really matter?), and (2) Heavy Metal is seen to be "not so bad." In other words, "You can listen to Heavy Metal as long as it talks about Jesus." This is the same deception that was used when "Jesus Christ Superstar" came out. Either Heavy Metal is harmless or it isn't — there's no middle ground. How can something be a little evil, or a little good? It's kind of like being a little pregnant, I guess.

My opinion is this: Either get out of Heavy Metal music or don't. Make a choice and stick to it, but make sure it's the right choice, because souls are at stake. Don't hang around waiting for more, hoping the music will get better; it won't. Heavy Metal is a style and an image, not just words. If you need further proof in the case of *Stryper,* examine one of their records or tapes and you will see that the name of their record company is "Enigma." An enigma, of course, is a perplexing or baffling problem, kind of like the question as to whether Heavy Metal belongs in Christian music. If you want the answer to that question, at least as far as *Stryper* is concerned, I would encourage you to check out some of the other albums in Enigma's catalog: albums like *Cirith Ungol's* "King Of The Dead." Ads for this album appeared in "Hit Parader" with the following description:

> "Heralding in a new age of true Metal . . . A churning
> maelstrom of chaos descending."[2]

Another Enigma LP is a hodgepodge of many different Metal bands. The cover of the record is a swift flowing black river full of human skulls. To receive Enigma's catalog, send $1.00 to Enigma Records, P.O. Box 2896, Torrance, California 90509. On the back of *Stryper's* "Soldiers Under Command" album, a mark of satanic "blessing" is found.

When secular Rock bands record their Devil-praising records, they sometimes invite witches into the studios with them to "bless" the music being produced. This "blessing" is actually a curse. By means of incantations, demons are called up to concentrate their power into the musicians and engineers at the recording session. Demons are also placed onto the tapes and records themselves. These "familiar objects" are then bought by kids and teens everywhere. Little do they realize that they have just paid for the privilege of bringing demons into their homes!

Sometimes the foul servants of Satan grow so bold they place small individualized marks of the "blessings" on the outside covers of the albums. *Venom, Black Sabbath* and *Grim Reaper* have all done this. In the case of *Stryper's* "Soldiers Under Command" LP, the blessing is a crescent with a small black blob next to it. (See figure 39.)

I spoke with a woman who was involved in Satanism at the highest levels for 17 years. As one of the most powerful witches in the United States, part of her dark work was to "bless" the studios and records of some of the biggest secular Rock groups around. She says the *Stryper* blessing represents moon worship with a drop of blood next to it. (See Appendix.)

II Corinthians 6:17 tells us to come out and be separate from the unrighteous. Why is *Stryper* part of a record label that produces satanic secular Heavy Metal? Were they more concerned with getting a recording contract, no matter what the cost, than they were with spreading the Gospel, aided and sustained by God alone? I certainly don't know the answer to such a question, brethren, but I do know this: I Corinthians 14:33 tells us that God is not a God of chaos, but of peace. Heavy Metal and Rock & Roll are filled with chaos, not peace. I don't think they have any place in the life of a believer, young or old. (See I Corinthians 15:33 and 10:21-22.)

4) The assertion that kids who buy Christian-Rock usually buy other praise records as well is really not very well thought out. My reply to that is, "Great! Now all you have to do is cut out the Christian-Rock and you'll be on the right track." If those record buyers didn't have a desire to purchase those other records in the first place, they wouldn't even be there to start with. I don't think Christian-Rock albums somehow made them buy better music as well. I

Figure 38

Whose side are they on?

Figure 39

Stryper — a dry cleaned Motley Crue.

know plenty of people who snap up every new secular Rock record as soon as it comes out who wouldn't be caught dead in a Gospel album store. That's just one more example of how incompatible these two styles of music are.

5) "The BEAT (or percussion), has Biblical relevance in the Old Testament, therefore the beat itself is not the problem." I'll agree with that statement, to a certain extent. The beat of percussive instruments as described in the Old Testament is not the problem; it's the beat of modern Rock & Roll that's the problem! The very idea of King David sitting behind an Alex Van Halen drum kit pounding out four beats to the measure is absurd and ridiculous. How can you compare apples and oranges? The music and percussive accompaniment of the ancient Jewish nation was meant to praise God Almighty. The music and percussive accompaniment of modern Rock & Roll is meant to praise Satan. Don't try to rationalize Rock by using the Bible; let it stand or fall on its own merits. (It hasn't got any.)

6) The idea that no one has the right to draw the line regarding the many interpretations, pros and cons of Rock music really makes me ill. YOU the parent draw the line! You decide the scope of the Rock problem within your own house! If you haven't got much of a problem to speak of, then praise God! If you've got an incredible difficulty on your hands, then start praying, and get to work on it. What DO you stand for, anyway? What are the goals and standards of your home and family? If you don't know, then is it any wonder your children don't either? If you don't care enough to clearly set those standards within your own household why should they care to obey them? To do anything less is a miserable cop-out.

7) "To take Rock & Roll away from children without giving them some kind of substitute will only serve to alienate them further and drive them away from you." There is much merit to this point of view. Please note, however, that there is a distinct difference between "no substitute," "a Christian-Rock substitute," and an entirely different

type of music substituted in Rock's place. Parents, you're walking on thin ice here. That's why you must go to the Father for guidance and wisdom in a situation like this; human beings just can't fight Satan alone! We're not strong enough. But be assured of one thing, when we send the Lord Jesus before us, we've tapped into an incredible power! (Read Mark 11:23-24, John 14:13-14 and also I John 4:4.)

Extreme care must be used to bring these young people through the flames without losing them altogether. By ourselves, we're totally helpless. Only with continual prayer, love, patience, understanding, and firm, steadfast, consistent commitment to the goal can anything positive be accomplished. Prayer is an indispensable tool for accomplishing this work. If you are reading these words, and you don't believe in the power of prayer, then you might as well toss this book in the trash right now, because you'll get nowhere fast without the awesome and mighty power of God through prayer. Try it! What have you got to lose? Just remember a couple of things before you start: If you're not doing anything for God in your life, why should He do anything for you? If you will only humble yourself to meekly petition the Father for help, not demand what you think He owes you, He WILL hear and respond, according to His Will and Grace.

8) "There's no escape from Rock. They'll just get it somewhere else." This is an old, old excuse for just about any problem no one wants to face. Young people may get those influences somewhere else, but they sure don't need to get them in their own house! Here's something many of us husbands and fathers don't realize: God is going to hold us personally responsible for the spiritual state of our respective families on Judgment Day. That's where all this "head of the house" business got started. (See Ephesians 5:22-33 and 6:4.) We haven't been given free rein to lord it over our wives and kids, barking out orders and administering discipline as we see fit. The Lord God has entrusted us

with an awesome responsibility as far as the spiritual growth and maintenance of our families is concerned. If we neglect or ignore that responsibility, we're going to have a lot of explaining to do to the Almighty someday soon. Husbands — Fathers — Let's get on the stick and run our families and households as the Lord intended. Let's not shuffle off our God-given responsibility onto the wife and kids, lazily hoping it will all turn out O.K. Take a stand. Draw the line. Get right with God and go to work where it counts — your own home. If worst comes to worst and the kids don't respond, at least you can meet your Maker with a clear conscience knowing you did your best.

Dear brothers and sisters, parents and young people: I maintain that there can be no such thing as Christian-Rock. To try to justify wedding something as seamy, seedy, shabby, and sick as secular Rock & Roll to praise music is just plain nonsense, in my opinion. As for deciding which groups may be too Rocky to deserve the name, "Gospel," that is simply a question you'll have to decide for yourself, on a case by case basis, after asking the Lord what He thinks about a particular group. Here are some things to look for, though: if the singer starts screaming, he's not singing, and if he's not singing, then he's not praising either. If the guitars start standing out to the point of being offensive to your ears, then maybe that music's not what it claims to be. YOU are the best judge of such things; if it sounds like Rock & Roll to you, then that's exactly what it is, and using the information provided in this book, you can act accordingly. But never forget that Satan is the master deceiver and the Father of Lies. You MUST NOT make your decisions about these groups and singers without taking the problem to the Lord first. Seek His Will through prayer, search His Word, THEN take action!

Keep in mind, parents, that the remedies to Rockitis that work in one family may not work in yours. In my own personal case, the only way to totally break free from the enslavement of Satan-Rock music was to quit listening to it entirely, to turn that stereo and car radio off and leave it off for good! (That's what on/off switches were made for.) That particular solution might be too radical for your children to handle at first. Only you and the Lord really know the inner workings of your offspring. Lean on Him, and the answers you need will come. (See Luke 11:9-13.)

I am well acquainted with a modern Christian family — father, mother, and two teenage daughters. These people aren't living in the past; the father is on his second marriage, and he's giving it everything he's got to make sure it works this time. Those parents watch very closely what their two girls see on television and hear on the radio and stereo. Some might call them censors, but what's wrong with being a censor where your precious children are concerned? This kind of attitude used to be called, "raising a family." It seems to me that today too many parents turn that particular job over to the TV set. It should also be noted that the two loving and Christian-conscious parents I'm talking about here don't just take away everything their daughters enjoy; they SELECT what those girls see and hear with their kids' well-being at heart. There's a lesson to be learned here, I think.

There's one very simple test for Christians to use to determine what is and what is not Godly music: Could you play that music as part of the Sunday morning worship service without offending God? I don't care if it's Rock, Christian Rock, Country, or Contemporary, if the music can't fit comfortably into Sunday morning worship, then it's not worth playing at all.

If such music cannot be used to praise the King, then why are you listening to it?

Is Christian-Rock more dangerous than secular Rock & Roll? My answer is yes. It's more deadly because it's disguised, and pulling blindfolds over Christian eyes is something in which Satan delights.

CHAPTER 12

Breaking Satan's Grip

"Children, obey your parents in the Lord: for this is right. Honour thy father and mother; (which is the first commandment with promise;) that it may be well with thee, and thou mayest live long on the earth. And, ye fathers, provoke not your children to wrath: but bring them up in the nurture and admonition of the Lord."

Ephesians 6:1-4

"I was completely hypnotized. The real Pied Piper was Rock & Roll. When I first heard it, I dropped everything else."

John Lennon[1]

The only real answer to any problem is Jesus Christ. As John 14:6 tells us:

"Jesus said unto him, 'I am the way, the truth, and the life: no man cometh unto the Father, but by me.'"

If you are reading these words right now and have never accepted Jesus Christ as your Lord and Savior, victory over whatever Rock & Roll problem you may be facing will be impossible to win. When you face Rock, you face Satan. Only the incredible and majestic power of Christ can knock the Devil back. None of us can do it alone.

How do you go about making Jesus your Lord? Believe He is what He claims to be — The Son of God. Accept Him. Throw away your pride and get down on your knees and tell Jesus Christ that you want Him and need Him to take complete control of your life. Pray a simple prayer in your own words asking Him to forgive your sins and accept you as His child.

After you have sincerely taken Jesus into your heart, READ GOD'S WORD — THE BIBLE — to find out how to live the way God wants you to. The first four books of the New Testament is a good place to start. Find and attend a church that preaches Jesus boldly and get baptized when you feel you're ready. Life without Christ is boring, dismal and full of hate and depression. Life with Him is exciting, powerful and full of joy. Best of all, living with Jesus goes on forever; it doesn't stop when we die.

The Son of God lived, died, and rose from the dead almost 2,000 years ago. He's alive right now, today, and He wants you to join Him in life eternal. The alternative is death and Hell.

Won't you please accept Him? Don't delay.

The information contained in this book is designed to be used by families and individuals who face the problem of Rock & Roll on a personal, one-to-one level, as I have. Too many parents watch in horror as the children they have lovingly raised for so many years in a good home squander their money on blasphemous Rock records, tapes, magazines, concerts, posters, T-shirts, buttons and other Rock-related junk.

The information in this book is also aimed at church, school, and community leaders who are watching an ever-soaring juvenile crime and drug abuse problem zoom totally out of control. All our major magazines and newspapers tell us that young people are using drugs and getting busted at an earlier age than ever before. Some of these kids start smoking Pot in the elementary schools! By the time they graduate, the vast majority have not only tried cocaine, marijuana, LSD, Speed, Quaaludes, and hard liquor, they have also built up sizeable physical and/or psychological addictions to these drugs. Why?

Rock & Roll is the single biggest reason why our young people seem to have completely lost their minds and their self control.

ALL the major Rock Stars from Mick Jagger to Ozzy Osbourne to David Lee Roth on down, not only endorse drugs, they openly BRAG about their narcotic addictions and abuses, in print and on records. When David Lee Roth screams, "I'm speeding down that line," in "Somebody Get Me A Doctor," (on the album "Van Halen II"), he's not talking about taking a train ride. He's talking about snorting Speed!

These are the heroes our young people adore so much.

An ABC News Special Report a few years ago detailed the tragic rise in pre-teen violent crimes in many of Los Angeles' simmering, war torn ghettoes. Rapes, muggings, thievery galore and senseless gunshot murders aren't being carried out just by hardened adult criminals anymore; these depraved acts of violence are being committed by children as young as 12 years old! (Usually while "high" on illicit drugs.) In an effort to come to grips with the staggering, shocking problem, L.A. law enforcement and social action agencies polled and researched kids and juvenile felons involved in the crimes, trying to dig into their heads and get at the roots of their rage. They asked these kids what plans they had for the future — what did they want to do with their lives — if given the chance, what did they want to become?

There were only two answers.

All the way down the line those young people, of all races, invariably said that they wanted to be sports heroes or Rock stars.

The Rock lifestyle looks pretty good to impressionable teens everywhere, whether they're starving in the ghetto, cruising down Main Street in the Midwest, or sitting around bored in their parents' $500,000 mansion. There's something in it for everybody.

Rock stars get all the women and sex they can handle, the biggest cars, the flashiest clothes, jewelry, and houses. They feed on only the best drugs and booze, not to mention millions of dollars in cash, fawning music magazine and radio station interviews, and a global network of screaming adoration and riches that would have rivaled King Solomon in all his glory.

There's also a heavy price to pay, and not even the biggest of Rock's royalty gets away cheap. Witness this interview with *Van Halen* drummer Alex Van Halen (who has lost 30% of his hearing thanks to Rock & Roll):

> "I'm hoping it will come back . . . I notice myself going 'Huh?' and 'What?' a lot more these days. It's annoying but if you dance, you gotta pay the piper. Remember I've been doing this since I was 12 years old, eleven years in this band . . . We had a doctor come in once to measure and he just said, 'Give me back my db meter. I don't ever want to see you again.'"[2]

Van Halen bassist Michael Anthony had this to say about Alex's live set-up, also taken from the same article:

> "If I was behind a kit like Al's — the level it has to be pumped just so he can hear the set — it would collapse my head."[3]

Rock stars have it all. They treat everyone outside their own small, closely knit circles with utter contempt. They don't HAVE to be polite, patient, or considerate. Their money allows them to bypass all the conventional rules of society that the rest of us lesser mortals must deal with every day. They can destroy plush hotel suites with insolence; they can vulgarly brutalize anyone they choose. They parade their foul mouths in public and vent their venom at innocent passersby. Their accountants can take care of the damages later. They persist in this satanic lifestyle till their brains rot and their souls decay. Their complete and utter degradation of themselves and their followers knows no bounds. What miserable, pathetic wretches these people are! They have the world at their feet, yet they don't know the meaning of the most elementary teaching of Jesus Christ: Love your neighbor as you would yourself. (See Matthew 22:38-39)

The only thing these people love is money. As the Bible tells us:

> "For the love of money is the root of all evil: which while some coveted after, they have erred from the faith, and pierced themselves through with many sorrows."   I Timothy 6:10.

As a matter of fact, the Bible describes today's typical Rock star to a "T." In Jude 17-19 we read:

> "But, beloved, remember ye the words which were spoken before of the apostles of our Lord Jesus Christ; How that they told you there should be mockers in the last time, who should walk after their own ungodly lusts. These be they who separate themselves, sensual, having not the Spirit."

And in II Timothy 3:1-9:

> "This know also, that in the last days perilous times shall come. For men shall be lovers of their own selves, covetous, boasters, proud, blasphemers, disobedient to parents, unthankful, unholy, without natural affection, truce-breakers, false accusers, incontinent, fierce, despisers of those that are good,

traitors, heady, highminded, lovers of pleasures more than lovers of God; having a form of godliness, but denying the power thereof: from such turn away. For of this sort are they which creep into houses, and lead captive silly women laden with sins, led away with divers lusts, ever learning, and never able to come to the knowledge of the truth. Now as Jannes and Jambres withstood Moses, so do these also resist the truth: men of corrupt minds, reprobate concerning the faith. But they shall proceed no further: for their folly shall be manifest unto all men, as theirs also was."

That day has certainly come!

As a reminder of just how evil and degenerate the Super Rock Stars of the Eighties have become, I offer these two quotes from *Van Halen's* David Lee Roth and *AC-DC's* Angus Young:

> **Roth** — "There will be two courses to choose from — intercourse and outercourse. Winners will receive a free half hour of sex with your favorite member of *Van Halen.* "[4]

> **Young** — " . . . I had one idiot trying to blast away in my earhole. He started with 'Do you believe in God?' and I said 'I've no interest in it so leave me alone . . . ' Some people are sick. If they want to go God-bothering they should go God-bother the Pope. He needs it. We don't."[5]

I Corinthians 1:18 has some wise advice pertaining to the David Lee Roths and Angus Youngs of this world:

> "For the preaching of the cross is to them that perish foolishness; but unto us which are saved it is the power of God."

We've sure come a long way since Elvis Presley. Why, Elvis looks like a shy, stuttering kid next to the rampaging, satanic, sex-stuffed Rock rapists around today!

Rock & Roll has turned our schools into battlegrounds. How many parents stop to think about the ways their hard-earned tax dollars are supporting this disgusting trend? Probably many of them don't realize that the schools their sons and daughters attend often play raucous Rock & Roll over the cafeteria intercoms at lunch time daily. This is quite common. At my own high school, deep in the heart of the conservative Midwest, a day didn't go by that we weren't subjected to loud, non-stop Rock & Roll music during the noon hour. A radio or borrowed stereo brought from home was simply placed in front of the main PA microphone in the principal's office, and so it went.

Parents, have you ever asked your children what kind of music they were hearing at school? At most American middle and high schools the halls echo with the jackhammer blast of Rock & Roll all day long. It is tolerated and forgotten by most administrators. THIS kind of attitude from our school system, the backbone of America, the hope for the future of our country! If you think it's not happening in YOUR schools, it might be worth your time to check it out. The answers might shock you. If your schools are some of the few left that refuse to pander to young people, in effect letting them run the school, you can consider yourself lucky, because there aren't many left.

"Of course," you say. "Rock & Roll is not for everybody. People older and less easily fooled than teenagers with too much time on their hands, often readily recognize Rock for what it is: loud, vulgar, raucous gutter music. The Devil's music. So common sense may tell you that listening to Rock is a strictly controlled matter of choice, just like television. If you don't want to expose yourself to such ear pollution, you can simply turn off the radio or stereo."

NOT TRUE.

Rock & Roll has become such an all-pervasive part of modern society that we literally CANNOT escape it. If you don't think that statement is valid, listen carefully to the piped in Muzak surrounding you the next time you visit the supermarket, your favorite restaurant or laundromat, or your doctor's office or your dentist's, or your lawyer's, or almost ANY professional place of business. Shopping malls and TV commercials also bombard us with reworked Rock at every turn. Some shopping malls even play MTV on their own televisions spread throughout the complex 12 hours a day!

Nearly the entire *Beatles'* catalog has been transposed and rearranged for Muzak, as well as hundreds of other Rock songs, both new and old. These tunes are consistently and efficiently being drilled into our brains and subconscious during every part of our work, play, and leisure activities. In the highly industrialized, ultra-complex, transistorized technocratic society that is today's America, one grim fact emerges from the din: it is impossible to escape Rock & Roll.

Until concerned people do something about it.

The Rock music industry is huge. In 1978, (their banner year), profits exceeded 4.1 BILLION dollars. Inflation and recession eroded that sum to a mere 3.6 billion in 1980, a figure corporate executives and industry analysts claim simply is not enough to make ends meet. Perhaps if these people quit spending millions of dollars on Cocaine, their profits would go up. We shouldn't let these numbers scare us, though. If enough Christian believers pool their massive resources of WILL together, even huge corporations such as these can be toppled. Without an audience to feed their drug-fueled furnace, these groups and companies would collapse of their own bloated dead weight.

This book won't save the world. It's not meant to. For those who have denied Christ and His power, only the wonderful gift of God's Holy Spirit can reverse their steps and show them the light. The information contained in this book is meant to be used by concerned mothers, fathers, brothers, sisters, pastors, teachers and friends to provide an alternative for young people, something besides Rock &

Roll. It is absolutely every parent's Christian right and responsibility to make this choice available for their children, to regain the authority let slip away for so many years as the fires of Rock have raged out of control. We must demystify the god-like status of the Rock industry. We need to show it for what it is: pure, satanic, money-grubbing garbage.

Satan's tactics haven't changed one bit since the Garden of Eden. He's still preying on human lust, pride, and the desire for equality with God. He's still spreading his web of lies and deceit, telling us poor humans that yes, we too can become like God if we only have enough money, enough fame, enough power and prestige.

He's doing it through the medium of Rock & Roll.

How do we know we're on the right track? How do we know for sure that these Rock groups and the industry they feed can be brought low by the righteous anger of Christians everywhere?

Let us examine a prominent Rock band, Todd Rundgren's *Utopia,* and their 1982 LP "Swing To The Right." The cover of "Swing" is a color retouched photograph of an actual record-burning fellowship from the 1960's. According to "Hit Parader," August, 1982, the photo is an actual "Beatle Burning" from around 1966, sparked by John Lennon's infamous "we're bigger than Jesus" remark. Men. Women. Children. They are all gathered around a bonfire of burning records. The haircuts are short; the clothes are conservative. One young man, probably the preacher of the congregation, or perhaps its youth leader, holds a microphone, a big smile on his face. In fact, smiles are everywhere, smiles of peace and contentment in doing God's work, smiles of satisfaction in a job well done. One young boy of about ten, grinning from ear to ear, is holding up a record ready to throw onto the fire, pausing to let the photographer capture the event. Todd Rundgren's art people have airbrushed away the original cover on the album the boy is holding ("Meet The Beatles"), and replaced it with the photograph of "Swing To The Right," sort of a picture within a picture.

The LP itself is filled with songs of defiance and refusal to obey authority, a statement of anarchy and rejection of the traditional moral values that have made America strong. By making fun of the new conservative mood of the country, Rock groups like *Utopia* are trying to down play and wish away the fact that good Christian people are wise to their tricks at last, and have finally had enough of the trash, filth, smut, and demonology they produce.

The flip side of "Swing To The Right's" cover shows two things: a Nazi book burning from the Forties, and what the August, 1982 issue of "Hit Parader" describes as young people in the Midwest holding their own record burning ceremony, "Instigated by some Moral Majority types."

And what's wrong with the "Moral Majority types" anyway? Thanks to the PMRC, all the major Rock-rag fanzines are currently jumping on this type of slanderous bandwagon in a big way. We have to remember that such periodicals make their living by plastering the ugly mugs of *Van Halen* and *AC-DC* all over their covers and pages. Their righteous indignation at finally being caught in the corruption of youngsters everywhere is truly pathetic. These people have no room to talk about being persecuted or taken advantage of.

In fact, guitarist-singer Eric Bloom of the satanic *Blue Oyster Cult* made these vicious comments about the backlash:

> "Hey I don't care if these self-styled preachers burn Cult records as long as they buy 'em first."[6]

"Hit Parader" writer Toby Goldstein said:

> "There's very little difference between the Ku Klux Klan raving on in 1956 against 'Nigra jungle music sold by Jews to promote anti-Christian behavior' and current preachers who see Rock's devilish overtones corrupting their own communities."[7]

298

Rock writers are now comparing valiant Christian ministers not afraid to do their moral duty to the KKK!

Let us examine this in an objective manner. Such shrill and hysterical accusations from these Rock groups and the parasites who make their living from Rock's table scraps should tell us something, if we look beyond the inflammatory words.

These people are scared!

In reality, they're running scared like spooked cattle on a stampede, fearful of losing their ill-gotten millions as more and more God-fearing Christian Americans make their voices heard. It's time to put a long delayed stop to the wellspring of the Devil left untouched for so many years. They're afraid of being stripped of their harems, Rolls Royces, heroin and cocaine.

These people are nothing. They're not powerful; they're pathetic. They have all the trappings of power, and they do have an insidious ability when used by Satan to warp and twist the minds and morals of innocent youngsters, but once the righteous might of our Lord Jesus Christ is brought into play, these pawns of the Devil run like leaves in the wind!

NOW is the time for all concerned Christians to increase the pressure and deliver the final death blow to this blight upon our society, before these Rockers get any richer and more powerful than they already are.

The first step is realizing that addiction to Rock & Roll is a form of demonic possession, and also seeing that those same demons can be thrown out of the hearts and minds of our young. Christ cast out demons all through the Gospels, as did his disciples.

One area that MUST be examined at this point is the spiritual warfare that you as parents are going to come up against as you try to remove the curse of Rock & Roll from your home. We can look at and debate the CULTURAL side of Rock all day long without ever making any real progress on the problem at hand. Why? Because Rock & Roll music is not just cultural in nature, it is SPIRITUAL as well. As a matter of fact, ALL music is spiritual. It doesn't matter whether we're talking about electric guitars or French horns; those instruments don't play themselves! The music produced first begins in the heart and mind of the musician; it flows out from his or her spirit and is then channeled through the instrument, finally reaching the ears of the listener.

Music is spiritual communication in the truest sense. What kind of spirits are communicating to your children via Rock & Roll?

The famous Bible verse from Ephesians 6:12 clearly tells us who our enemy is and exactly what we're up against when we begin our fight. There's a lot more going on here than just a distasteful social phenomenon called Rock & Roll. Kids have grown out of adolescent phases for generations. Rock & Roll is something quite different, and rare is the young person who reaches adulthood without carrying some of the soul-searing scars inflicted by Rock.

I'm trying to make a simple point here, parents: until you see the problem of Rock & Roll in a spiritual light, you and your children can fire opinions back and forth at each other for a year and still get nowhere fast. For example, Dad says to Junior: "How can you stand to listen to that loud screamin' stuff? It's disgusting. Turn it off. That one guy in the band looks like he has a feather duster on his head."

The angry son takes Dad's comments personally and comes back with both guns blazing: "You don't understand this kind of music. Just because you didn't listen to this stuff when YOU were young, don't put me down for doing it. What do you want me to do, listen to Frank Sinatra?"

The above scene is an example of debating the cultural merits and demerits of Rock & Roll. Parents, if you take this approach without the benefit of the Holy Spirit, Scripture, and Prayer, Satan and his ravenous pet called Rock & Roll will chew you up and spit you out in little pieces.

What's the solution, then? Get a clear understanding of the problem.

I'm going to say this as simply as I can: demons are afflicting your household and your children through the medium of Rock music. They are far more powerful than we humans, and it is only by tapping into the greatest power source in the universe, Jesus Christ, that we can overcome such tremendous oppression.

Mom and Dad, have you already talked yourselves blue in the face with your kids about their obsession with Rock? Does it seem like they just don't hear a word you're saying? Or perhaps if they do listen, does it seem as if nothing ever sinks in? Read II Corinthians 4:4 and you'll begin to see why your kids' heads have suddenly gotten so hard. Satan has blinded their minds!

For parents who have put on and professed Christ in every way, especially within their families, II Corinthians 4:4 may leave you saying, "Hey! Hold on just a minute. My kids aren't unbelievers; I've raised them up in the Lord!" To you mothers and fathers I suggest reading Ephesians 4:18 and Leviticus 19:31. Satan has darkened your kids' understanding and blinded their hearts through the callous brutality of Rock & Roll.

So what can you do about this demon power which is slowly (or perhaps quickly) stealing your children away from you?

TAKE AUTHORITY OVER IT.

We can claim that power of deliverance only through Jesus Christ. We are utterly helpless on our own, but through Him and in Him, we CAN cast Satan out. Scripture tells us this in Luke 10:17-20 wherein Jesus was speaking to 70 of his disciples. Are His words any less true today to those of us who have also chosen to follow Him?

When I began writing this book I had a close friend (unsaved) tell me, "Leave out this demon possession stuff. Nobody believes in that kind of thing. Why, I don't even know any Christians who believe in it."

Well, believe in it or not, Mom or Dad, brother or sister, SOMETHING is turning ever younger kids into Rock & Roll addicts. SOMETHING is turning family homes into shell-shocked battlegrounds, and something mighty powerful is preparing a whole generation of teenagers and pre-teens for the mushroom clouds of Doomsday. They'll march off into the flames singing all the way down into the Pit.

Rock & Roll is doing this. Satan is doing this.

I'm not talking about Hollywood here. Fifteen years worth of popular occult movies and books have left us trembling at the thought of "mighty" Satan and his demon hordes, rising from the exploding smoke and flames to SMITE and DE-STROY the helpless, weak-kneed humans. (Sounds kind of like the average Rock concert, doesn't it?) No, Satan is much more subtle than Tinseltown special effects would have us believe, and THEREIN lies the strength of demon power: in our unbelief and our do-nothing attitude.

So exactly how can Christian mothers and fathers take the authority over Satan that the Lord has entrusted to us?

Use the Scriptures as your example. Rebuke those demons out loud. (Matthew 8:16, Matthew 8:31-32, Matthew 10:1, Matthew 16:23, Matthew 17:18.) Jesus didn't wish them away, He CAST them out, and COMMANDED them to leave. You also should order them out of your house and out of your children's minds by the Name and Power and Blood of Jesus Christ alone. Bind them by that same Power and Blood and Name. Don't undertake such a Crusade without heavy prayer. Fasting combined with prayer may be helpful. (Mark 9:16-29) Believe in what you're doing and believe in the Power of Almighty God to work such a miracle. (Hebrews 11:6) Any type of frivolous or "Let's try it, we've got nothing to lose" attitude could be disastrous. (Acts 19:13-16) Finally, get rid of all the Rock & Roll residue left in your child's room. Burn that stuff up in the trash can! (Acts 19:19 & 20) Much study of all four Gospel accounts pertaining to Jesus' deliverance ministry MUST be done before beginning any of these tasks.

You need to understand one more very important concept, parents. Satan is accusing and petitioning God for control of YOUR children! The best example of this is found in Job 1:6-12, & 2:2-7. You have God-given spiritual responsibilities for the care and upbringing of your children (I Timothy 3:2-5 & 3:12, also Ephesians 6:1-4). Since these children are YOUR spiritual responsibility, entrusted to you by God, you also have the right to counter-petition Satan for their control. You have the right to enter the very throne room of God through prayer in order to break Satan's grip! (See Hebrews 4:16, & 7:25.) Use your God-given rights!

Who is mightier, Satan or God, demons or Christ? I take comfort and joyful assurance in many Scriptures, especially Romans 16:20, and Colossians 2:15.

How do the demons do their dirty work on your kids?

First, a teenager becomes OBSESSED with Rock groups and the mystique surrounding them. He may have heard some friend's tapes, or become curious after listening to a particularly catchy song on the radio. Perhaps he has just attended his first Rock concert, returning home with a new perspective of just how vile and smutty the real world can be. The brutal, degraded reality behind Rock & Roll has been hidden beneath those exploding flashpots, bright shiny guitars, mountain moving music, and strobing laser lights, especially to an impressionable young person's unawakened mind. The seed has been planted. The "seed" is a demon who will later manifest more and more power and control over the person.

Soon enough the young girl or boy's Rock obsessions begin steadily increasing. Allowances and job money start flowing out as 45s, albums, magazines, tapes and posters start rushing in. Drawn by the weird occult symbols and shocking pictures on those Rock record covers, thousands of fresh teens fall victim to Satan's song every year.

In more extreme cases (such as my own), simply ingesting Rock & Roll records and magazines twenty-four hours a day is not enough. A desire to actually MAKE Rock music manifests itself, and even more hard earned dollars are traded for expensive guitars, amplifiers, PA and recording equipment and accessories. From my own personal experience, I can say with absolute conviction and certainty that anyone reaching this stage of Rock & Roll obsession is deep in the throes of demon possessed addiction. NOTHING is more important than that next practice session, that weekend club date, that new Rock album. The ONLY priority is Rock & Roll. Nothing else matters. That brass ring is just hanging there, waiting to be grabbed, if only you can be more disgusting, rude, and obnoxious than that band down the block.

Obsession.

Once all the Rock magazines have been bought and read, and the records listened to over and over until memorized, demonic control takes a major leap forward. Those hideous, garish, occult album covers and posters scattered around the typical teenager's room all serve to focus human attention on inhuman concepts such as torture, magic, and insanity. We have actually invited the evil into our home! It will lie there festering, its power over us growing, if we let it. Those things are "familiar objects," dedicated to the Devil. They give Satan legal right to enter and afflict anyone in the house. Burn them! The scriptural basis for familiar objects is found in Deuteronomy 7:25-26 and I Corinthians 10:19-20.

Ever notice how hard it is to get some Rock tunes out of your head? Perhaps you've only heard the song once on the radio, but those "hooks" are still there long after the song is over, drilling deep into your subconscious, locked away for future reference. Such is the nature of Demon Rock. It's goal: Paralyze the thought processes and begin instituting major changes in attitudes, concepts, and tolerances — satanic changes.

Ask any father of a screaming, defiant, demanding teenager if Rock hasn't had something to do with the increase of tensions in that particular home. All families have problems and arguments, but can it be denied that Rock & Roll has fanned the flames? Its endorsement of druggish freedom and denial of all authority, especially parental authority, is a nightmare that won't go away.

For example: Junior has an argument with Dad and storms off to his room, slamming the door. Now he can be alone with his tapes and headphones. Now he can listen to Ozzy Osbourne and reinforce his feelings of isolation, frustration, and inadequacy. The communication line, the only real way to solve whatever basic problems exist, has been cut. Now the demons' thoughts can slip into the innermost areas of the confused teenager's brain. Now they can whisper their commands and messages of hate through the lips of Rock singers, through the choruses of Rock songs. Now the hidden backmasks do their dirty work. Here's what they say: "Your Dad's a fool. He's not cool. YOU are in control of your own destiny. Don't listen to him. Fight back!"

For too many teens, drugs quickly come into the scene once the relationship with Rock has been firmly established. When family tensions keep mounting, and meaningful communication dries up, the frustrated, angry young people too often turn to drugs to blot out their misery. And don't think it can't happen to your child, no matter what his age. It may already be happening. Drugs are easy to get. Students sell them at school, and at work, in hallways between classes, and downstairs in gym locker-rooms. It's easy if you've got the money. That's all a kid needs to get his first (or 250th) high.

I know this is true because I've seen it.

Drugs aren't just a by-product of Rock & Roll; they're a very basic part of the whole devilish machine. Ask any young person who's not afraid to admit it: when stoned to the gills on marijuana, his senses roaring, and his ears ringing, he can really get into that music; it's like riding a jet plane with the distorted guitars meshing like rippling buzzsaws, and the drum beats and snare shots crisply cracking behind the fluid bass lines that whoosh and thud.

Rock & Roll and hallucinogenic drugs go together like sugar and molasses.

LSD is the ultimate extension of this psycho-sensory joy ride. When "tripping," the intense young Rock listener can actually hear the hiss of the studio master tapes beginning their tracks, not to mention that wheezy cackle and evil command from Ozzy Osbourne buried way back in the mix. Under LSD's influence, it's all there: the secret messages, the subliminal voices and whisperings, the weird instructions. Drugs like LSD bring it all out into the open. Drugs also dull the mind and kill the spirit. Just because your child listens to Rock & Roll doesn't mean that he or she will become addicted to drugs, but they could very easily become addicted to Rock, and that's a sure step in the wrong direction.

Demonic control continues with an unbridled, pagan lust for sex. Once the drugs have "liberated" the mind, it's time to follow suit with the body. After all, isn't that Rock's two biggest drawing cards, drugs and sex? Once parents have given up their disciplinary authority by allowing Rock & Roll trash and smut into their home for fear of alienating their children, there is no one left to make the rules but the Rock stars. And their rules clearly state: brutal, dehumanized sex is 100% OK with them.

When Rock stars aren't singing about jabbing needles into their veins, they're crowing about their latest multiple sexual conquests. They wallow in the perverse. They bathe themselves in homosexuality and lesbianism. Your friend or child may not BECOME a homosexual by listening to Rock trash do their disgusting thing, but they could easily come to accept these perversions as normal, if somewhat unusual, modes of human sexual behavior. The next step will be to experiment with some of these perversions. Is YOUR kid strong enough to hold out? Is anyone's?

Today all that sex, smut, and druggy behavior is as close

as the TV set. After all, this is the 20th century. Satan isn't going to waste his time snaring souls only through records and books when he can use the universal medium of television to marshall his forces for the end. TV has become the worst type of exposure for our kids, worming its way into virtually every American's home. With the exploding increase in Rock & Roll video programming, and the expansion of cable TV, Rock has attained instant credibility and landed feet first into our very living rooms. The snot-nosed defiance begun by a greasy haired, hip wiggling Elvis thirty years ago has grown up and gotten smarter; no more struggling to separate the "hip" from the "square." No more attempts to widen the "generation gap." This time it's that great equalizer the television set that is completing the process of Rock & Roll demonism in the hearts and minds of our youth. Rock & Roll will soon be playing in the background of 50 million American homes, thanks to cable TV and Rock & Roll videos. Surely the F.C.C. wouldn't allow anything on our TV sets that could hurt us, would they?

Perhaps they aren't aware of the problem.

Perhaps someone should tell them.

Modern Punk groups with names like *New Math* and *Christian Death* ooze into record stores every month with albums titled "Only Theatre Of Pain" and "They Walk Among You." Here are some of *New Math's* lyrics:

> "White hot iron it burns my skin
> Like the Mark Of The Beast upon my head
> Loss of reputation
> I'm a public disgrace
> Everybody knows me for my infamous name . . . "

So how do we cast out the demons? How do we free ourselves and our friends and our children from the chains of Rock & Roll that have held us prisoner for so long? Let us examine a comprehensive plan to deal with this problem.

We must take ACTION in order to see some positive results. No more complacency. No more letting our kids' confused desires run our homes. There's a lot more at stake here than hot tempers and disappointed teenagers. Every Christian parent, pastor, and church administrator has a sacred duty to bring up their young people in the ways of Jesus Christ, to take some control and responsibility, use some initiative, and guide them in Godly steps to Salvation. Our young people, the next generations, are the only hope for the future of our country, our families, our churches, and our entire social structure. We MUST get involved, and we must do it NOW. Satan has had almost 30 years to work his mischief on our youngsters. It's high time we took the Devil by the horns and put a stop to it.

Here is the plan:

A uthority
C ommunication
T ime
I nspiration
O rganization
N ormalcy

By reasserting our AUTHORITY, and meaningfully COMMUNICATING with our young people, over a period of TIME we can teach them the difference between the ways of the Devil, and the ways of Christ. The INSPIRATION and direction for such a project must come from the Scriptures followed by lots of prayer. We can then ORGANIZE to help bring about a return to NORMALCY, a return to Christ Jesus.

The first step is to reassert our AUTHORITY — authority in the home and in the schools. After all, our children's tax dollars didn't pay for those things. It was our own sweat and desire for a better life for our kids that made those homes and schools possible. It is our sacred duty in Jesus Christ to provide them with guidance, to give them a better role model than some drugged up, homosexual Rock star.

Parental authority in the home seemed like an endangered species for a while, but thank God that situation is now beginning to change. Some parents, victims of the many "progressive" theories about child rearing, may ask themselves this question: "What right do I have to interfere in my child's life and take away something he loves so dearly?"

Look at it this way: When your son or daughter was a baby, you wouldn't hesitate to jerk the sharp knife or cleaning solvent out of their little hands before they hurt themselves, would you? The same situation holds true for a teenager and Rock & Roll. Ultimately, Rock is going to be as dangerous to their souls and lives as knives and light sockets were to their baby bodies.

Here is what the Bible tells us about this matter:

> "Foolishness is bound in the heart of a child; but the rod of correction shall drive it far from him."
> Proverbs 22:15

> "Withhold not correction from the child: for if thou beatest him with the rod, he shall not die. Thou shalt beat him with the rod, and shalt deliver his soul from hell." Proverbs 23:13-14

> "For rebellion is as the sin of witchcraft, and stubbornness is as iniquity and idolatry." I Samuel 15:23

These are strong words, but the meaning behind them should be crystal clear: Get involved! Don't be afraid to stop their use of things contrary to God.

One of those things is Rock & Roll.

Besides, what has Rock got going for it? Demons, occultism, homosexuality and lesbianism, sexual perversions, anarchy, Communist and humanist themes that deny the existence of God, drugs that destroy mind and body, naked women on album covers, "kiddie porn," and violence galore — THAT'S what Rock & Roll is about!

No one needs to be subjected to this.

You should first identify the scope of the problem in

your own individual situation. How serious is it? Does your child just listen to the radio a lot and buy 45s with his weekly allowance? Or is he beginning to bring home posters and Rock magazines more and more frequently? Is he starting to spend more time listening to music, and less with the family, more money for records and less saved for college and the church? Or is he firmly in the grip of Rock, talking constantly about groups and records, going to concerts and watching the bands on T.V.? Is he thinking about buying a guitar in order to learn to play some of his favorite songs himself?

Another factor to carefully consider is the age of your child. It's not in the best interests of anyone to treat a 16 year old the same as you would his 9 year old brother or sister. In the case of very small children just beginning to walk down Rock's rotten path, the parent should become the censor. If you have determined that the records and tapes your children are buying are not in their best spiritual interest and development, you must simply put a stop to it and take those records and tapes away. Every parent has a sacred Christian right and duty to do this. Put your foot down. Be firm, but make it clear that you are taking this step out of love, not some kind of "power trip." Remember, YOU are the parent in this situation. YOU are in charge of your household.

This censorship can usually be continued until the child reaches his early teens. After that, the parent must change tactics and begin reasoning with the child. The key word here is COMMUNICATION. You must ask your teenager, on a one-to-one basis, "Why do you like Rock so much?"

One of the most common answers will probably be, "I like Rock because of the beat. It makes me want to dance." This is very true, but you should point out to your child that Rock & Roll, especially Heavy Metal Rock & Roll, is based on the Blues, a song style begun by the post Civil War American Negro sitting amidst destroyed plantations and burned out cities. Death and destruction was

310

everywhere. It is a style filled with smutty sexual references and a "things will never get better" mentality. Both the *Rolling Stones* and *Led Zeppelin* started out as Blues bands. The Blues itself, with its churning twelve-bar changes stopping and starting in the same hypnotic sequence time after time, evolved from African voodoo beats and tribal music. Black slaves carried it with them on the Dutch and British ships heading for America. By the end of the Civil War, the Blues were born.

Rolling Stones' bassist Bill Wyman made these chilling comments about just how important the Blues are to HIS band:

> " . . . Whenever we rehearse and learn new numbers, every other thing we play is a jam of an old Elmore James or Muddy Waters or Chuck Berry thing. I know a lot of people say, 'What are you playing that old stuff for?' But we're not doing it for sentimental reasons — we're doing it to retain the FEELING of those blues and R & B (Rhythm & Blues) things."[8]

That's why kids like the beat so much. That's why the music makes them want to start dancing. Over a century later, those evil African voodoo influences are still weaving their primitive spell on a whole new generation of American young people.

You must make it clear that you are sincere in learning more about this Rock phenomenon that affects your children so deeply. You must be prepared to listen thoughtfully to their reasons before making the statement that, from the beginning, Rock & Roll has been based on self-destruction. Instant self-gratification, rejection of godly things, AND musical accompaniment to chants both to worship demons and to call up demons are what Rock is all about.

Here are a few positive steps you as a parent can take within the framework of your own family: The first step is the parents' own relationship with God. If you have not made Jesus Christ your personal Lord and Savior and

Master, you will not have the power necessary to deal with the situation. Only the power and authority of Jesus Christ can overcome the mighty influence the demons of Rock music have on your children. Those parents who are Christians need to start using the authority Jesus has given to them. Daily, they should, in prayer, bind the demons afflicting their children in the name of Jesus.

> "But if our gospel be hid, it is hid to them that are lost: In whom the god of this world hath blinded the minds of them which believe not, lest the light of the glorious gospel of Christ, who is the image of God, should shine unto them."   II Corinthians 4:3-4

The minds of kids involved in Rock music are literally demonically bound. Unless the parents stop those demons from functioning, their children will never be able to understand what is being said to them about the evils of Rock music and their need for Jesus Christ.

You should also take time out of your own busy schedules to budget family hours and activities to examine Rock & Roll. Actually WATCH some of those Rock videos on the tube together, you and your children. Explain to them just how those shots, lighting, and special effects are set up. Show them that the whole affair is a minutely detailed and painstakingly produced piece of film designed to project an image — sex, the occult, science fiction, and so on. Look for any subliminal things that are there — background sets, signs, clothes. You'll be surprised at just how many things ARE concealed in the average Rock video. Expose them! (It's interesting to note the fact that NONE of the groups or singers in these video productions are actually singing or playing anything! In the studios where these things are made, huge monitor speakers are set up out of camera range. They blast out the song being produced at ear splitting volume while the Rock stars jump around with their guitars and pretend to sing the words. All this noise is later erased from the sound track and substituted with the original recorded version of the song.)

The same goes for listening to records and examining the covers of Rock albums together, as a family. One thing's for sure: if you, the parent, can convince your child or children to play their records for you and scrutinize their covers and lyric sheets closely, those children will be embarassed! Why? Because they know, deep in their hearts and souls, that all the cursing, the sex, the drug references, and the lyrics about Satan — are WRONG. God has put this knowledge in every human. Witness this passage from Romans 1:18-20:

> "For the wrath of God is revealed from heaven against all ungodliness and unrighteousness of men, who hold the truth in unrighteousness; Because that which may be known of God is manifest in them; for God hath shewed it unto them. For the invisible things of him from the creation of the world are clearly seen, being understood by the things that are made, even his eternal power and Godhead; so that they are without excuse."

By using your children's own conscience in this way, you will be driving the message about Rock's destructive power home in a way that will leave a lasting impression on them — one that they'll never forget. Also, you as a parent will not be seen as FORCING them to accept your opinions on the subject; they'll see it for themselves! By approaching the problem in this way, your kids won't feel that you're invading their privacy by trying to get too close to them. This, though unpleasant, is every parent's duty to God.

After showing your willingness to communicate with your children, you must have as good a grip on the facts and figures as they do if you want to show Rock for what it is. You need to know something about those songs and groups, and you must know the history of Rock & Roll if you're to make a difference in their attitude. This book was designed to help you in that task.

Another excellent and constantly updated source of information about the current state of affairs in Rock are the dozens of Rock & Roll magazines that flood the news stands and grocery stores twice a month. Why not use those trashy rags to the best advantage, and get the information you need from Satan's own garbage dump? You may get some strange looks from the checkout clerk, probably because they don't often see middle-aged Moms and Dads buying the latest Rock fanzines, but so what? Burn those magazines after you've read them.

Most Rock magazines carry ads in their back pages for witchcraft paraphernalia, fake IDs, tons of expensive Rock-related junk, and something called "barbaric jewelry," (strands of barbed wire worn as necklaces and bracelets.) What kind of concentration camp mentality is being developed here, anyway? What's next, autographed pictures from Auschwitz? Ads for fake IDs encourage kids to break the law, and the witchcraft stuff speaks for itself.

These magazines have the same grotesque Heavy Metal gurus on their covers month after month, year after year. Since they all depend on Rock for their livelihood, they should share in our general condemnation. In the meantime they can be used as instructive tools for parents wanting to learn more about their kids' addiction. Many times it's those magazines themselves that start the ball rolling. Youngsters may bring home such stuff even before they start buying the records and getting into the groups pictured there. If you see any of the garbage mentioned above lying around your house, you can be sure you've already got a problem on your hands as far as your kids and Rock are concerned.

You need to relate to your children. Talk to them about your own fascinations with music when you were their age, whether it was Be-Bop, Jazz, Swing, or the early Rock of the Fifties. Show them that you liked music then, and still do. It's not the love of music that's the problem; it's the cursing, the blatant sex descriptions, the calls on the Devil

314

that abound in all of modern Rock & Roll that is dangerous to the hearts, minds and souls of its listeners.

If you want to get some positive results, you must meaningfully relate to your child's point of view. Make clear to them the fact that you fully realize that as maturing adults they have the right to spend time and energy on various things, but Rock & Roll should not be one of them. Show them that Rock is a phase — a deadly phase — and that you're only trying to help them find their way out of it. The power of prayer cannot be emphasized strongly enough in handling situations like this. Someday your child may thank you for your concern and patient understanding. Even if he doesn't, at least you'll know that you did your best, humbly asking God for guidance.

Don't be worried; be confident! But also never lose sight of the fact that YOU, guided by the Lord, are making the rules in your house, not your children.

Also — and this is very important — keep in mind that it's going to take some TIME to bring about meaningful changes in your children's points of view about Rock & Roll. You could, of course, just walk into your teenager's room, demand that he or she quit listening to Rock, and throw away all their records and tapes — that is your right as a parent — but what would that accomplish? You might find yourself with more hateful, insolent rebellion on your hands than ever before. Have some patience. Your teenager may have spent years listening to Rock music. Their addiction may be far too advanced to cut off overnight without disastrous consequences. The book of Proverbs holds some wise advice for parents and children, such as:

> 12:1 "Who so loveth instruction loveth knowledge: but he that hateth reproof is brutish."

> 1:8-9 "My son, hear the instruction of thy father, and forsake not the law of thy mother: for they shall be an ornament of grace unto thy head, and chains about thy neck."

29:15 "The rod and reproof give wisdom: but a child left to himself bringeth his mother to shame."

17:25 "A foolish son is a grief to his father, and bitterness to her that bare him."

25:15 "By long forbearing is a prince persuaded, and a soft tongue breaketh the bone."

Let us not fool ourselves. There really are no musical substitutes which will COMPLETELY take the place of Rock & Roll for today's craving teens. The Pop, Blues, and Heavy Metal all inspire laziness and self-indulgence. They are opiates for young minds. They encourage drug taking and "no future" Doomsday thinking. There is no substitution for their sickness, and they need to be completely cut out of every Christian young person's life.

Many people automatically feel that Gospel music is the natural alternative to Rock & Roll. I can't think of a better way to turn young minds from the hate and selfishness of Heavy Metal to the love and abundant joy of Jesus. No longer will they be listening to prayers to the Devil, but praises to the King! Parents should keep something in mind, though. Gospel artists aren't angels on Earth. They stumble and fall occasionally as we all do in our quest to come near the blameless Presence of God. Though it doesn't begin to compare with the sleazy, disgusting, dollar-and-drug-filled empire that is modern Rock & Roll, Gospel music is still big business. We must not forget that it is also SHOW BUSINESS, and by definition that's not always as sincere as it should be. Some Gospel stars are reformed alcoholics and drug addicts who have seen the Light and turned to Christ. Under the intense pressures of that show business environment, they may backslide at times.

Don't get me wrong, friends. We're all sinners. I'm a sinner of the first degree. There's not one of us worthy of the Kingdom Of God, and that includes me. The only point I'm making is this: Don't just shove a pile of Gospel records at your child in exchange for his Rock collection and then expect miracles to happen. No one knows the needs and inner workings of your child better than you except the Lord God. If you've already done your homework about Rock & Roll, the least you can do is apply the same methods to Gospel.

The entire thrust of this book in a nutshell is to get to know your child better; don't give up your awesome responsibility for his or her up-bringing to anyone, not to the stars of Rock, nor the kings of Gospel.

Another alternative to Rock & Roll not usually thought of is the majestic beauty of old church hymns. Can anything surpass the soaring grandeur of those wonderful praises in word and song? Such lovely anthems properly sung can send a tingle up the spine just like the best Rock has to offer, and they don't need screaming guitars and foul-mouthed singers in chains to do it, either!

I can see some of you young people groaning now. When faced with this alternative, you might feel embarassed to be caught listening to such "straight" music. Maybe you think it's ridiculous, or stupid, or just plain boring. Well, if that's the way you feel, that's just tough. You'd better change your head around and do it soon, because if you think singing and listening to hymns praising the Lord God is boring or embarassing, you're not far from the Kingdom Of Hell. Who do you think invented music, anyway, Satan? Who gave us the tongues and throats and ears and minds to listen and sing with in the first place, the Devil?

> "Let the word of Christ dwell in you richly in all wisdom; teaching and admonishing one another in psalms and hymns and spiritual songs, singing with grace in your hearts to the Lord."   Colossians 3:16

If God intended music to be used as a means of joyful praise to His Grace and Glory, then where does modern Rock & Roll fit in?

There aren't many former Satanists around willing to

317

talk about their experiences, but Mike Warnke is one. In his 1972 book, *The Satan Seller,* he shows us exactly where Rock & Roll's real home is: Hell. As a high priest of the Devil during the 1960's, Warnke was personally responsible for bringing new souls to damnation through membership and participation in ceremonies of satanic worship. A real go-getter for the cause, he modernized the ancient ritual in order to attract more members to the Devil. ONE OF THE KEY CHANGES HE MADE WAS THE INTRODUCTION OF SCREAMING ROCK MUSIC TO THE WORSHIP CEREMONY. Before he repented and escaped from Satan's clutches, 1,000 new souls had embraced Lucifer!

I also suggest you carefully read the personal testimony written for this book by Elaine. She was once one of the top witches in the U.S. I think you will find what she has to say about Rock music in the Appendix of this book very sobering.

There's yet another alternative to Rock & Roll, and it's the most overlooked of all: Silence. How can parents and children meaningfully communicate when the doorbell's ringing, the telephone's jangling, the TVs blaring, the radio's roaring, and the stereo's blasting? In order to communicate, you must first be able to hear yourself think and the other person talk. Try some SILENCE for a change in your house and see if things don't calm down just a little bit. I'm not talking about living the life of a monk and doing without all our modern conveniences; just a couple of hours a day set aside for real give-and-take co-communication, quiet prayerful reflection and contemplation of God. These things plus devotional family Bible reading could make all the difference between a home filled with blaring Rock & Roll, and one filled with the blissful Peace of God.

Can you afford not to try?

Over a period of time, after teaching our youth all we can about Rock's rottenness, we must encourage them to begin pulling themselves out of the quick sand they have been stuck in for so long. The INSPIRATION for this must come from the Scriptures and prolonged prayer. For example:

Young people, don't let Rock rule your life. Assert your own authority over yourself. The Rock stars that make this musical muck don't care about you. They only want your money. Their lifestyles insulate them from the common people that made them rich; they live in a dream world.

> "For what is a man profited, if he shall gain the whole world, and lose his own soul?"　　　Matthew 16:26

Tell your friends about these disgusting Rockers who are raping the youth of the world. Don't let them continue to get away with it. Rock stars are making fools of everyone who support them, and they're laughing the whole time they're doing it. Tell your friends. Spread the news. Show some individuality for a change. Tell it like it is.

> "But these, as natural brute beasts, made to be taken and destroyed, speak evil of the things that they understand not; and shall utterly perish in their own corruption; and shall receive the reward of unrighteousness, as they that count it pleasure to riot in the day time. Spots they are and blemishes, sporting themselves with their own deceivings while they feast with you. Having eyes full of adultery, and that cannot cease from sin; beguiling unstable souls: an heart they have exercised with covetous practices; cursed children . . . "　　　II Peter 2:12-14

It used to be that young people wanted to be left alone to "do their own thing." Well now they're doing "someone else's thing," and it's no longer "cool" to be an individual who turns his back on Rock. Stand up for yourself and take the heat. You owe it to yourself, mentally, emotionally and spiritually to call the shots in your own life, not take orders from some scummy, demented Rock group.

And as for parents, the entire struggle of guiding your children away from Rock should be looked upon as a duty to your kids and to God.

In general, you should follow these four steps: (1) Identify the scope of the problem in your individual situation, (2) Bind the demons, (3) Pick a strategy to deal with it, and (4) Follow through in a firm, consistent, caring manner.

There are plenty of other art forms for young people to become interested in besides Rock & Roll. If your plan isn't working, go back to the Bible with an open heart and mind, and keep learning! If constant prayer and petitions for help from our Lord Jesus Christ are lacking, you'll get nowhere fast.

You shouldn't be using this program of ACTION because you see yourself as being totally in control of every move your children make, or because you think you're better than the Rock stars they worship. You should do it out of loving concern for the spiritual, mental, and emotional well-being of your precious children. If through the grace of God, your kids believe at once what you're telling them about Rock, and wholeheartedly want to change their lifestyle, you had better have a concrete plan ready and waiting for them to use. I pray that this book may help you in that regard.

In I Timothy 3:4-5 the Bible tells us what a Godly man's family must be like:

> "One that ruleth well his own house, having his children in subjection with all gravity. For if a man know not how to rule his own house, how shall he take care of the church of God?"

In Deutronomy 6, verses 6 and 7, the atmosphere of the Godfearing home is described. Music, TV, conversation, or attitudes of people, anything which does not fit into this atmosphere, must be diligently resisted in prayer and by loving parental authority.

How does YOUR family compare to these verses?

CHAPTER 13

Pulling Down Strongholds

"For though we walk in the flesh, we do not war after the flesh: For the weapons of our warfare are not carnal, but mighty through God to the pulling down of strong holds." II Corinthians 10:3-4

"You can't kill Rock & Roll. It's here to stay ... " Ozzy Osbourne[1]

ORGANIZATION is probably the most important part of our plan of ACTION. We can all yell and complain about Rock & Roll until we turn blue in the face. That's easy. But what good is all that hot air unless we DO something about it?

You may be saying to yourself, "But I'm only one person; what can I do to change a 3 billion dollar a year conglomerate like the Rock music industry? What difference can I make?"

Well, first of all, we need to lower our sights a little. We must take things one step at a time, and that first step should be on the family level, putting our own house in order. After that, we can move on into the local and national areas to get things done.

As far as your own family is concerned, you as parents can use a variety of organized tactics to put a stop to Rock in your house. We've already looked at a few. One sure way for parents to keep closer track of where their children are headed spiritually is to watch where their money goes. Find out exactly how much your teenager is earning from his allowance and part time job, and then see precisely how he spends it. If too much money seems to be going nowhere, you may be forced to put your teenager on a budget. In this way you'll have a little more control over the dollars being wasted on Rock, (or possibly drugs).

Another logical place to start community action on a local level is in the Church. Why not get the youth groups involved in something worthwhile, like going to arcades where teenagers and pre-teens "hang out?" Take a listen to the music that is usually blasting out of the stereo speakers at such places. It will consist of the same groups and songs that we have been talking about all through this book. Get a group of kids, parents, ministers, or all three, to go to a few arcades and take notes on what is going on there. Take your findings to the local newspaper. Do the same thing with school dances that feature live Rock bands, as well as movie theaters showing Rock flicks, and "street dances" where large numbers of young people meet. (They used to be called "Record Hops.")

Church members and youth leaders alike NEED such projects in any congregation. It would give them a fresh outlook and a new approach to stopping Rock & Roll filth in its tracks. The educational value for younger, more impressionable boys and girls who don't yet know about the dangers of Rock is priceless. There's tons of room for discussions in Sunday School classes and youth group meetings , using the information contained in this book. There are all kinds of opportunities for pastors to prepare sermons on this subject. They MUST educate the congregation and make them aware of the deadly peril their sons and daughters are facing.

Through ORGANIZATION, a public forum on Rock & Roll can be established, at least in the Church. Rock can finally be brought out of the dark, cobwebby closet it has hidden in for so many years. Examine it in the light. When you've exposed Satan, throw his filth in the trash and tell others what you know. Major movements and shifts in social tastes and public opinion are started in just this way. Organize letter writing campaigns and lobbying groups to make legislators and F.C.C. people aware that we will no longer stand for the trash we've been bombarded with for so many years.

The best place to begin anti-Rock campaigns and lobbying efforts is at your own local level. Start with your own community. After all, that's where you and your neighbors live; shouldn't it reflect the values that YOU hold dear? Start with the local radio stations. Monitor the songs being played. Do you find any of them offensive?

Remember, YOU HAVE CLOUT! U.S. Code Title 18, Section 1464 states:

> "Whoever utters any obscene, indecent or profane language by means of radio communication, shall be fined not more than $10,000 or imprisoned not more than 2 years or both."

Those people have to apply for F.C.C. licenses and renewals every so often in order to continue running their stations in the public interest. If your group or spokesman cannot get a satisfactory response from the people in charge, go over their heads.

If your city is large enough to have big name Rock concerts appear regularly, contact your City Council and arrange personal meetings with its members, or appear with friends, supporters, and petitions at the regular public meetings to state your case. You might be pleasantly surprised to find that a lot of the people that make up those organizations have kids of their own, and they don't like them listening to Rock garbage any more than you do! The City Council is a direct link to the mayor, and if you can get the mayor on your side, you'll start seeing changes made!

If you are unfortunate enough to have a City Council of foot dragging professional politicians who don't like to make waves of any kind, go to the meetings and present your case anyway. There's usually a newspaper reporter or two there who would like nothing better than a good story about sparks flying at the usually dull and routine courthouse. Don't be afraid of publicity; spread the word!

At this point you might be saying to yourself, "I can present a case to those people, all right, but just what is my case? What good will it do to simply say I and my neighbors don't like Rock & Roll?"

What we're talking about specifically here is banning Rock bands from coming to your town to play. If you as a collective group make it difficult for them to appear in your city, they won't! They'll just move on to their next stop and thumb their noses at you. If enough cities band together to exclude the group or groups, especially in a regional sense, you'll be hitting those jerks right where it hurts, in their big, fat wallets! That's when they'll start sitting up and taking notice, and that's when you'll know you've got them running scared.

Big time Rock tours of America are always planned months in advance, and mapped out by regions: Northeast, South, Deep South, Midwest, West Coast, Canada-U.S. Frontier. Touring is incredibly expensive for even the biggest Rock bands to undertake; if an entire region or regions are denied them, it may not be worth their time to tour at all. At the very least, they won't be close enough for your kids to see them.

How can you as a concerned parent and citizen convince your mayor or City Council to ban a specific band's performance from your area, that's the question.

Try health hazard and common nuisance on for size.

What it boils down to is this: there's not a big time Rock band in the world that will play a live concert much under 90 db's. If you can cause a city ordinance to be enacted limiting such performances to way below that number, with hefty fines for violations, you will have effectively shut down Rock & Roll in that venue. (To the bands and fans, a concert at less than 90 db's would sound like it was being played on a little kid's toy record player.) In addition to this type of ordinance, lay very heavy cash security deposits against damage and/or deaths to fans on the most notorious groups. They'll waste no time in scratching your city off their tour list!

This brings up another good reason for a ban on live Rock in your area: the common nuisance factor. I don't see how any self-respecting city administrator, mayor, or council member can weigh the potential problems of a big Rock show against the potential revenues and come out even.

Let's compare sporting events with Rock concerts. At a big basketball or hockey game there's going to be traffic and crowd control problems — that comes with the territory. But there's not going to be numbers of people vomiting and overdosing all over the place. The parking lot will not have turned into one big illegal drug store. There's not going to be mass riots and destruction of the hall later, as happened in 1984 at New York's Madison Square Garden during a *Judas Priest* show. And there's certainly not going to be the necessity of making structural repairs to the building!

That's right, over a period of time the constant booming barrage of blitzkrieg Rock & Roll has actually caused damage to the foundation and understructure of the buildings where regular concerts are held. That should give you some idea of the sound level in those places: music so loud it cracks concrete!

Fire codes in the building? Forget it. Everyone smokes and lights matches. Where would a Satan worship service be without flames, anyway? Also, when you're dealing with bands like *KISS,* it is a wonder they don't burn the place down themselves with their own special effects!

What about the dangers of lawsuits against the city when a death or disaster occurs at such affairs, as at Cincinnati? The possibility of an accidental death is always a problem with any mass meeting of thousands of people, but don't the odds go up drastically when put into the context of a Rock event? Those drunk and drugged people jump in their cars after being pounded in the face for hours with the sonic booms of Satan-Rock. How would you like to be sitting in the the car in front of them when they hit the gas pedal?

Try laying all the points mentioned above on your city administrators, and if they still refuse to take note there's one sure fire way to get their attention and keep it. The word is "Smut." There's not a politician anywhere in the United States who wants to be seen as being in favor of a lewd or dirty public display, and that's just what a Rock concert is.

Are you wondering where that foul language is coming from that Junior or daughter is starting to pick up? Go to a Rock concert and you'll hear things said over the microphone that you haven't heard since the Service. The Supreme Court has allowed individual communities to decide for themselves what is and is not pornographic. If your City Council poo-poohs the idea that live Rock & Roll is the same thing as smut, challenge those people publicly to go see for themselves. If they didn't think the show was too bad, and you did, then maybe your town's ready for a change round about election time.

Don't give up! The Bible tells us throughout the Old Testament not to be discouraged or afraid, even in the face of overwhelming odds.

And what about all those disgusting album covers sitting out in plain sight at your local record store, just waiting for some youngster to come in and look at them? Do you find any of these offensive? Get your group to talk with the store's district manager about continuing to stock such trash. There's a very good recent example of just how effective this kind of pressuring can be, and it runs all the way back up the pipeline to the groups themselves and their managers.

In 1982 Joan Jett put out a record which included a version (on cassette) of an old *Rolling Stones'* tune called "Starf_____." With a title like that, she should have known better, but Rock stars think they can get away with anything as long as we let them. When the *Stones* tried to market the same tune, their record label made them change the title to "Star Star" and mumble their way through the offensive lyrics, which they did.

Joan didn't bother, and boy, was she sorry! When the K-Mart chain found out about the song, they refused to handle the product, and started shipping back the tapes. Since cassettes now outsell albums, that hurt! Jett manager Kenny Laguna says they lost $225,000 in sales the first two weeks of the boycott. As other retailers heard of K-Mart's action, they also followed suit, and before long Joan Jett's new album was stalled on the charts and falling.

Moves like that by concerned consumers can really put the crunch on Rock stars who thought nothing could touch them. For her "Glorious Results Of A Misspent Youth" record, Jett first submitted the tapes to K-Mart to make sure they weren't offended. If they had been, Laguna says the words would have been changed. If YOU are offended by certain Rock records or songs for whatever reason, bring your group and petitions to the offices of retail chain managers, or higher, if need be. You'll get results!

The above outline is just a few ways to organize your youth, your church, and your community in such a fashion as to finally be a real threat to the multi-million dollar power hungry drug addicts behind Rock & Roll. As far as national efforts are concerned, here are a few tips: Why not contact the Parents Music Resource Center? Though sneered at in the liberal press, these people have access to Senators, Congressmen, and other even bigger lobbying groups, in the grassroots, and in the Capitol Building.

You also might want to actually MEET with your Congressman or Representative. They are no doubt very busy people, but they're still accessible to the common voter, especially if he has a briefcase full of letters, petitions, and signatures in his hand. After all, this isn't the Soviet Union. We elected those people! If you do secure a meeting with someone in national government, you need only have a well-documented representation of the facts of whatever case you wish to make. Try it!

The hottest music-related topic of 1985 and best example of citizens' groups making a difference, was the Parents Music Resource Center, a Washington, D.C. based coalition of citizens concerned about the vulgar pornography, Satanism, and drug/alcohol aspects of modern Rock. The PMRC single-handedly took on the Recording Industry Association Of America (RIAA) in September of 1985 and shook that powerful organization to its roots. The National Music Review Council of Dallas, Texas as well as the National P.T.A. rallied round the PMRC, creating a sizeable constituency of angry parents almost overnight. How did this very successful grassroots campaign begin?

With only 3 people: Tipper Gore, Susan Baker, and Pam Howar. These women are not just Main Street housewives, however. They are all wives of senior officials in the Reagan Administration and other powerful D.C. businessmen. As women and mothers, they became disgusted and alarmed by attitudes and songs from the likes of *Prince, Motley Crue, Twisted Sister, Van Halen* and *Judas Priest.* They took advantage of their sizeable mailing list of the most powerful and influential names in Washington, and began a mailing campaign and media blitz in April of 1985 which quickly gathered momentum and national attention. It all began at a church meeting.

Their goal? Rate those Rock records. Put a letter on each

album and tape just like the movie ratings system already in effect for many years. They also demanded printed song lyrics on outer record sleeves, separate displays for albums with offensive covers, rated Rock concerts, closer supervision of MTV videos, printed lyric sheets sent to radio station DJs, and an end to the use of backmasking techniques in Rock recordings.

Stanley Gortikov, president of the RIAA, claims that he has never experienced backmasks in his quarter century career in recording. I happen to have an hour long tape of backmasks reversed that Stanley might find interesting and educational.

When the PMRC's demands and the RIAA's refusals hit the news wires, people all over the country went nuts. "Censorship! We won't have it!" screamed some. "God bless those women! It's about time someone spoke up!" shouted others. Some cynics smugly smirked, "If those women didn't have famous and powerful husbands, they wouldn't have gotten anywhere."

Well, famous or not, the fact of the matter is that Mmes. Gore, Howar, Baker, and friends did what any citizens' group can do: they organized, they aired their concerns publicly, they initiated a massive letter writing campaign to friends, supporters, and adversaries, (lots and lots of letters were written and sent to Gortikov and the presidents of the biggest record companies in America), and finally, THEY GOT RESULTS!

They may have achieved their results more quickly than others less well known, but achieve them they did. The PMRC did it, and so can any other group concerned about "Porn-Rock."

A Congressional hearing was called for September 19, 1985 with the Senate Committee on Commerce, Science and Transportation in attendance. This meeting became a media event, (circus would be a better word). Rock stars like Dee Snider and Frank Zappa went head-to-head with senators and congressmen. The end result was a public airing of the "Porn-Rock" problem, with a militant Snider and snide Zappa mouthing a mile of mush about misguided Christian principles and Freedom of Speech. When the dust had settled, the RIAA backed off and gave in, though not by much. With Congressional regulation hanging over their heads, the Industry half-heartedly agreed to put small warning stickers on albums that might be considered offensive.

The PMRC vowed to continue their fight until their entire revised agenda had been met. As of January, 1986, that is where the situation stands.

If I may, I would like to inject an opinion or two. In the middle of all the yells about censorship, free speech, artists' rights, and keeping big government off business' back, one thing is being overlooked.

If PMRC didn't have the support of thousands of Moms and Dads just like the ones reading these words right now, the whole issue of Rock censorship would not exist. The fact that it does exist should tell us something. Parents are as mad as can be about what Rock is doing to their kids, and they're not going to take it anymore! They shouldn't have to. The PMRC is trying to give parents some warning before Rock trash is brought into the home. If censorship does occur, it will be because the Rock stars and Record Industry have finally gone too far.

Attempting to legislate morality never works. It never has and I don't believe it ever will. I applaud the PMRC and other groups like them for their courage, ceaseless effort, and outspoken position. It's about time someone took a stand. But the HOME is the real center of our lives. That's the way God designed it, and that's why Satan wants to wreck it. Mom and Dad, don't let the Devil steal your childrens' souls through the altars to Satan in their bedrooms. Young people — open up and really LISTEN to what your parents are trying to tell you.

National boycotts by concerned consumer groups of a number of varying causes have also proven to be a very effective lobbying tool. Boycott is a dirty word to national TV

330

sponsors. Just the threat of an organized, united effort by citizen's groups to quit buying sponsor's products is usually enough to get things straightened around. The same principle can easily be applied to cable TV stations that specialize in Rock programming.

The F.C.C. is the key to approaching radio stations about their programming.

The F.C.C. has a clear responsibility to guard the listening public from the kind of Rock & Roll trash we hear each and every day. Pressure needs to be brought on the people in charge of such responsibilities to conduct their jobs with more careful vigilance.

This kind of voter pressure on elected and appointed representatives can be very effective. The backwards masking scandal which caused California Assemblyman Phil Wyman to introduce his bill to the California Assembly Committee on Consumer Protection and Toxic Materials in Sacramento is one such case, not to mention the PMRC's success in September of 1985.

This clipping appeared shortly before Easter in the 1982 issue of "The Indianapolis Star," filed under the caption, "NO Rock."

> "Rock group *Black Sabbath* won't be performing at Phoenix, Arizona Easter Sunday because a lawmaker objected that their act was 'absolutely degrading.' Arizona State Representative Tony West complained about the performance at the state-owned Veteran's Memorial Coliseum, saying 'apparently they have a propensity to be demonic, to ridicule the Christian religions and they actually burn crosses . . . '"

In the February 27, 1986 edition of the Bloomington, Indiana Herald-Telephone Newspaper, it was reported that a Councilman from Corpus Christi, Texas is pushing for a city ordinance against disgusting Rock concerts in his town. Councilman Leo Guerrero said this about the *KISS/W.A.S.P.* show he personally attended:

"You can smell the pot. This is the biggest bunch of trash they've ever allowed in a municipal building here."

Decibel levels at the concert were measured at 110 dbs. Guerrero's ordinance wants to enforce an age limit of 14 for kids attending Rock concerts, as well as a reduction in the noise levels and a crackdown on drugs.

We could use more representatives like Phil Wyman, Tony West and Councilman Guerrero. They're out there in your district, just waiting to hear from you.

Only by following the steps already outlined can we hope to dispose of Rock & Roll once and for all. Only then can we have a return to NORMALCY, where Jesus Christ will hold first place in our children's hearts and minds, instead of Mick Jagger.

It's not Satan that's totally responsible for the mess we're in today. It's our own inactivity! We're the ones who have let ourselves down, by not keeping a closer watch on the course Rock & Roll was taking all through the Sixties and Seventies. Well now it's the Eighties, and it's high time we all took a sober interest in this matter. It's our children who are the stakes in this hellish game. We can't afford to lose them.

As Psalm 18:2 tells us:

"The Lord is my rock, and my fortress, and my deliverer; whom I will trust; my buckler, and the horn of my salvation, and my high tower."

And in Romans 9:33 we read:

"As it is written, Behold, I lay in Zion a stumbling stone and rock of offense: and whosoever believeth on him shall not be ashamed."

Satan is trying to roll away The Rock. The Rock & Roll he so delights in is trying to blind us to his plan. but we can

332

stop him. We can stop this thing in its tracks. Let's get started.

These human demons and gutter scum have long deserved having the magic carpet jerked rudely from beneath their snakeskin boots. It's time they took a fall instead of another dollar from our kids' pockets.

Any steps we take to break the back of Rock & Roll must be taken with love in our hearts, not hate or jealousy. As God's word tells us:

> " . . . Though I speak with the tongues of men and of angels, and have not charity [love], I am become as sounding brass, or a tinkling cymbal. And though I have the gift of prophecy, and understand all mysteries, and all knowledge; and though I have all faith, so that I could remove mountains, and have not charity, I am nothing. And though I bestow all my goods to feed the poor, and though I give my body to be burned, and have not charity, it profiteth me nothing." 1 Corinthians 13:1-3

Just realizing that a problem exists is not enough. What are we going to DO about it? As the Bible directs us in James 2:19-24:

> "Thou believest that there is one God; thou doest well: the devils also believe, and tremble. But wilt thou know, O vain man, that faith without works is dead? Was not Abraham our father justified by works, when he had offered Isaac his son upon the altar? Seest thou how faith wrought with his works, and by works was faith made perfect? And the scripture was fulfilled which saith, Abraham believed God, and it was imputed unto him for righteousness: and he was called the Friend of God. Ye see then how that by works a man is justified, and not by faith only."

333

INDEX OF ADDRESSES

Parents Music Resource Center

> PMRC
> 1500 Arlington Blvd.
> Arlington, VA 22209
> 703-527-9466

Federal Communications Commission

> Ms. Edythe Wise
> F.C.C.
> Mass Media Bureau
> Chief of Complaints
> 1919 "M" Street, N.W.
> Washington, D.C. 20554

National Association Of Broadcasters

> N.A.B.
> Mr. Eddie Fritts
> President and Chief
> Executive Officer
> 1771 "N" Street, N.W.
> Washington, D.C. 20036

Recording Industry Association of America

> RIAA
> Mr. Stanley Gortikov
> President
> 888 Seventh Ave., 9th Floor
> New York, NY 10106

National Cable Television Association

NCTA
Mr. Jim Mooney
Executive Director
1724 Massachusetts Ave., N.W.
Washington, D.C. 20036

MTV

MTV
Mr. David Horowitz
President
1133 Avenue of the Americas
New York, NY 10036

Congressman

The Honorable (Name)
U.S. House of Representatives
Washington, D.C. 20515

Senator

The Honorable (Name)
U.S. Senate
Washington, D.C. 20510

Networks

CBS-TV
Entertainment Division
51 W. 52nd Street
New York, NY 10019

ABC-TV
Audience Information
1330 Sixth Avenue
New York, NY 10019

NBC-TV
Audience Services
30 Rockefeller Plaza
New York, NY 10020

The above is for you to use to mount letter-writing campaigns. Tell these people how you feel about Rock music.

POSTSCRIPT

One question that many parents and young people are sure to ask after reading this book is: "If he was so heavily involved in Rock & Roll, just how did Jeff Godwin finally get out of it? Was it through prayer, or Christian friends, or loving parents, or a powerful, emotion-packed deliverance? How did it happen?"

My only answer to that very valid question is that it was none of those things yet it was all of those things. My deliverance from the demonic and all-consuming spell of the Rock & Roll curse quite simply came about through the Will of God and the saving Grace of Jesus Christ. My experience cannot and should not be a blueprint for every young person and parent to follow. All of us are far too unique and different for that. I AM sure of one thing, however, the further you delve into the music of Rock & Roll, the further you'll drift away from the true Rock and spiritual anchor of us all: Christ Jesus.

Young people, please allow me to tell you what Rock music did to me, and then you examine your own lives and see if some of the same things don't hold true for you also.

(1) ROCK MUSIC TOOK ALMOST ALL MY MONEY FOR MANY, MANY YEARS. I spent literally thousands of dollars on records and tapes and books and magazines and radios and stereos and tape decks and posters and concert tickets and, finally, guitars and amplifiers and microphones and PA systems and speaker cabinets and even a van to haul it all in!

Heavy Metal left me penniless, and the Rock stars I worshiped that much richer for my foolish bankruptcy.

(2) ROCK MUSIC STOLE MY MIND AND TRIED TO SNATCH MY SOUL AS WELL. It's only because of the Grace of God that I'm here to tell you about these things today. I wanted to be a Rock star so badly I began acting like one. That means I became foul mouthed, foul minded, vile and deceitful, a braggart, and a violent troublemaker and brawler. And those were my good points! You see, as Peter says in II Peter 2:19: " . . . For of whom a man is overcome, of the same is he brought in bondage." In other words, a man is a slave to whatever has mastered him. Rock & Roll mastered me, and I became its slave.

The Rock stars took drugs — I took drugs. (Although I have never put a needle in my veins nor have I ever taken heroin.) The Rock stars bragged of treating their women like dogs — I did the same. The Rock stars boozed it up like there was no tomorrow — and I teetered on the brink of alcoholism for many years. And what was it all for? A mindless pursuit of an empty and deceitful dream that eventually leads to 2 things: spiritual and physical death.

You've got to realize something, young people. When you give your allegiance to Rock & Roll, you're turning your back on Jesus Christ.

> "Love not the world, neither the things that are in the world. If any man love the world, the love of the Father is not in him. For all that is in the world, the lust of the flesh, and the lust of the eyes, and the pride of life, is not of the Father, but is of the world."
>
> I John 2:15-16

And who is the Prince of this world?

> (Jesus speaking) "Hereafter I will not talk much with you: for the prince of this world cometh, and hath nothing in me."　　　　John 14:30

> "And the devil said unto him, all this power will I give thee, and the glory of them: for that is delivered unto me; and to whomsoever I will I give it."   Luke 4:6

Do you really want to do that, to turn your back on Jesus? You can't have it both ways, you know. You must make a choice.

> "I know thy works, that thou are neither cold nor hot: I would thou wert cold or hot. So then because thou are lukewarm, and neither cold nor hot, I will spue thee out of my mouth." (Jesus speaking.)
> Revelation 3:15-16

As I hungrily galloped after the Heavy Metal monsters of modern Rock, fueled by booze and dope, my mind began to degenerate. The Lord had turned me over to my own device, a prisoner of Satan and the self-destructive attitude that is the mainstay of Metalmania. God was allowing me to destroy myself; since I had deserted Him, He withdrew His Presence from me.

> "And even as they did not like to retain God in their knowledge, God gave them over to a reprobate mind, to do those things which are not convenient; being filled with all unrighteousness, fornication, wickedness, covetousness, maliciousness; full of envy, murder, debate, deceit, malignity; whisperers, backbiters, haters of God, despiteful, proud, boasters, inventors of evil things, disobedient to parents, without understanding, convenantbreakers, without natural affection, implacable, unmerciful: who knowing the judgment of God, that they which commit such things are worthy of death, not only do the same, but have pleasure in them that do them."   Romans 1:28-32

(3) ROCK & ROLL TAKES EVERYTHING, BUT GIVES NOTHING IN RETURN. When you say you get hours of pleasure from listening to Rock music, you're only fooling yourself. Think about it: what makes you part with your hard earned money just to buy one "good" tape or record

out of five "bad" ones, your own generosity? At nine bucks a shot, that's pretty generous, indeed. That same music that you love so much holds you bound like a puppet in chains. It makes you dance because you can't sit still and listen to it at the same time. It makes your heart race and your blood pump hot like a steam engine in a boiler room. The music controls you, beloved, just like it controlled me!

What makes you play those records and tapes again and again until they wear out, your own free choice? What burns those words and music into your brain until you can't get the songs out of your head, your own free will?

I propose a test, young people. If you don't think Rock & Roll has a hold on you, do without it for a week. COMPLETELY without it. Don't play it at home, in the car, or at school, and stay away from those who do. Turn the stereo and radio off and leave it off all day, every day, for a week. You may say what every cigarette smoker and drug addict and alcoholic says, "I can quit any time I want to; I just don't want to right now." If you can quit Rock, I want you to prove it. By the way, try some prayers for wisdom, guidance, and forgiveness during the time you would have spent listening to music. If 7 days without prayer makes one weak, then I guarantee 7 days without Rock will make you spiritually stronger than when you started.

If you can cut Rock & Roll completely out of your life like I have, then you'll have won a great victory. What gives me the right to put down Rock? I've BEEN there, brother and sister. I don't listen to Rock music any more; I read the Bible instead. I sold all my guitars and amps; today I tithe for the Lord instead. I don't do drugs and booze anymore, and never will; I keep my head clear so I can pray to the God who knew me before I was even born.

Can you do the same? Can you do without Rock? Or does it control your wallet AND your will, your money AND your mind? Why don't you find out starting today; begin by pulling that plug right out of the wall and leaving it where it lays.

In conclusion: How was I delivered from the power of Satan and Rock & Roll? (They're the same thing, incidentally.) There was no magic solution and there was no instant cure. The Lord let me dig myself down so far that I finally had nowhere to go but up. And when I looked up, I saw the hand of Jesus Christ reaching out to bridge the gap. This process took years, mainly because of my own stubborness and the incredible hardness of my calloused heart.

In the end, the waters of baptism are what really did it for me; that was the final stage of real acceptance of the King Of Kings and Lord Of Lords, Jesus Christ. And oh, what a sweet, sweet feeling to come out of those waters washed clean in the Blood, a new creature, God's child, and an heir to the Kingdom Of Heaven! Praise God for such a priceless gift!

I'm not one in a million, dear friends, just one out of many. My story's not unique, just sad because I waited so long. You can find Jesus, and you can find peace, and you can find Life, if you'll only seek Him wholeheartedly. As the Word Of God so richly proves,

> "In all thy ways acknowledge him, and he shall direct
> thy paths."   Proverbs 3:6

Jeff Godwin
The Rock Ministries
P.O. Box 2181
Bloomington, IN 47401

APPENDIX A

My name is Elaine, and I am, at the author's request, adding my personal testimony to this book. I was, for 17 years, a servant of Satan. I became involved in witchcraft at the age of 17 and joined a cult of Satan worshipers which is little known publicly, but exists nation-wide. I rapidly climbed the ladder to power and before I was 30 years old, I had reached the position of high priestess in my local area. In addition to that I was also one of the 5-10 regional brides of Satan in this country and was in a position of national leadership within the group. I held that position for several years.

During those years, I traveled the world as Satan's representative to coordinate efforts with Satanists in other nations and also worked with many people in high governmental positions within the U.S. I had much power, as much money as I wanted, and was treated with great respect. But all that time the demons I had deliberately asked to come and live inside me to give me this power, were eating away at my very soul and planning for my destruction.

Through a series of events, too long to detail here, I came against some people who had truly made Jesus Christ their Lord and Savior and Master. One of them I tried to kill, but was unable to do so. For the first time in my life I had come up against a power that was greater than anything Satan could give me. I was very shaken. The person I tried to kill, and a number of other true born-again believers in our Lord Jesus Christ, loved me in spite of who and what I was, and prayed for me intensively. They also showed me that they loved me with the love of Jesus just as I was. I became hungry to know more about this unusual love and power. Finally, 6 years ago, I rejected Satan and everything to do with him, and asked Jesus Christ to wash me clean from all that sin with His precious blood, and to become my Lord and Savior, and Master. I have been serving the one true God, Jesus Christ, ever since. Believe me, the difference is wonderful!

Because of the high position I held for so many years, I was involved in the planning of many of the destructive influences Satan has brought into the U.S. and other countries. Satan is REAL! Demons are REAL! I can tell you from my own personal experience, but you don't have to take my word for this, simply read God's word, the Bible.

Like so many other things, the whole movement of Rock music was carefully planned and carried out by Satan and his servants from its very beginning. Rock music didn't "just happen," it was a carefully masterminded plan by none other than Satan himself.

I have personally met a great number of the Rock stars. They have ALL agreed to serve Satan in return for money and fame. They have received all they wanted, but also so much more that they didn't expect. Their very lives and souls are, and in many cases have been, destroyed. These Rock stars KNOW exactly what they are doing. They are, step by step, teaching untold millions of young people to worship and serve Satan.

I attended special ceremonies at various recording studios throughout the U.S. for the specific purpose of placing satanic blessings on the Rock music recorded. We did incantations which placed demons on EVERY record and tape of rock music that was sold. At times we also called up special demons who spoke on the recordings — the various back-masked messages. ALSO, in many many of the recordings, we were ourselves recorded in the background (masked by the over-all noise of the music) doing chants and incantations to summon up more demons every time one of the records or tapes is played. As the music is played, these demons are summoned into the room to afflict the person playing the music, and anyone else who is listening. The purpose of all of this? MIND CONTROL! Mind control not only to give the listeners understanding of the messages about Satan conveyed to them by the music, but also to prevent them from recognizing their need for Jesus. (See II Corinthians 4:4).

Many of the song lyrics are themselves actual incantations calling up demons when the song is sung. The purpose of this is two fold: to exert control over the listener, and to provide the listener with actual incantations he or she can use to send demons upon another person to gain revenge by afflicting them with illness, accidents, etc, and also to help influence another person into the bondage of Rock music itself. A good example of this is the lyrics to the "Doom Song" by the *Plasmatics* which are quoted in Chapter 4.

The reference to people coming in robes with candles to hear *Black Sabbath's* music by Ozzy Osbourne on page 104, makes reference to the ceremonies held by the Satanists to "bless" the Rock music. The reference made to a "subliminal rhythm track" by Paul Rothschild on page 131, refers not only to back-masking, but also to the chanted incantations by Satanists in the background of the music.

If you don't think there is a supernatural power behind Rock music, you just try to stop listening to it (if you normally do so), or try to get someone else to stop listening to it. You will quickly experience the power behind the music!

Parents, young people, you MUST understand that any time you come against Rock music you are coming directly against demonic powers. The ONLY power that is greater than Satan and these demonic powers is Jesus Christ! NO human being is stronger or smarter than Satan and his demons. It is only through the power and authority given to us by God in the name of our Lord Jesus Christ that those of us who have made Jesus our Lord and Savior and Master can defeat and overcome these demonic powers.

Young people, I don't care what your Rock stars tell you, they and Satan hate your guts and are all planning for one thing — your destruction. Jesus loved you enough to die for you, would any of your Rock stars do so???

FOOTNOTES

CHAPTER 1
1. *Faces Magazine,* February, 1985, p. 53.
2. *Rolling Stone Magazine,* February 12, 1976, Issue No. 206, p. 83.

CHAPTER 2
1. A frequent live stage utterance by the Columbus, Ohio, Rock group The Godz.
2. *BAM,* November 6, 1981, Issue No. 116, p. 27. As reported by Blair Jackson on seeing the Rolling Stones at San Francisco's Candlestick Park.

CHAPTER 3
1. Lyrics from the AC-DC song "Hells Bells."
2. *Hit Parader,* February, 1985, p. 17.
3. *Faces,* February, 1985, p. 21.
4. David Dalton, *The Rolling Stones — The First Twenty Years,* (Knopf, 1981), p. 148.
5. Ibid.
6. George Tremlett, *The Rolling Stones,* (Warner Books, 75 Rockefeller Plaza, NY, NY 10019, 1975), p. 14.
7. Ibid., p. 16.
8. Tony Sanchez, *Up And Down With The Rolling Stones,* (Morrow-Quill, 1979), p. 158.
9. Ibid., p. 157.
10. David Dalton, *Rolling Stones,* (Amsco Publishing Co., 1972), p. 38.
11. Roy Carr, *Rolling Stones — An Illustrated Record,* (Harmony Books, 1976), p. 81.

12. Dalton, (Amsco), p. 119.
13. *Rolling Stone Magazine,* August 21, 1980, Issue No. 324, p. 42.
14. Dalton, (Knopf), p. 111.
15. Carr, p. 102.
16. *The Globe Newspaper,* Vol. 27, No. 53, December 30, 1980, p. 23.
17. Stanley Booth, *Dance With The Devil,* (Random House, 1984), p. 109.
18. Ibid., p. 25.
19. *Hit Parader 1981 Yearbook,* p. 70.
20. *Circus,* November 30, 1980, p. 31.
21. Ibid., p. 34.
22. James Douglas Morrison, *The Lords And New Creatures,* (Simon & Schuster, 1970).
23. *Led Zep Special,* (Modern Day Perodicals, Inc., 1980), p. 46.
24. Ibid.
25. Ibid.
26. Ibid.
27. Ritchie Yorke, *The Led Zeppelin Biography,* (Methuen Publications, A Division of The Carswell Co., Ltd., 1976), p. 183.
28. *Creem,* November, 1979, p. 47.
29. Yorke, p. 183.
30. *Circus,* June 9, 1977, p. 40.
31. *Creem,* April, 1977, pp. 70-71.
32. *Circus,* June 9, 1977, p. 40.
33. Ibid., p. 41.
34. *Circus,* September 18, 1979, p. 29.
35. Ibid.
36. Stephen Davis, *Hammer of The Gods,* (William Morrow & Co., 1985).
37. *Creem,* April, 1977, p. 41.
38. Ibid., July, 1977, p. 47.
39. Yorke, p. 86.
40. Ibid., p. 138.
41. *Creem,* July, 1977, p. 47.
42. Ibid., November, 1979, p. 48.

CHAPTER 4

1. Lyrics from the song "Sing This Song All Together" by The Rolling Stones.
2. *Lennon Remembers,* by Jann Wenner, Straight Arrow Books, 1971, p. 97.
3. *Rolling Stone Magazine,* October 15, 1981, Issue No. 354, p. 15.

4. Ibid.

5. *Hit Parader,* October, 1976, p. 14.

6. Ibid, February, 1985, p. 42.

7. *Hit Parader 1981 Yearbook,* p. 28.

8. *Circus,* August 26, 1980, p. 26.

9. Ibid.

10. Ibid.

11. Ibid.

12. Ibid.

13. Ibid., June 30, 1981, p. 28.

14. Ibid., March 31, 1985, p. 56.

15. Ibid.

16. Ibid.

17. Ibid.

18. *Hit Parader,* April, 1985, pp. 74-75.

19. Ibid., March, 1985, p. 52.

20. Ibid.

21. Ibid., p. 54.

22. *BAM,* July 3, 1981, Issue No. 107, p. 18.

23. *World War II — The Nazis,* by Robert Edwin Herzstein and the editors of Time-Life books, printed in Alexandria, Virginia, by Time, Inc., p. 89.

24. *Circus,* September 13, 1976, p. 41.

CHAPTER 5

1. *Creem Magazine,* May, 1982, p. 58.

CHAPTER 6

1. Lyrics from the song "Generation Landslide" by Alice Cooper.

CHAPTER 7

1. Roy Carr, *The Rolling Stones — An Illustrated Record,* (Harmony Books, New York, 1976), p. 82.

2. Curtis Knight, *Jimi,* (Praeger Publishers Inc., New York, 1974), p. 59.

3. Ibid., p. 108.

4. Ibid., p. 127.

5. Ibid., p. 207.

6. Ibid.

7. David Dalton, *The Rolling Stones, The First 20 Years,* (Knopf, 1981), p. 115.

8. Ibid., p. 116.

9. Tony Sanchez, *Up And Down With The Rolling Stones,* (Morrow-Quill, 1979).

10. Ibid.

11. *Circus,* October 28, 1980, p. 39.

12. Ibid., p. 40.

13. George Tremlett, *The Who,* (Warner Books, New York, 1975), p. 61.

14. Ibid., pp. 61-62.

15. Jann Wenner, *Lennon Remembers,* (Straight Arrow Books, 1971), p. 76.

16. Ibid.

17. Ibid., p. 77.

18. Ibid., p. 38.

19. *Rolling Stone Magazine,* October 1, 1981, Issue No. 353, p. 100.

20. Ibid.

21. *Creem,* November, 1979, p. 30.

22. Ibid., p. 27.

23. Ibid., p. 29.

24. Ibid., p. 30.

25. Ibid.

26. Ibid.

27. Ibid.

28. *BAM,* September 11, 1981, Issue No. 112, p. 20.

29. Ibid.

30. Ibid.

31. Wenner, p. 78.

32. Ibid., p. 76.

33. Ibid., p. 82.

CHAPTER 8

1. *Musician Magazine,* June 1984, Issue No. 68, p. 52.

2. *Rolling Stone Magazine,* October 7, 1976, Issue No. 223, p. 17.

3. Ibid., February 12, 1976, Issue No. 206, p. 80.

4. Ibid.

5. Ibid.

6. Ibid., p. 83.

7. Ibid.

8. Ibid.

9. Ibid.

10. Ibid.

11. Jann Wenner, *Lennon Remembers,* (Straight Arrow Books, 1971), p. 86.
12. *Musician Player,* February 1982, Issue No. 40, p. 48.
13. *Time Magazine,* October 7, 1966.
14. Tony Sanchez, *Up And Down With The Rolling Stones,* (Morrow-Quill, 1979).

CHAPTER 9
1. Lyrics from their song "Turn On Your Receiver," by Nazareth.
2. *Creem,* April, 1982, p. 37.
3. *BAM,* January 29, 1982, Issue No. 122, p. 13.
4. Ibid., p. 22.
5. Ibid.
6. *Musician Player,* August, 1980, Issue No. 26, p. 49.
7. *Rolling Stone Magazine,* June 26, 1980, Issue No. 320, p. 38.
8. Ibid.

CHAPTER 10
1. Lyrics from the song "Anarchy In The U.K," by The Sex Pistols.
2. John Lennon, *Lennon Remembers,* (Straight Arrow Books), pp. 12 & 14.
3. *Trouser Press Magazine,* July, 1980, Issue No. 52, p. 23.
4. *Hit Parader,* May, 1982, p. 6.
5. Yorke, p. 146.
6. *Trouser Press Magazine,* July, 1980, Issue No. 52, p. 25.
7. *Rolling Stone,* October 20, 1977, Issue No. 250, p. 72.
8. Ibid., p. 71.
9. Ibid., p. 72.
10. Ibid., p. 73.
11. Ibid., p. 74.
12. Ibid., p. 73.
13. Ibid., p. 75.
14. Ibid., p. 73.
15. *BAM,* September 25, 1981, Issue No. 113, p. 24.
16. *Creem,* March, 1985, p. 64.
17. Ibid.
18. *BAM,* September 25, 1981, Issue No. 113, p. 23.
19. *Creem,* January, 1982, p. 43.
20. Ibid., p. 43.
21. Ibid., p. 62.
22. *BAM,* September 25, 1981, Issue No. 113, p. 23.

23. Ibid., p. 25.
24. Ibid.
25. Ibid.
26. Ibid.
27. Sanchez, p. 122.
28. *Playboy Magazine,* January 1981, p. 101.
29. Vincent Bugliosi & Curt Gentry, *Helter Skelter,* (Bantam, 1974), p. 155.
30. *BAM,* July 31, 1981, Issue No. 109, p. 19.
31. Ibid.
32. Dalton, p. 183.
33. Ibid.
34. *Faces,* May, 1985, pp. 21 & 25.

CHAPTER 11
1. Lyrics from the song "Sympathy For The Devil," by The Rolling Stones.
2. *Hit Parader,* March, 1985, p. 39.

CHAPTER 12
1. Anthony Fawcett, *One Day At A Time,* Revised Edition, (Grove Press, Inc., N.Y., 1981), p. 153.
2. *Musician,* June, 1984, Issue No. 68, p. 52.
3. Ibid., p. 54.
4. *Hit Parader,* May, 1982, p. 4.
5. *Creem,* May, 1982, p. 58.
6. *Hit Parader,* August 1982, p. 27.
7. Ibid., p. 26.
8. *Musician Player,* November, 1981, Issue No. 37, p. 56.

CHAPTER 13
1. Lyrics from the song "You Can't Kill Rock & Roll," by Ozzy Osbourne.

ADDITIONAL SOURCE MATERIAL

1. Priscilla Beaulieu Presley with Sandra Harmon, *Elvis And Me,* (Putnam, 200 Madison Ave., N.Y., NY 10016, 1985, by Graceland Enterprises).
2. Peter Brown and Steven Gaines, *The Love You Make,* (McGraw-Hill, 1983).
3. Ray Coleman, *Lennon,* (McGraw-Hill, 1984).
4. Stanley Booth, *Dance With The Devil,* (Random House, 1984).
5. Dave Marsh, *Before I Get Old, The Story Of The Who,* (St. Martin's Press, New York, 1983 by Duke & Duchess Ventures, Inc.).
6. Stephen Davis, *Hammer Of The Gods, The Led Zeppelin Saga,* (William Morrow & Co., 105 Madison Ave., New York, NY 10016, 1985).
7. Curtis Knight, *Jimi,* (Praeger Publishers, Inc., 111 Fourth Ave., New York, NY 1003, 1974).
8. John Green, *Dakota Days,* (St. Martin's Press, New York, 1983).
9. David Sheff, edited by G. Barry Golson, *The Playboy Interviews With John Lennon and Yoko Ono,* (Berkley Books, by Playboy, 1981).
10. May Pang and Henry Edwards, *Loving John,* (Warner Books, Inc., 666 Fifth Ave., New York, NY 10103, by May Pang and Literary Ventures Association, 1983).
11. Jacob Aranza, *Backward Masking Unmasked,* (Huntington House, Inc., 1200 No Market Street, Suite G, Shreveport, Louisiana 71107 by Huntington House, Inc., 1983).
12. Bob Greene, *Billion Dollar Baby,* (Atheneum Publishers, 122 East 42nd St., New York, NY 10017, by Bob Greene, 1974).
13. Jerry Hopkins and Danny Sugarman, *No One Here Gets Out Alive,* (Warner Books, Inc., 75 Rockefeller Plaza, New York, NY 10019 by Jerry Hopkins, 1980).
14. Red West, Sonny West, Dave Hebler as told by Steve Dunleavy, *Elvis-What Happened?,* (Ballantine Books, New York, by World News Corporation, 1977).
15. Albert Goldman, *Elvis,* (Avon Books, A Division of the Hearst Corporation, 959 Eighth Ave., New York, NY 10019, by Albert Goldman, Kevin Egge and Lamar Fike, 1981).
16. Jerry Hopkins, *Elvis — The Final Years,* (Berkley Books, New York, by Jerry Hopkins).